Mac OS® X
Snow Leopard™
PORTABLE GENIUS

Mac OS® X
Snow Leopard™
PORTABLE GENIUS

by Dwight Spivey

WILEY

Wiley Publishing, Inc.

Mac OS® X Snow Leopard™ Portable Genius

Published by
Wiley Publishing, Inc.
10475 Crosspoint Blvd.
Indianapolis, IN 46256
www.wiley.com

WILEY

About the Author

Dwight Spivey is the author of several Mac books, including *Mac Bible* and *Mac OS X Leopard Portable Genius*. He is also a software and support engineer for Konica Minolta, where he specializes in working with Mac operating systems, applications, and hardware, as well as color and monochrome laser printers. He teaches classes on Mac usage, writes training and support materials for Konica Minolta, and is a Mac OS X beta tester for Apple. Dwight lives on the Gulf Coast of Alabama with his wife, Cindy, and their three beautiful children, Victoria, Devyn, and Emi. He studies theology, draws comic strips, and roots for the Auburn Tigers in his ever-decreasing spare time.

Credits

Executive Editor
Jody Lefevere

Project Editor
Sarah Cisco

Technical Editor
Brian Joseph

Copy Editor
Kim Heusel

Editorial Director
Robyn Siesky

Editorial Manager
Cricket Krengel

Vice President and Executive Group Publisher
Richard Swadley

Vice President and Executive Publisher
Barry Pruett

Business Manager
Amy Knies

Senior Marketing Manager
Sandy Smith

Project Coordinator
Patrick Redmond

Graphics and Production Specialists
Jennifer Henry
Andrea Hornberger

Quality Control Technician
Susan Moritz

Proofreading
Melissa D. Buddendeck

Indexing
Valerie Haynes Perry

To my wife, Cindy: I love you very much.
I told you marrying a geek would pay off!

Acknowledgments

Super thanks to super agent, Carole Jelen McClendon. I'm so glad I fell into your sphere!

Sincere appreciation goes to Cricket Krengel, Sarah Cisco, and Jody Lefevere, my editorial manager, project editor, and acquisitions editor, respectively. Thank you all for being so good to me from start to finish of this book.

Thanks and salutations go to my technical editor, Brian Joseph, for his expertise and keeping me honest.

Thank you to all the wonderful people who helped get this book from my Mac to the store shelves. You are too numerous to mention here, but I extend my heartfelt appreciation to each one of you for your hard work. You've all done a fantastic job!

I cannot forget to thank my kids, Victoria, Devyn, and Emi, who are so good to put up with Dad's absences when he's writing these tomes. Thanks as well to Mom, Dad, Kelli, Keith, Kelsey, Keaton, Kelen, and Kooper. I love you with all my heart!

Contents

chapter 2

chapter 3

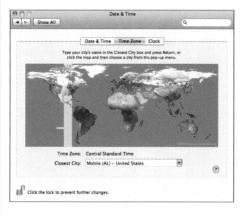

How Do I Manage User Accounts?   82

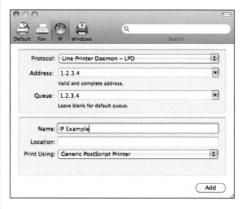

chapter 7

How Do I Work with PDFs and Images?   146

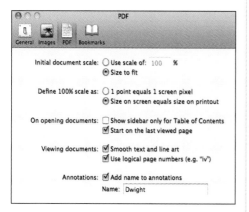

chapter 8

How Do I Organize My Life with iCal and Address Book?   160

chapter 9

How Do I Master the Web
with Safari?   190

chapter 10

How Do I Stay Connected
with Mail?   214

chapter 11

What Are iTunes' Coolest Features?   234

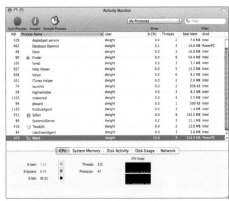

Introduction

Thank you, Apple! Once again you've raised the bar for your competitors and knocked the socks off the rest of us. Snow Leopard isn't only the best-looking operating system around, it's also the most functional and easy to use.

Some of you may be rolling your eyes right now; all computers use the file and folder concept and some sort of colorful user interface, so there couldn't be that much difference between Mac OS X and its competitors, right? Wrong! I don't just say this because of some blind devotion to all things Apple; I've actually used different flavors of Windows and Linux for more than 14 years, right alongside my trusty Mac, so experience has been my teacher. If I have any devotion to Apple, there are plenty of good reasons why, the subject of this book being the first.

Readers of this book who are already Mac users understand exactly what I'm talking about. For those of you moving from other computing platforms, it's my desire that by the end of this book you will have a whole new perspective on computing and see what it means to really have fun while working with your computer.

In *Mac OS X Snow Leopard Portable Genius* you learn much more than just basics; you learn the subtle nuances and little tips and tricks that make using your Mac that much easier. I've covered the gamut, from printing files, surfing the Internet, and using e-mail, to partitioning your hard drive, automating repetitive tasks, and using UNIX commands, with just a little bit of geeky humor thrown in for good measure.

I hope this book will do justice to Mac OS X Snow Leopard, which isn't just a computer operating system; it's an art form.

You are about to embark on the world's most advanced operating system experience, courtesy of Apple Inc. In this chapter, I show you how to get Mac OS X Snow Leopard up and running, as well as how to navigate Snow Leopard using the Finder application, which helps you find just about anything on your Mac.

System Requirements for Installing Snow Leopard

As anxious as you probably are to get started, make sure that your Mac meets all the necessary hardware requirements for properly installing and running Snow Leopard. Table 1.1 lists the requirements, which are straight from Apple.

Table 1.1 Requirements for Installing Snow Leopard

Requirement	Minimum Specifications
Processor	Intel processor
Memory	512MB of RAM just to get Snow Leopard up and going. 2GB is needed to run all the bells and whistles at a decent speed
Media	An internal, external, or shared DVD drive
Hard drive space	At least 9GB of free space

What's New in Snow Leopard?

A great deal of Snow Leopard's improvements to Mac OS X are under the hood. You won't notice too many differences cosmetically between Snow Leopard and its predecessor, Leopard. Let's check out some of Snow Leopard's more prominent goodies:

- **Greatly reduced footprint.** Snow Leopard requires considerably less hard drive space than previous versions of Mac OS X.

- **64-bit extension.** Apple has extended the capabilities of its 64-bit technology so that Mac OS X can now accommodate insane amounts of RAM (memory). As a matter of fact, theoretically your Mac could now support up to 16 terabytes of memory, which is about 500 times more than in Leopard (the previous version of Mac OS X).

- **Microsoft Exchange support.** Snow Leopard has built-in support for Microsoft Exchange 2007. This means that applications such as Mail, Address Book, and iCal can use the Exchange Web Services protocol to access your e-mails, contacts, and calendars.

- **Grand Central.** All new Macs have multicore processors, and now with a new set of technologies called Grand Central, your Mac can make full use of these processors by making the entire operating system multicore aware. If you're a regular guy like me, this means your Mac is going to speed up dramatically.

- **QuickTime X.** This is a brand-new iteration of what is already the best media platform on the Internet. Media playback and JavaScript are greatly improved, making Web applications zip along like never before.

Choosing an Installation Method

Only you can decide how to install Snow Leopard. Should you upgrade or wipe everything clean on your hard drive and start all over with a fresh OS install? Let's look at the options.

Upgrading from a previous version of the Mac OS has its advantages, to be sure:

- **There is no need to create new user accounts for every user.**
- **You don't have to reload all of your applications and documents.**
- **The Snow Leopard installer does all the difficult work, migrating user account information such as passwords, e-mail accounts, and Safari bookmarks.**

These are compelling reasons to simply upgrade and be done with it. However, there are also a couple of good reasons to wipe the drive clean and start fresh:

- **If you have Mac OS X 10.2 or earlier, you can't upgrade to Snow Leopard.** You must have 10.3 or 10.4.
- **If your Mac has been exhibiting some weird behavior lately, it is most likely system related.** It's best to start over if this is the case.
- **You may want to simply start over, especially if your Mac has become bloated with extraneous applications and documents that you've forgotten about or neglected to maintain.**

Weigh the six points I just listed and decide for yourself whether to upgrade or wipe the drive clean. If you choose to upgrade, simply continue on to the next section. Should you decide to wipe the drive clean and start fresh, skip to the "Custom Installations" section to get going quickly.

Upgrading to Snow Leopard

Let's get started with your upgrade to the newest feline from Apple. Follow these steps:

1. **Insert the Snow Leopard installation disc into your Mac.**
2. **When the disc mounts, the Mac OS X Install DVD automatically opens, as shown in figure 1.1.**

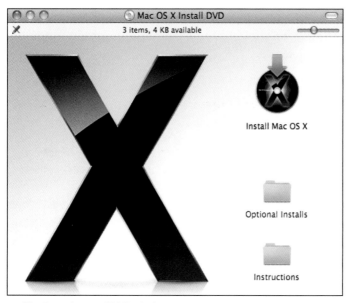

1.1 The Snow Leopard DVD window

3. **Double-click the Install Mac OS X icon.**

4. **Click Continue in the Install Mac OS X window.**

5. **Select the hard drive on which you want to install Snow Leopard.**

6. **Click Install in the Install Mac OS X window, as shown in figure 1.2.**

1.2 Click Install to begin the installation process.

7. **After your Mac reboots, select the language you want to use for the installation process and click the forward arrow.**

8. **Click Continue at the Welcome screen.**

9. **Agree to the software license agreement.**

10. **Choose the hard drive on which you want to install Snow Leopard and click Continue.**

11. **Click Install in the Install Summary window.**

12. **Sit back, get a cup of your favorite beverage, read the Welcome to Snow Leopard manual that came in the Mac OS X Snow Leopard retail box, and when the installation is finished, you will be fully Snow Leopardized!**

Caution If you are installing Snow Leopard on your startup disk, do not stop the installation process! If the process doesn't finish, you may not be able to start up from your hard drive. If you are installing on a laptop, make sure the power supply is connected before beginning the installation so that the process isn't stopped due to low battery power.

Custom Installations

Should you decide to completely start over with your Mac, you've come to the right section of this chapter. To "start over" means to completely install a fresh operating system and not upgrade over an existing one. Follow these steps:

Caution Back up your files before performing this kind of installation! Otherwise, you will lose all the data on your drive! If you don't back up, it's almost inevitable that after the process is complete, you will slap your forehead in disgust, realizing you just erased Grandma's recipes that have been passed down for generations.

1. **Insert the installation disc and reboot your Mac.**

2. **Immediately after the startup sound, hold down the C key to boot from the installation disc.** Continue to hold C until you see the gray Apple logo.

3. **Choose the language you want to use for the installation process and click the forward arrow.**

4. **Select the drive on which you want to install Snow Leopard.**

5. **Click Install to install the default system and files, or skip to step 6 and customize the installation.**

6. Click **Customize** to choose a particular set of files and alternative system resources.

7. Select the check boxes next to the applications and utilities that you want to include in the installation.

8. Click **OK** when you finish with the customization, and then click **Install**.

Advanced Installation Options

There are a couple of other things I want to show you that can help customize your Snow Leopard installation.

Partitioning your hard drive

If you have a large hard drive, you can partition it, meaning that you can divide the physical drive with software to make the drive appear and even operate as if it were multiple disks. This is advantageous if you plan to install Windows on your Mac using Boot Camp (see Chapter 16), using part of your drive for the OS and other parts for storing your documents and information, or if you want to install multiple versions of Mac OS X on one computer. Of course, there are many more reasons you would partition your drive, but you get the idea.

To partition your drive, follow these steps:

1. **Insert the installation disc into your Mac and restart the computer.**

2. **Immediately after you hear the startup sound, hold down the C key to boot from the installation disc.** Continue to hold the C key until you see the gray Apple logo on the screen.

3. **Select the language you want to use for the installation process and click the forward arrow.**

4. **Choose Utilities ⇨ Disk Utility from the menu.**

5. **Select the disk in the volume list on the left side of the Disk Utility window, as shown in figure 1.3.**

6. **Click the Partition tab in the window and then click the + button in the lower-left corner to begin adding partitions to the Volume Scheme.**

7. **Select a format for each partition using the Format menu.**

8. **You can resize each partition by typing a size into the Size box.**

9. **Click Apply when you are ready to partition the drive.**

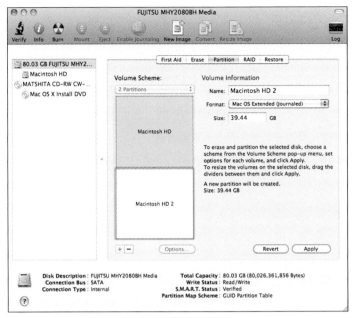

1.3 Partitioning a drive with Disk Utility is a breeze.

Installing the Xcode developer tools

The Snow Leopard installation disc comes with all the tools that application developers need to get started with programming for Mac OS X. These tools, called Xcode developer tools, can easily be installed from the Mac OS X Install DVD. They are found in the Optional Installs folder on the disc; the path to the installer is shown in figure 1.4.

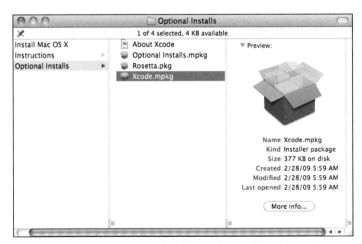

1.4 You have to search a little to find the Xcode installer on the DVD.

9

To install the Xcode developer tools, follow these steps:

1. **Double-click the Xcode.mpkg file to launch the installer and click Continue.**

2. **Click Continue again in the Software License Agreement window and then agree to the license agreement.**

3. **Select the hard drive on which Xcode will be installed and click Continue.**

4. **Choose the items you want to install and click Continue again.**

5. **Click Install in the Standard Install on "Macintosh HD" window to begin the installation (see figure 1.5).**

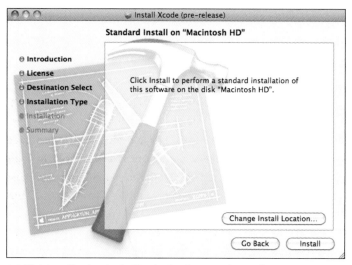

1.5 Click Install to begin the Xcode developer tools installer process.

Working with Finder

After your Mac has booted or when you first log in, take a look at that smiley-face guy grinning at you near the bottom-left corner of your screen. That's the Finder (see figure 1.6), and it's one of the most important items in all of Mac OS X Snow Leopard.

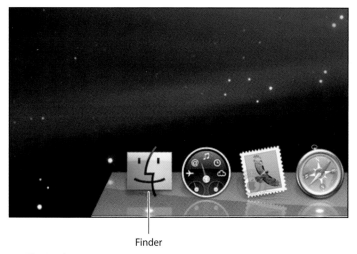

Finder

1.6 The Finder icon

The Finder is an application that always runs in Snow Leopard, and it has been a part of the Mac OS since its inception. The Finder is what Mac fans have used for decades to browse their computers' drives and discs, and it has evolved into a great tool that I can't imagine not having (especially as you can't view the contents of your hard drive without it!). For the Windows converts in the audience, think of the Finder as the Mac OS X equivalent to Windows Explorer. In this section, I show you how to use the Finder's basic features, and I also give you tips that I've learned to make the Finder even easier and more productive to use.

The Snow Leopard Desktop at a glance

The Desktop is what you see when you first start up or log in to your Mac; this area is where all the action in your applications takes place. The Desktop is a major part, and is actually the starting point, of the Finder.

Desktop

Figure 1.7 should mirror your own Mac's screen very closely after you log in; it shows the major parts that you see when the Finder first comes up.

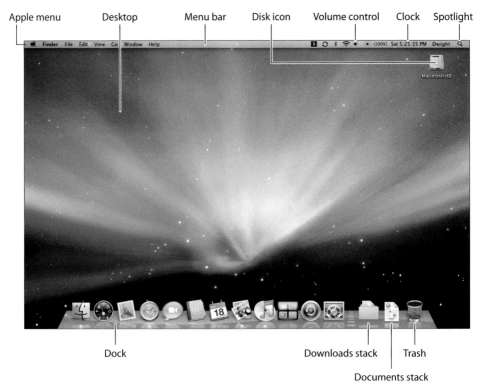

1.7 The Finder's Desktop, in all its default glory

Now that you know the names of the items you see in the Finder, you can use Table 1.2 to decipher what functionality they provide.

Table 1.2 Finder Items

Item	Function
Apple menu	Provides quick access to functions such as Sleep, Restart, Shut Down, Recent Items, and System Preferences. Windows users will find that it functions similarly to the Start menu that they are used to.
Menu bar	Use the menu bar in the Finder and in other applications to print, copy and paste, and change application preferences.
Desktop	Functions like the desktop on your desk; it's where everything else (such as documents and applications) sits while you are working on it. You can easily change the Desktop picture; see Chapter 2 for more details.
Volume control	Adjusts your Mac's volume.
Clock	Displays the current date and time.
Spotlight	Searches your Mac for files and folders. More on this later in the chapter.

Item	Function
Disk icon	The Macintosh HD icon shown in figure 1.7 is my hard drive's icon, but if you have more than one drive on your Mac, you will also see them here.
Dock	Houses icons that link to applications and other items that you use most frequently. You can modify the Dock, as you'll see later in this chapter.
Trash	Contains files and folders that you want to remove from your Mac. Former Windows users will find it similar to the Recycle Bin.
Downloads stack	Provides fast access to items in your Home folder's Downloads folder.
Documents stack	Provides fast access to items in your Home folder's Documents folder.

Finder windows

Now that you are more familiar with the features of the Desktop, let's examine a Finder window, which is the mechanism you will need to view files and folders on your disks. Figure 1.8 shows a default Finder window, and Table 1.3 gives a brief breakdown of each noteworthy item.

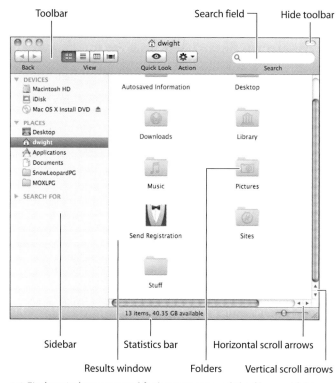

1.8 Finder windows are used for browsing your disks, files, and folders.

Table 1.3 Finder Window Components

Component	Description
Folders	Used to store files and other subfolders.
Toolbar	Contains tools for accessing files and folders.
Sidebar	Provides quick links to disks, favorite folders, shared folders, and preconfigured searches.
Statistics bar	Displays information about the current folder.
Hide toolbar	Click to hide the toolbar and sidebar from view; click again to bring the button toolbar and side bar back.
Search field	Type a search term to look for the item in the current folder.
Results window	Shows the files and subfolders that reside in a folder, and also displays search results.
Vertical/Horizontal arrows	Drag the bars or click the arrows to navigate to areas of a window that has scroll bars and are hidden from view.

Setting the Finder preferences

As you'll notice throughout this book, you can modify most things in Snow Leopard to match your personal preferences and tastes (to one degree or another), and that's the way I like it. The Finder is no exception to this rule (see Chapter 2 for a lot of Finder customization tips), giving you access to its preferences by choosing Finder ⇨ Preferences, or by pressing ⌘+,. Let's take a look at the preferences that the Finder allows you to control.

General

The options listed in the General tab of the Finder Preferences window (as shown in Figure 1.9) are fairly self-explanatory, with the exception of spring-loaded folders and windows, which are so cool that they get their own sidebar. The other three options allow you to do the following:

- **Show certain types of items on the Desktop.**

- **Choose which folder automatically opens when you open a new Finder window.**

- **Decide whether to always open folders in new (separate) windows.** I do not recommend that you use this feature unless you are someone who just can't get enough open windows on his or her Desktop.

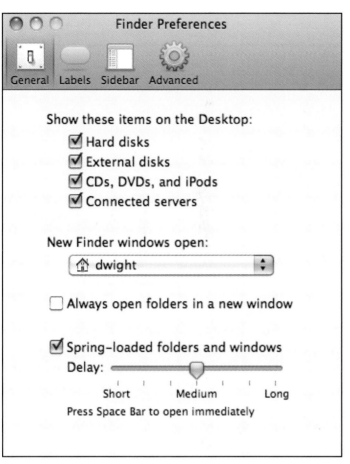

1.9 Options available in the General tab

Spring-Loaded Folders and Windows

Spring-loaded folders and windows are a neat feature of the Finder but are foreign to many Mac users, especially the new recruits, so I'll take a minute to mention them separately. Enabling spring-loaded folders and windows lets you move items between folders and disks with minimal effort. With this feature enabled, you can drag an item over any folder, hold it there for just a split second, and the folder automatically opens. Continue to hold down the mouse button while you position the item over each subfolder, and they will all behave accordingly, automatically opening and allowing you to drill down into the subfolders as far as you need to. Finally, drop the item into the folder you want to move it to by letting go of the mouse button. Reading a description of this feature can be pretty boring, so give it a try on your own so that you can master this nifty little trick.

Labels and Sidebar

The Labels tab of the Finder Preferences window allows you to assign colored labels to categories that you determine. You can then assign these labels to files and folders by right-clicking them (or Ctrl+clicking if you don't have a two-button mouse), and then selecting a label from the list, as shown in figure 1.10.

The Sidebar tab of the Finder Preferences window simply lets you choose which types of items to display in the Sidebar of every Finder window.

Advanced

Table 1.4 explains the options that are available in the Advanced tab of the Finder Preferences window.

Open

Move to Trash

Get Info
Compress "Important Stuff"
Burn "Important Stuff" to Disc...
Duplicate
Make Alias
Quick Look "Important Stuff"

Copy "Important Stuff"

Label:
× ▪ ▪ ▪ ▪ ▪ ▪
"Big Time Important"

Convert Selected Simplified Chinese File
Convert Selected Traditional Chinese File
Send File

1.10 Assigning a label to a folder

Table 1.4 Advanced Tab Options

Option	Function
Show all file extensions	Each file has an extension on the end of its name that is hidden by default. This extension helps Snow Leopard know what type of document the file is, and what application it is associated with. Unless you understand these extensions, it is best to leave this option deselected.
Show warning before changing an extension	Snow Leopard warns you that you are about to change the extension of a file. This warning is beneficial so that you won't accidentally change an extension, which could cause your document to open in a different application than intended, or not open at all.
Show warning before emptying the Trash	Snow Leopard prompts you to confirm that you mean to empty the Trash before allowing you to do so.
Empty Trash securely	Select this option to make certain that all traces of a file are removed from the hard drive when you empty the Trash. This is a feature security nuts will love, but it prevents you from ever recovering any files you may have accidentally deleted. Use this option with caution.
When performing a search	Determine the default location for searches by selecting an option from this pop-up menu.

Genius You can securely empty the Trash on a case-by-case basis instead of enabling it all the time. To do so, place the item you want to permanently delete in the Trash, and then choose Finder ⇨ Secure Empty Trash.

Moving around in the Finder

Mac OS X employs the same basic navigation techniques as any other graphical operating system, such as double-clicking to open files and folders, right-clicking (or Ctrl+clicking) items to see contextual menus that can alter or perform an action on an item (like the Labels example you saw earlier in this chapter), and clicking and dragging items to move them to and fro. I'm sure you're all experienced at the basics of mouse operations, so I'll move on to more Finder-centric tasks and options.

Finder viewing options

You can change the way files and folders are displayed in Finder windows by choosing one of the four View options in the toolbar — icons, list, columns, and cover flow. Let's look at how each option displays the contents of the same folder so that you can see the clear differences between each view.

Icons

Icons view shows each file and folder as large icons in the window, as shown in figure 1.11.

1.11 A folder as seen in Icons view

Genius Are the default icons too large or small for your liking? Click and drag the Icon size slider in the lower-right corner of the Finder window to enlarge or reduce the icon sizes in the current folder.

17

Quickly Open Commonly Used Folders

I can't speak for other Mac users, but the Finder menu that I most wish I had discovered years ago is the Go menu, which you see in the menu bar when Finder is active. The Go menu gives you instant access to the most commonly used folders in Snow Leopard, but for some reason I overlooked it for most of the eight-plus years I've used Mac OS X. Click the Go menu to quickly go to the Applications folder, the Utilities folder, your Network, and more.

Better yet, familiarize yourself with the keyboard shortcuts that are used to access those items (the keyboard shortcuts are listed to the right of each command in the Go menu). If an item you want to jump to isn't in the Go menu, press ⌘+Shift+G to open the Go to Folder window, then type the path of the folder you want, and click the Go button to jump over to it.

List

List view does just what it says: It displays the files and folders in a list. You can arrange the list by filenames, the date the files were modified, the size of the file or folder, and the kind of item it is.

Columns

My personal favorite is Columns view. This view arranges the contents of a folder into columns, with each column displaying the contents of the subsequent folder.

Cover Flow

Cover Flow is hands-down the coolest viewing option at your disposal. Figure 1.12 shows that the files and folders are displayed as they really appear when opened in an application, which can be a great help when searching for a particular document or picture.

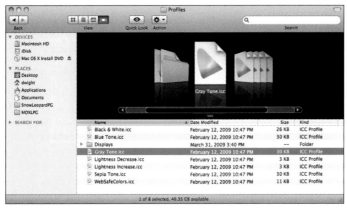

1.12 Cover Flow is really neat to use. Click and drag the slider back and forth to see how effortlessly the Finder zooms through the files in the folder.

Getting Information on Files and Folders

You can never have too much information, and Mac OS X is more than happy to provide you with what you need to know about your computer's files and folders. To find out what there is to know about an item, follow these steps:

1. **Click (once) the file or folder you want information about.**

2. **Press ⌘+I, or choose File ⇨ Get Info.**

Figure 1.13 shows you a typical Get Info window, and Table 1.5 explains the categories that are available in the window.

To quickly get information on multiple items without having to open separate Get Info windows for each one, you can use the Inspector, which is a floating version of the Get Info window. To do this

1. **Open a folder that contains the items you want to see information about.**

2. **Press ⌘+Option+I to open the Inspector window (it looks just like a standard Get Info window).**

3. **Click each file in the folder to see its information in the Inspector window.** The Inspector changes information for each file you select. You can move between files by using the arrow keys on the keyboard.

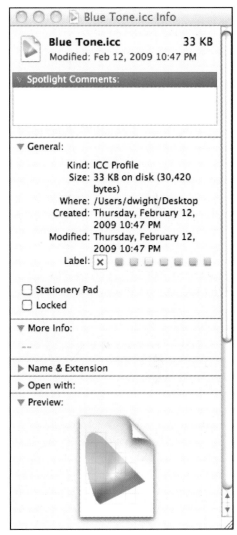

1.13 A Get Info window with most of the categories expanded

19

Table 1.5 Information Categories

Category	Information displayed
Spotlight Comments	Type information about the file that will help you find it using a Spotlight search. More on this later in the chapter.
General	Tells you information such as what kind of item you're viewing, its size, where it's located, and when it was created and/or modified.
More Info	The additional information shown here will vary, depending on the type of item this is. For example, for the folder in figure 1.13, you can see when the folder was last opened. If the file were an image, you might see its dimensions and color space.
Name & Extension	Allows you to change the name and extension of the file, and to hide the extension.
Open with	Select the default application that you want to open this type of file with. This option only displays when getting info about a file.
Preview	Shows a small thumbnail version of the file.
Sharing & Permissions	Allows you to change access permissions for the item. Click the lock icon in the bottom-right corner to change the permissions. Click the + or – buttons to add or remove users from the permissions list.

Using Quick Look

Quick Look is one of the best features in Snow Leopard. It allows you to see the contents of a file without actually opening it in its native application. For example, you can see every page of a Word document without having to open Word itself. This makes it really easy to find a document if you've forgotten its name but know the content that you're looking for, or when you're looking for just the right image but don't want to have to wait for Photoshop to load. To use Quick Look, follow these steps:

1. **Find the file you want to view and click it once to highlight it.**

2. **Click the Quick Look button or press the space bar to open the file in Quick Look view, an example of which is given in figure 1.14.**

3. **To see the item in Full Screen mode, click the arrows at the bottom of the window.** To exit Full Screen mode, click the arrows again.

4. **Close the Quick Look window by clicking the X in the upper-left corner.**

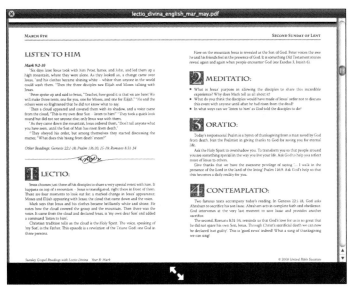

1.14 A document previewed using Quick Look

Working with Removable Media

When you insert or connect removable media, such as CDs, DVDs, external hard drives, and USB flash drives, Snow Leopard automatically mounts them, making them immediately available for use. The media's icon appears on your Desktop, in a Finder window, or both, depending on how you have configured your Finder preferences. Figure 1.15 shows a flash drive (Kingston) and a DVD (Mac OS X Install DVD) on both the Desktop and in the Sidebar of the Finder window under Devices. Double-click the icon to see the media's contents, just as you would any other hard drive or folder.

Perform one of the following steps to disconnect or eject removable media:

- **Click the Eject icon to the right of the media icon in the Sidebar of the Finder window.**

- **Click and drag the media icon from the Desktop and drop it on the Trash icon in the Dock.**

- **Right-click or Ctrl+click the media icon on the Desktop or in the Sidebar, and then select Eject from the contextual menu.**

- **Click the icon for the media once to highlight it and press ⌘+E.**

Eject icon

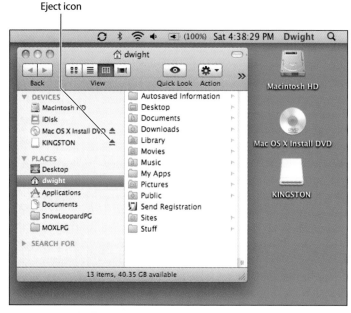

1.15 A DVD and a flash drive as they appear on the Desktop and in the Sidebar of the Finder window

Utilizing the Dock

Ah, the Dock: loved by most, tolerated by some, and loathed by a few. Regardless of how you feel about the Dock (personally, I can't imagine working without it), it is an integral part of your Snow Leopard experience. The Dock is where you keep aliases (or shortcuts) to applications, utilities, and folders that you use or access more frequently than others. It also displays icons for all your currently running applications, and even some processes, like print jobs. Currently running applications have a bright dot underneath their icons.

The Dock is divided into two sections by a divider line. Applications and utilities reside on the left side of the divider line, while folders reside on the right with the Trash icon. Right-click, or Ctrl+click, the divider line to see display options for the Dock.

Adding and removing items

You can add and remove items to and from the Dock as you please, and it's really easy to do:

- **To add an item to the Dock, simply click and drag its icon to the Dock and drop it in where you want it to go.** You can reposition an item in the Dock by simply dragging and dropping it to its new location.

- **If you have an application open that you want to keep in the Dock, click and hold its icon (as shown in figure 1.16), and select Keep in Dock from the contextual menu that appears.**

- **To remove an item, click and drag its icon from the Dock and let go of the mouse button.** The icon disappears in a puff of smoke! Don't worry: the original item is still in its location; you've only removed the alias (shortcut) for the item.

1.16 Keep an icon in the Dock if you need to use it often.

Setting the Dock's preferences

You can tame the Dock by setting its preferences to meet your needs. Open the Dock's preferences by right-clicking, or Ctrl+clicking, the divider line, and select Dock Preferences.

The Dock preferences window lets you make several changes:

- **Increase or decrease the size of the Dock by moving the Size slider.**

- **If your icons are too small to see clearly, select the Magnification check box and adjust the slider to increase or decrease the amount of magnification.**

- **The Dock can be positioned on the left or right side of the window, or at the bottom, which is its default setting.**

- **The Minimize using option lets you choose the special effect that occurs when you minimize a window into the Dock.** To minimize a window, click the yellow button in its upper-left corner.

- **Select the Animate opening applications check box to cause the icon of an item you are opening to bounce up and down in the Dock.** I leave this option deselected; the bouncing annoys the heck out of me.

- **If you don't like the Dock cramping your style — or your Desktop space, for that matter — you can hide it from view by selecting the check box next to Automatically hide and show the Dock.** When you inevitably have to use the Dock again, hold your mouse pointer at the very bottom of your window for just a second, and the Dock temporarily pops back up into view, only to go back into hiding when you're finished.

Searching for Items

Apple introduced Spotlight in Mac OS X Tiger and instantly changed the way Mac users look for items on their computers. Spotlight finds things on your Mac much faster than you or I could if we were poking around every file and folder, and it's the quickest way to find things that I've ever seen on a computer.

When you first log in to your Mac, OS X creates an index of every file and folder it contains; Snow Leopard knows everything there is to know about every single thing that occupies your Mac's space, whether the item is visible or invisible. Snow Leopard stores this information, or metadata, and Spotlight uses the information, along with filenames and content, to find what you are looking for. Every time you add or remove an item, or add or remove something within that item (like text within a document), Snow Leopard updates its index files, thereby keeping all your searches up-to-the-minute accurate.

You might think that with all this information to look through a search could take forever, but that's not the case at all. Spotlight can find items containing your search words almost as quickly as you can type them.

Searching with Spotlight

Chances are good that no matter how long it's been since you've seen the file you're looking for, Spotlight can dig it up for you again. Let's see how to use this amazing feature:

1. **Click the Spotlight icon (the magnifying glass) in the upper-right corner of your Mac's window to reveal the Search text field, as shown in figure 1.17.**

1.17 Type your search words into Spotlight.

2. **Type your search criteria in the text field.** Some applications have Spotlight Search fields in their toolbars, which you can use to type search words when specifically searching for items within that application (for example, when searching for an e-mail within Mail).

3. **Spotlight immediately begins searching your Mac and displays the information it finds that matches the criteria you typed in step 2.**

4. **Scan the list to find the item you are specifically looking for and then click to open it in its default application.** Spotlight only shows the top matches in each category; in order to see all the matches click Show All at the top of the list.

Genius

Did you notice that Spotlight isn't just showing you items such as documents and folders that contain your search words? Spotlight literally searches every file on your Mac for your search criteria, including e-mails, Web pages you've visited, contacts, music, movies, images, and PDF files. Spotlight can even search other Macs on your network that you have connected to if they have file sharing enabled.

Setting Spotlight preferences

You can easily modify Spotlight to search where and how you want it to, using its preferences. Choose Apple menu ⇨ System Preferences, and then click the Spotlight icon in the Personal section to access the Spotlight preferences pane, as shown in figure 1.18.

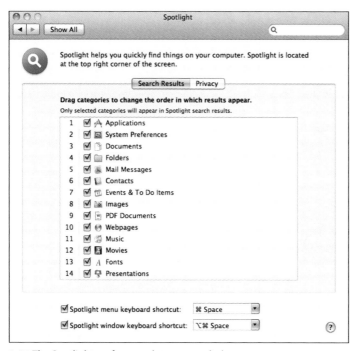

1.18 The Spotlight preferences let you search the way you want.

Figure 1.18 shows the Search Results section of the preferences pane. This section lists the categories of files that appear in the search results window. Select the check box next to those categories you want Spotlight to search, and deselect those you want it to leave alone.

25

For example, if you don't want Spotlight to check your e-mail when performing a search, simply deselect the Mail Messages check box. You can also click and drag the categories into the order you prefer the results to be displayed in.

Click the Privacy tab at the top of the preferences pane to reveal the Privacy list. This section allows you to specify directories (folders) on your Mac that you want to exclude from any searches.

To modify the Privacy list, follow these steps:

1. **Click the + button under the bottom-left corner of the list.**

2. **Browse your Mac for the folder you want to exclude from searches, highlight the folder, and then click Choose.** The folder is now shown in the Privacy list.

3. **You can remove a folder from the list by highlighting it and then clicking the – button under the bottom-left corner of the list.**

The two check boxes at the bottom of the preferences pane allow you to enable Spotlight keyboard shortcuts for opening a Spotlight menu or window with the stroke of a couple of keys, as shown in Table 1.6. You can also select which keys perform these functions by selecting a key combination from the pop-up menus associated with each one.

Table 1.6 Spotlight Keyboard Shortcuts

Function	Keys
Open the Spotlight menu	⌘+space bar
Open the Spotlight (Finder) window	⌘+Option+space bar
Open the top search result	⌘+Return
Jump to the first item in the next heading	⌘+Down arrow
Jump to the first item in the prior heading	⌘+Up arrow
Jump to the first item in the menu	Ctrl+Up arrow
Jump to the last item in the menu	Ctrl+Down arrow
Show an item in the Finder	Click the item while holding down ⌘

Searching with the Spotlight menu is certainly fast and easy, but it doesn't always yield the best results, as it may give you so many results that you could never realistically search them all in a reasonable amount of time. To remedy this situation, Spotlight brings in your trusty friend, the Finder.

Searching within a Finder window

The Finder gives you much more leverage to enhance your search beyond the Spotlight menu's capabilities.

To perform a basic Spotlight search within a Finder window, follow these steps:

1. **Open a Finder window by pressing ⌘+N while the Finder is activated (click the Finder icon on the left side of the Dock if the Finder isn't the activated, or foremost, application).**

2. **Browse your Mac for the folder that you know includes the files you are looking for or through, and click the folder to highlight it.**

3. **Type the search criteria into the Search text field in the upper-right corner of the Finder window, and you see your results displayed in the Finder.**

Any search utility worth using will allow a lot of flexibility to narrow searches, and Spotlight is as flexible as they come.

Figure 1.19 shows a Finder search window that has been assigned several search attributes, which act as filters for your search results. These attributes allow you to specify the type of file you want, when it was last modified, whether the file is visible or not, and many, many other attribute types.

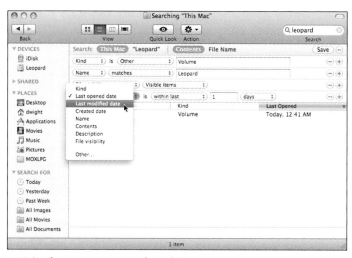

1.19 Attributes narrow a search in a big way.

To add attributes to a search, follow these steps:

1. **Click the + button next to the Save button in the upper-right area of the Finder window to add the first attribute.**

2. **Choose the type of attribute to use by clicking the pop-up menu, as shown in figure 1.19.** There are many more attributes preconfigured by Apple that you can access by choosing Other from the attribute list. You can also add other conditions (specifically, the "All, Any, or None of the following are true" criteria) to the search by holding down the Option button while clicking the + button. Also, some attributes have several pop-up menus that you can change to customize it.

3. **Make any setting changes to the attribute to narrow your search.**

4. **Your new filtered search results are displayed almost instantly after you add an attribute.**

5. **Continue to add as many attributes as necessary, or remove attributes by clicking the – buttons to their far right.**

Genius

Use Boolean operators such as AND, OR, and NOT to logically narrow your search. You may also use quotes around text to specify that the words in the quotes must be found in exactly the order you typed them.

Managing Windows with Exposé

Exposé is a great feature for helping to clear up the jumbled mess of windows that can grind your productivity to a halt. Exposé arranges your windows in one of three ways using three of the function keys at the top of your keyboard: F9, F10, and F11.

Manipulating open windows

Press F9 to arrange the open windows so that they can all be seen, as shown in figure 1.20. Move the mouse pointer over the windows to see what applications they belong to. Click the window you want to bring to the forefront, or press F9 to return to the Finder's previous state.

The F10 key brings all the open windows for the current application to the forefront. A press of the F11 key causes all open windows to scram out of the way so that you can see the Desktop. To return the windows to their previous position, press either F10 or F11, depending on which one you used to move the windows.

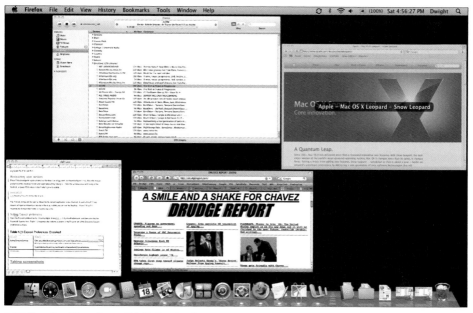

1.20 Pressing F9 performs this little miracle.

Setting Exposé preferences

Open the Exposé preferences by choosing Apple menu ⇨ System Preferences, and then selecting the Exposé & Spaces icon. Table 1.7 explains the options available in the Exposé tab of the Exposé & Spaces preferences window.

Table 1.7 Exposé Preferences Explained

Section	Options
Active Screen Corners	Click any of the four pop-up menus to choose what actions Snow Leopard takes when you move your mouse pointer to a corner of your screen.
Exposé	Customize the keys or key combinations that perform Exposé actions.
Dashboard	Choose which function key will cause Dashboard to open and close.

Taking Screenshots

At some point during your Mac adventure you may need to take a shot of your screen so that you can share information about your system with someone else, or to take a quick snap of some settings you've made; the reasons for taking a screenshot are many. You can take screenshots manually with just a couple of key presses, or you can take a little more control over the shots using the Grab utility that ships as part of Snow Leopard.

Capture screenshots manually

The quick and easy way to take screenshots is to incorporate a little manual dexterity:

● **Take a shot of the entire screen by pressing ⌘+Shift+3.**

● **Narrow the scope of your shot by pressing ⌘+Shift+4.** This maneuver turns your cursor into a crosshair. Drag the crosshair over the section of your screen that you want to take the shot of. As soon as you let go of the mouse or trackpad button a screenshot will be taken of the area you highlighted.

Genius

You can also take a shot of an individual window. Press ⌘+Shift+4 again, but don't drag the crosshair. Instead, press the spacebar and the crosshair changes to a camera! Position the camera over the window you want the shot of and click your mouse or trackpad button.

Using Grab to capture screenshots

Grab is a utility that helps you take screenshots that include various types of mouse pointers, take timed screenshots, and more. Grab can be found in the /Applications/ Utilities folder. Double-click to open Grab, and use the Capture menu to choose the type of screen capture to perform.

Grab's preferences, shown in figure 1.21, let you choose from a variety of mouse pointers.

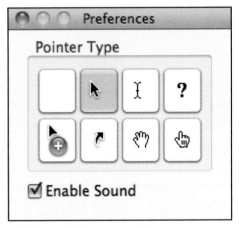

1.21 Select which mouse pointer to use depending on the task you will perform during the screenshot.

Using Multiple Desktops with Spaces

Spaces is an addition to Mac OS X. It is an organizational tool that lets you create multiple spaces for certain tasks. Spaces are essentially additional desktops. You could have a space for surfing the Web and checking e-mail, another space to watch your stocks, a third space to work on a spreadsheet, and so on.

Setting Spaces preferences

Choose Apple menu⇨System Preferences, and then click the Exposé & Spaces icon. Click the Spaces tab to see the Spaces preferences, as shown in figure 1.22.

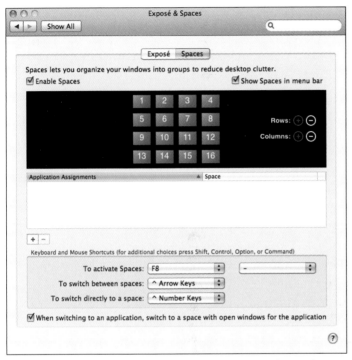

1.22 Spaces preferences allow you to alter how the Spaces feature functions.

To use the Spaces feature, you must enable it by selecting the Enable Spaces check box in the preferences window.

Adding and removing spaces

You can have as many as 16 spaces at any one time. There's nothing magical about adding or removing spaces: Just click the + or – buttons next to the Rows and Columns options, as shown in figure 1.22.

Moving between spaces

There are a few ways to jump from space to space:

1. **Press F8 and click the space to which you want to move, as shown in figure 1.23.**

2. **Select the Show Spaces in menu bar check box in the Spaces preferences (as shown in figure 1.22).** Click the Spaces icon (it looks like four small boxes with a number super-imposed over them) in the menu bar and choose the number of the space to which you want to jump.

3. **To scroll through the spaces, hold down the Control key and press one of the arrow keys.**

Genius

The easiest method for moving between spaces is to simultaneously press the Control key and the number key that corresponds to the space you want to navigate to.

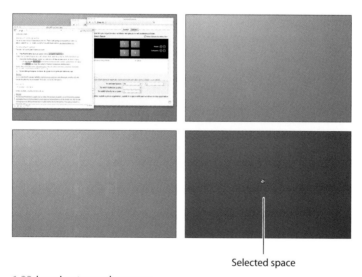

Selected space

1.23 Jumping to another space

Genius

To quickly move windows from one space to another, press F8 and then click and drag a window from its current space and drop it onto the desired one. You can also rearrange spaces by clicking the blue area of a space and moving it to the location of the space you want it to trade places with.

Assigning applications to spaces

One feature I love in Spaces is the ability to assign applications to always open in a specific space.

To assign applications to spaces, follow these steps:

1. **Click the + button under the Application Assignments window in the Spaces tab of the Exposé & Spaces preferences.**

2. **Browse your hard drive for the applications or utilities you want to assign, select them, and click the Add button.**

3. **You can change the space that an application opens in by clicking the space selection column for that application, as shown in figure 1.24.**

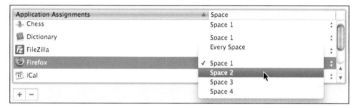

1.24 Choose the space in which your applications are assigned to open.

Can I Customize Snow Leopard?

As attractive as Snow Leopard's spots already are, it's always fun to customize the appearance and functionality of your Mac to match your personality and preferences. Customizing your Mac makes for a more enjoyable work and play environment, just as you get more enjoyment from your home once you've decorated it to your tastes. One of the slickest ways that Snow Leopard lets you customize your Mac experience is Dashboard and its widgets. These miniature applications are designed for your convenience and can do a multitude of things, such as stay up to speed with the weather or flight information. This chapter explores the numerous ways you can tweak Snow Leopard so that you feel as comfortable in front of your computer as you do when sitting in your living room.

The Appearance Preferences Pane

The Appearance preferences pane, shown in figure 2.1, is your first stop on the Mac customization tour. This Appearance pane allows you to modify basic color and textual elements of your Finder windows. To open this pane, click the System Preferences icon in the Dock, or choose Apple menu⇨System Preferences. Then click the Appearance icon in the Personal category of the System Preferences window.

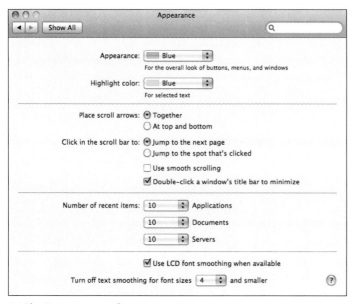

2.1 The Appearance preferences pane

Color modifications

The Appearance menu lets you choose the color you prefer for your systemwide menus and buttons. I hope either blue or graphite suits your taste because those are your only options.

You can change the default color used to highlight text with the Highlight color menu. Thankfully there's a lengthy list of color choices that are available to you here.

Scrolling options

The options shown in Table 2.1 allow you to control how your Mac scrolls through documents or Web pages that are too large to fit onto the screen in their entirety.

Table 2.1 Scrolling Options

Option	Description
Place scroll arrows	Scroll arrows, like those in figure 2.2, can be placed together at the bottom of the scroll bar, or separately, with an arrow on each end of the scroll bar.
	My personal preference is to keep them together because this placement keeps me from having to move my mouse very much.
Click in the scroll bar to	This lets your Mac know how it should behave when you click inside the scroll bar.
	Select the Jump to the next page option to cause each click in the scroll bar to advance you one page-length in the document.
	The Jump to the spot that's clicked option moves you to the spot in the document that you are clicking; if you click the top of the scroll bar, then you jump to the first page of the document.
Use smooth scrolling	Scroll through your documents or Web pages smoothly instead of jumping from page to page.
Double-click a window's title bar to minimize	Select this check box to cause windows to minimize to the Dock when you double-click their title bar.

Genius

You can switch between the Jump to the next page and Jump to the spot that's clicked options by holding down the Option key while clicking in the scroll bar.

Accessing recently used items

A very handy way to see and quickly access applications, documents, and servers that you've used in the recent past is by clicking the Apple menu and holding your mouse over Recent Items, as shown in figure 2.3. The Number of Recent Items pop-up menus in the Appearance preferences pane let you choose how many of each item type you want to list.

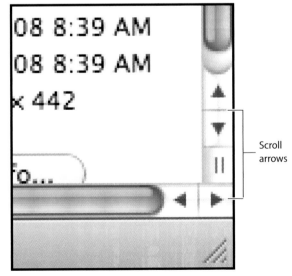

2.2 Scroll arrows grouped together in the scroll bar

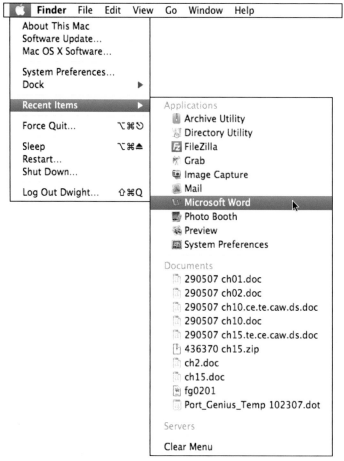

2.3 Looking at items that you've recently used

Viewing fonts

Mac OS X uses a technique called anti-aliasing, or font smoothing, to help fonts appear without jagged edges.

There are several font-smoothing methods employed by Mac OS X; each one is designed to improve how fonts look on different display types. Select the style that you prefer from the Font smoothing style pop-up menu.

The only possible downside to font smoothing is that some fonts may appear fuzzy. Smaller font sizes can be almost impossible to read, and so the Appearance pane offers the option to turn off font smoothing for fonts smaller than the size you choose at the bottom of the pane.

Changing the Desktop

No two things personalize your Mac quite like great desktop pictures and really cool screen savers. From photos of the kids to fantastic paintings of faraway space battles, or from extreme close-ups of beautiful flowers to a constant-streaming news feed, desktop pictures and screen savers can be very personal displays of individual tastes and styles.

Choosing a desktop picture

Open System Preferences by clicking its icon in the Dock or by choosing Apple menu⇨ System Preferences. Click the Desktop & Screen Saver icon in the Personal category, and then click the Desktop tab at the top of the pane.

The left side of the Desktop tab, shown in figure 2.4, lists the desktop pictures available on your system. Apple has taken the liberty of supplying you with a lot of different pictures and has even arranged them into subject folders.

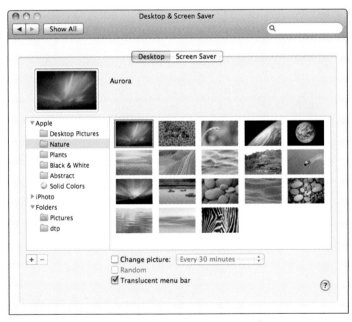

2.4 The Desktop tab of the Desktop & Screen Saver preferences pane

You can also add your personal collection of desktop pictures to this list by following these steps:

1. **Click the + button below the list.**
2. **Browse your Mac's hard drive for the folder that contains the desktop pictures you want to use.**
3. **Click Choose.**

To remove folders from the list, simply highlight the folder to be removed, and then click the − button below the list.

Browse the list for the desktop picture you want to use, and just click it once to set it as your Mac's default desktop picture.

Should you get quickly bored with your choice of desktop picture or if it's just too hard to decide which one you like best, select the Change picture check box at the bottom of the pane. Use the pop-up menu next to this check box to determine how often you want your Mac to change its desktop background. To add even more spice to your desktop selection, select the Random order check box, which allows your Mac to use its own discretion when choosing a desktop picture.

Selecting a screen saver

Screen savers look really great on your Mac's screen and they are somewhat useful for security purposes, but if not for these factors, screen savers would be obsolete in today's computing world. At one time, screen savers were a necessary tool that prevented burn-in from occurring on CRT-based monitors. New monitors are typically LCD or plasma, and burn-in just isn't a concern any longer.

Finding Desktop Pictures on the Web

The Internet is chock-full of great Websites for downloading desktop pictures. You can find a desktop picture to suit just about any mood or taste by performing a search on Google for the terms "desktop picture" or "wallpaper." If you want to find Mac-specific desktop pictures, simply add "Mac OS X" or "Mac" to your search criteria.

Here are a few sites you may want to check out:

- **www.macdesktops.com**
- **www.theapplecollection.com/desktop/**

- **http://interfacelift.com/wallpaper**
- **www.pixelgirlpresents.com/desktops.php**
- **http://browse.deviantart.com/customization/wallpaper/**

Genius

Mac OS X comes loaded with several really neat screen savers, but because there are plenty of screen savers that can be downloaded from the Web, you can personalize to your heart's content. Open Safari and search for "Mac OS X screen savers" on Google to find more screen savers than you can shake a stick at.

To choose a screen saver that meets your personal standards of coolness, do the following:

1. **Open the Desktop & Screen Saver pane in System Preferences (Apple menu ⇨ System Preferences ⇨ Desktop & Screen Saver), and click the Screen Saver tab.**
2. **Browse the list of screen savers on the left side of the pane and find the one that grabs your attention.**
3. **Click Test to see the screen saver as it will look when engaged during normal use.** Move the mouse or press any key on your keyboard to exit the test.
4. **To let Mac OS X choose the screen saver it uses, select the Use random screen saver check box.**
5. **Select the Show with clock check box if you want a digital clock to be displayed on-screen with the screen saver.**
6. **Click and drag the Start screen saver slider to set the amount of time that your Mac is idle before the screen saver starts.**
7. **Close the System Preferences after you finalize your selection.**

Set the screen saver's options

Some screen savers allow you to change the way they behave by supplying an Options button underneath the Preview window, as shown in figure 2.5. Click Options to make adjustments to the look and feel of the chosen screen saver.

Take the Flurry screen saver as an example; select it from the screen saver list on the left of the pane. Click Options to see the options that are specific to your selected screen saver.

Usually options for screen savers are very straightforward. Choose an option from the Color pop-up menu to change the color of the streams and move the sliders to change the number of streams, the thickness of the streams, and the speed at which the streams move.

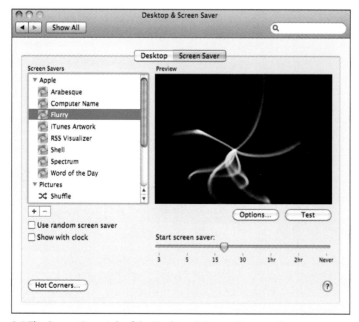

2.5 The Screen Saver tab of the Desktop & Screen Saver preferences pane

Using hot corners

Have you noticed the Hot Corners button in the bottom-left corner of the pane? Click that button to see the Hot Corners preferences sheet, similar to the one in figure 2.6. Hot corners allow you to set actions for your Mac to take when you move the mouse pointer to one of the four corners of your screen.

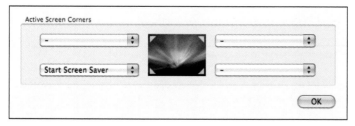

2.6 The Hot Corners preferences sheet, also known as Active Screen Corners

Click one of the four pop-up menus to select an action for the corresponding screen corner. Table 2.2 lists actions that you can use for hot corners.

Table 2.2 Hot Corner Actions

Action	Result
Start Screen Saver and Disable Screen Saver	These two options speak quite clearly for themselves.
All Windows	All open windows are arranged in the screen so that they can all be seen. This is the same function that Exposé performs with the F9 key, as described in Chapter 1.
Application Windows	All open windows for the currently active application are neatly arranged so that each of their contents can be displayed at once. This is also achieved with the F10 key and Exposé, as discussed in Chapter 1.
Desktop	This is yet another feature of Exposé (using the F11 key), which causes all open windows to zoom off the screen so the desktop can be clearly seen. On current keyboards, this feature is mapped to ⌘+F3; on laptops, it's Fn+F11.
Dashboard	Dashboard opens when the mouse is moved to the hot corner. See sections later in this chapter for more information on Dashboard.
Put Display to Sleep	Causes the Mac's monitor to go into sleep mode.
- (minus sign)	Disables the hot corner.

Customizing the Finder

The Finder is the application you will use most often on your Mac, and so you may as well customize it to fit your needs and likes. Mac OS X gives you a lot of latitude when it comes to customizing the Finder, and I'll show you a few of my favorite tweaks to this quintessential Mac OS standby in this section. While Chapter 1 covers the ins and outs of using the Finder, in this chapter you can discover how to give the Finder that personal touch.

Finder windows

The Finder is a great tool for navigating your Mac, but I like to take full advantage of the customization available so that I can make the Finder work for me.

Figure 2.7 is an example of the Finder modified to my specs. The biggest differences between my customized Finder window and the default window configuration are that the toolbar and sidebar have been changed significantly to give me quick access to the tools and folders that I use the most in my daily activities, and that I've changed my view from Icons to Columns. There's also a new addition to the bottom of the window, known as the path bar.

Path bar

2.7 The Finder done my way

In the rest of this section, I show you how I went about customizing Finder. Of course, you don't have to make the same changes to your Finder that I have made to mine; in fact, I encourage you to experiment with all the options the Finder affords, even those I may not touch on, so that you can find what combination works best for you.

Note The path bar is an easy way to see where you've been and to be able to quickly get back there. Enable the path bar by opening a new Finder window, and then choose View ⇨ Show Path Bar; the path bar appears in the bottom of the Finder window, exactly as shown in Figure 2.7. The folders in the path bar change as you browse your Mac's hard drive. Click one of the folders in the path bar to zoom back to one of the previous folders in your path. It's sort of like taking a tiny step back in time!

Modifying the toolbar

The toolbar gives you fast access to common tasks and actions, and helps you to navigate your Mac more efficiently. You can change the default set of tools in the toolbar to add items that you use more than others and remove those items that you don't need, by using the Customize Toolbar sheet (see figure 2.8).

Follow these steps to customize your Finder's toolbar:

1. **Activate the Finder by clicking its icon on the left side of the Dock.**
2. **Open a new Finder window by pressing ⌘+N.**

3. **Choose View ⇨ Customize Toolbar to open the Customize Toolbar sheet.**

4. **To add an item to the toolbar, drag and drop the item from the sheet to the position in the toolbar you desire.**

5. **To remove an item from the toolbar, simply drag and drop its icon anywhere outside of the Finder window, and it disappears in a puff of smoke!**

6. **If the arrangement of the icons in the toolbar doesn't suit you, just click and drag them to the spot where they work best.** As you drag an icon, the other icons move automatically to make room for it.

7. **Once you have everything just right, click Done to close the sheet.**

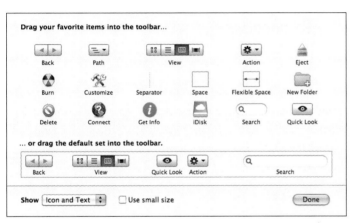

2.8 The Customize Toolbar sheet allows you to edit the tools available in the toolbar.

Genius

The fastest way to alter items already on the toolbar, or even the toolbar itself, without using the Customize Toolbar sheet, is by using the trusty ⌘ key. To quickly rearrange items on the toolbar, hold down the ⌘ key and click and drag the item to its new location. To remove an item, simply ⌘-click-and-drag it out of the toolbar, and then drop it. Cycle through the toolbar's Show options by holding down the ⌘ key and clicking the oval button in the upper-right corner of the Finder window. Continue clicking the oval button to see the various options. You can also hide the toolbar completely by simply clicking the oval button, without using the ⌘ key.

Table 2.3 gives an overview of each item's function to help you make an informed decision about which ones you want to include.

Table 2.3 Customize Toolbar Sheet Items

Item	Description/Action
Back	Navigate forward or backward in the folder path.
Path	Click to see the current folder path.
View	Quickly change the view for the current Finder window.
Action	Choose from a list of common actions, such as creating a new folder or getting information on an item.
Eject	Eject a disc or other removable media.
Burn	Burn a CD or DVD.
Customize	Provides quick access to the Customize Toolbar sheet.
Separator, Space, and Flexible Space	Use to separate items and groups of items.
New Folder	Creates a new folder in the current folder.
Delete	Moves the selected file or folder to the Trash.
Connect	Opens the Connect to Server window, allowing you to quickly connect to other computers.
Get Info	Shows all information relative to the selected file or folder.
iDisk	Connects to your iDisk (a subscription to Apple's .MobileMe service is required).
Search	Type the names of items you need to find on your Mac's hard drive.
Quick Look	Provides a glance at the contents of a file without having to open the application that created it.
Show	Choose how to display the items in the toolbar using the pop-up menu and the Use small size check box.

Change the sidebar

The sidebar contains links, or shortcuts, to folders, discs, and servers that you often need to access. You can modify the sidebar's contents in a number of ways:

- **To remove an item you don't use, click and drag the item out of the sidebar, and then drop it.**

- **Add your favorite folders by dragging their icons into the sidebar under the Places section (see figure 2.9).** The other items in the sidebar shift as necessary to make room for their new neighbor.

- **Adjust the size of the sidebar by clicking and dragging the divider bar (see figure 2.9).**

- **Hide the sidebar from view altogether by clicking the oval button in the upper-right corner of the window.**

- **Rearrange items in the sidebar by clicking and dragging them to their new location.**

Genius   See the Set Finder's preferences section of Chapter 1 to discover how to choose which Devices, Shared, Places, and Search For items are displayed by default in your sidebar.

2.9 Make the sidebar conform to your needs!

Add a background image or color

One trick that adds a touch of class and functionality to your Finder windows is to add a background picture or color to them. The background pictures or colors can be used for simple decoration or to differentiate the contents of each folder. For example, if you keep records of your children's homework on your Mac, you could assign a picture of each individual child to the particular folder containing the homework. When you open each child's folder in a Finder window, a light background picture of your little darling instantly identifies whose homework you're checking; this is especially helpful if you have multiple windows open at once. To add a background image or color to your Finder windows, do the following:

1.   **Open the folder to which you want to add the image or color.**

2.   **Choose View ➪ Show View Options, or press ⌘+J.**

3. **Select the Color option in the Background section to add a color to the window, or select the Picture option to place an image in the background (see figure 2.10).** You must be in Icon view to see these options.

- **If you choose to use a color, click inside the white square to the right of the radio button to open the Colors palette.** Select the color that you want to use for the background and click OK.

- **If you select a picture, click the Select button to the right of the radio button, browse your Mac for the image you need, highlight it, and click Select to apply the image to the window.**

Caution A potential "oops" when using an image is that if the image is too large to fit in the window, you only see the part of it that does fit. The Preview application that is loaded with Mac OS X Snow Leopard is a great tool for easily resizing images. See Chapter 7 for step-by-step instructions.

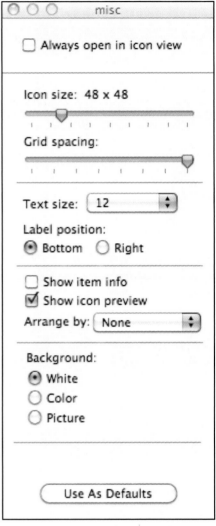

2.10 Make changes to a folder's window background by using the Background section of the View Options window.

Changing icons

A very popular method for redecorating your Mac is using custom icons for applications, folders, and files. You could change a plain folder icon to something more suitable to its contents, such as using an icon of a football for the folder that you use to keep your son's practice and game schedules. I've seen many a Mac whose icons had been changed systemwide from top to bottom; every default Mac OS X folder had been modified!

Here's how to change any item's icon in Mac OS X:

1. **Highlight the icon you want to use and press ⌘+I (Get Info) to open its Info window.**

2. **Click the icon picture in the upper-left corner of the Info window (see figure 2.11), and then copy the icon by pressing ⌘+C or choosing Edit⇨Copy.**

3. **Close the Info window.**

2.11 Change an item's icon from within its Info window.

4. **Highlight the item whose icon you want to change, and open its Info window by pressing ⌘+I.**

5. **Click the icon picture in the upper-left corner of the Info window and paste the new icon there by pressing ⌘+V or choosing Edit ⇨ Paste.**

6. **Close the changed item's Info window.**

Genius

There are utilities that you can purchase on the Internet that can greatly ease your icon revamping. One such tool is called CandyBar (www.panic.com/candybar), which makes icon customization and organization a breeze.

Adding and removing items in the Dock

You can add and remove items to and from the Dock as you please, and it's really easy to do:

- **To add an item to the Dock, simply drag its icon to the Dock and drop it in where you want it.** You can reposition an item in the Dock by simply dragging and dropping it in its new location.

- **If you have an application open that you want to keep in the Dock, click and hold its icon (as shown in figure 2.12), and select Keep in Dock from the contextual menu that appears.**

- **To remove an item, drag its icon from the Dock and let go of the mouse button.** The icon disappears in a puff of smoke! Don't worry: the original item is still in its location; you've only removed the alias for the item.

2.12 Keep an icon in the Dock if you need to use it often.

Change the Dock's appearance and placement

You can tame the Dock by setting its preferences to meet your needs. Open the Dock's preferences by right-clicking, or Ctrl+clicking, the divider line, and select Dock Preferences.

The Dock preferences window lets you make several changes:

- **Increase or decrease the size of the Dock by moving the Size slider.**

- **If your icons are too small to see clearly, select the Magnification check box and adjust the slider to increase or decrease the amount of magnification.**

- **The Dock can be positioned on the left or right side of the window, or at the bottom, which is its default setting.**

- **The Minimize using option lets you choose the special effect that occurs when you minimize a window into the Dock.** To minimize a window, click the yellow button in its upper-left corner.

- **Select the Animate opening applications check box to cause the icon of an item you are opening to bounce up and down in the Dock.** I leave this option unchecked; the bouncing annoys the heck out of me.

- **If you don't like the Dock cramping your style — or your Desktop space, for that matter — you can hide it from view by selecting the check box next to Automatically hide and show the Dock.** When you inevitably have to use the Dock again, hold your mouse pointer at the very bottom of your window for just a second, and the Dock will temporarily pop back up into view, only to go back into hiding when you finish.

Working with Widgets

Snow Leopard includes an application called Dashboard that affords you another fun way to customize your Mac. Dashboard lets you access and manage a multitude of widgets that you can use for tracking packages, getting driving directions, browsing the Yellow Pages, checking your stocks, seeing the latest weather forecasts, finding out what movies are playing at your local multiplex, playing Sudoku, and the list goes on and on. Widgets are among those rare things that make your life easier and are really, really cool to use at the same time! In the next few sections, I show you how to access, use, customize, and even create your own widgets.

To open Dashboard and see the default set of running widgets, do one of the following:

- **Click the Dashboard icon in your Dock.**
- **Press F12.**

Note Newer Mac keyboards and those on the newest laptops may use different F keys to invoke Dashboard. These keyboards use F4 instead of F12, but on laptops you can use Fn+F12 to achieve the same functionality. Consult the documentation that came with your keyboard or laptop for more information.

In the main body of the screen, you see the four widgets that Snow Leopard is running out of the gate: Calculator, iCal, Weather, and World Clock. These are very basic widgets that you can use to get your feet wet in the world of widgetry (yes, I just coined that term!). To get a quick feel for using a widget, click the Calculator to bring it to the forefront, and then use your mouse to perform calculations on the widget's virtual keypad, or use your keyboard to type information.

Genius

Don't like the placement of the widgets on the screen? To move a widget wherever you want, simply click anywhere on the widget and drag it to your preferred location.

Take notice of the + within the small circle that appears in the lower-left corner of the screen when you activate Dashboard. Click the + to open the widget bar, which grants access to all the widgets that Snow Leopard so graciously includes as well as allows you to change the widgets you have running.

Peruse the Widget bar until you see a widget that strikes your fancy, and then click to open it. When you click the widget you want to open, Dashboard drops the widget on your screen, which causes an amazing ripple effect to occur, similar to that of dropping a rock in a still pond. That little trick, shown in figure 2.13, will enthrall even the most steadfast Mac skeptic!

2.13 The ripple effect caused by opening a new widget has only one use: to look very, very cool!

To close any widget, click the X located in its upper-left corner. Dashboard even has a neat effect for this action: The widget is sucked into the X until it disappears! If that's not neat enough for you, hold down the Shift key while clicking the X to see it disappear in slow motion.

Snow Leopard widgets

Because there are quite a few widgets that come preinstalled in Snow Leopard, I thought it would be a good idea to give you a quick synopsis of what's available and what these widgets can do. Table 2.4 spells out the details of these widgets.

Table 2.4 Snow Leopard Widgets

Widget	Functions
Widgets	Opens the Widget Manager.
Address Book	Lets you quickly search your Address Book and displays information for the contact.
Business	Searches your local Yellow Pages for business listings.
Calculator	Performs basic mathematical computations.
Dictionary	A fast way to access the meanings of words. Also doubles as a thesaurus.
ESPN	Finds all the latest scores and sports news.
Flight Tracker	When you type a flight number, Flight Tracker details its status. This little widget does some really cool stuff. Check it out, whether you have a flight to track or not!
Google	Supplies you with a Google search window at a press of the F12 key.
iCal	Displays your schedule for the day selected.
iTunes	Provides a tiny remote control for using iTunes. iTunes must be open for this one to work.
Movies	Gives you the showtimes for the movies currently playing in local theaters. You can also view the trailer for the film, as well as buy tickets online.
People	Finds people by their name and city.
Ski Report	You can type the name of your favorite ski resort to get the latest information on skiing conditions.
Stickies	You can use them just like you would the real thing: to keep little notes all over your Mac!
Stocks	Keeps up with all the latest Wall Street comings and goings for stocks that you specify.
Tile Game	Keeps a really, really bored person occupied for a while.
Translation	Instantly translates words or phrases from one language to another.
Unit Converter	Converts units for several different measurements, such as time, length, currency, and pressure.

continued

Table 2.4 continued

Widget	Functions
Weather	Provides the latest weather prognostications for your neck of the woods. Covered in detail later in this chapter.
Web Clip	Lets you create your own widgets. More on this feature later in this chapter.
World Clock	Displays an analog clock that can give you the time of day for hundreds of locations around the world.

Managing widgets

Snow Leopard comes fully stocked with a great set of widgets, but there are a lot of them, and the ones you never use just seem to be taking up real estate on your screen unnecessarily. If you install other widgets, as discussed later in this chapter, there will be still more widget icons to browse through in the widget bar. Dashboard provides a handy way to disable the widgets that you hardly ever use without actually uninstalling them; this comes in handy should you decide to try one of them in the future.

To disable, or enable, widgets, do the following:

1. **Press F12 to open Dashboard.**
2. **Click the + in the lower-left corner of your screen to open the Widget bar.**
3. **Click the Manage Widgets button to open the Widget Manager, as shown in figure 2.14.**
4. **Deselect the check boxes next to widgets that you want to disable, and select the check boxes for those you want to enable.**
5. **Close the Widget Manager window when finished.**

How to Uninstall Widgets

You can easily uninstall widgets that you have added to Dashboard by opening the Widget Manager and clicking the remove symbol (which looks like a red circle with a horizontal white line in the middle of it) to the right of the widget's name.

But what if you want to uninstall a widget that came with Snow Leopard? There are no red uninstall symbols next to their names, so what is one to do? Snow Leopard's default widgets are located in Hard Drive ⇨ Library ⇨ Widgets. To remove one of these widgets, drag it to the Trash and type your administrator password.

2.14 The Widget manager helps you organize your Widget bar.

Setting preferences in widgets

Many widgets require a bit of customization to utilize them effectively. For example, Movies doesn't do you much good if you live in Sevierville, Tennessee, but it's giving you showtimes and theaters in Cupertino, California. As another example, Stocks won't be of much assistance if you want to see what the hot new stock you just bought into is doing, but all you see are the default stocks that are set up in the widget.

Let's use Weather to illustrate how to edit the preferences of a widget:

1. **Press F12 to open Dashboard.**

2. **Position your mouse pointer over the lower-right corner of the Weather widget to see the Information button, which looks like a small "i" (see figure 2.15).**

Information button

2.15 Click the Information button to open a widget's preferences, if available.

3. **Click the Information button to flip over the widget so that you can see its avail-able preferences.** Make the preference changes you desire, and then click Done.

4. **The widget should now reflect the changes you made to its preferences.**

Note

Not all widgets give you the option of adjusting their preferences; don't beat your-self up if you can't seem to find the elusive Information button in a given widget.

Finding more cool widgets

So far, the only widgets you've been privy to are those that come with Snow Leopard, but I'm about to change that. There are hundreds of widgets that have been developed, and some of them are exactly what you're looking for.

The best place to find new widgets is Apple's own Web site (more on that in a moment), but you can also find a lot of other widgets by simply performing a search on Google for "Mac OS X Widgets."

To get new widgets the quick and easy way, do the following:

1. **Press F12 to open Dashboard.**

2. **Click the + in the lower-left corner of your screen to open the Widget bar.**

3. **Click the Manage Widgets button to open the Widget Manager, and then click the More Widgets button at the bottom of the window.** Safari automatically whisks you away to Apple's Dashboard Widgets Web site, shown in figure 2.16, where you can browse the massive amounts of available widgets that have been created by developers and regular users alike.

4. **Find a widget that you want to try by using the Widget Browser.** You may need to scroll down slightly on the page to see the browser.

5. **Click the Download link to have Safari download the widget.**

6. **Click the Install button when prompted to open your new widget in Dashboard.** If you like what you see, click the Keep button; if not, click Delete.

Top Widgets List

2.16 Apple's Web site is your one-stop shop for your Dashboard widget needs.

Create your own widgets using Web Clips

A neat feature in Dashboard is the ability to create your own widgets using clips of Web pages. This is a great feature for tracking information from a certain Web site without having to constantly navigate to that Web site to check its status. I'll use the Top Widgets list on Apple's Dashboard Widgets Web site for this example, which allows you to see the most popular widgets available without having to open Safari and browse to the site. You can simply view the list in Dashboard by pressing F12 (see figure 2.16).

To create a widget using Web Clips, do the following:

1. **Press F12 to open Dashboard.**

2. **Click the + in the lower-left corner of the screen, and click the Web Clip icon in the Widget bar.**

3. **Click the Safari icon in the Web Clip Widget window to open Safari.**

4. **Type the address of the site you want to use to create your widget.** In this example, I use www.apple.com/downloads/dashboard/.

5. **Choose File ➪ Open in Dashboard.** The Web page darkens and you are presented with a selection box, as shown in figure 2.17.

6. **Position the selection box over the section of the Web page you want to use for your Widget, and then click to select the area.** You can drag the handles that appear around the selection box to adjust the area that is selected.

2.17 Place the selection box over the part of the Web page that you want to use for your widget.

7. **Click the Add button in the upper-right corner of Safari's window (in the purple bar).** Safari passes the selection on to Dashboard, where your new widget is created.

How Do I Change Snow Leopard's System Preferences?

By this point you are familiar with my affinity for making your Mac behave like you want it to. No other place in Snow Leopard gives you more control over your Mac than System Preferences. This is where you get to assert yourself as the alpha user, firmly establishing yourself as the ruler of your personal computing domain. System Preferences is the central location in Mac OS X for making both local and systemwide changes to networking, security, software and hardware, sound, and Snow Leopard's appearance. This chapter shows you how to tame Snow Leopard by explaining what preferences are available and how you can change them if you need to, or just simply want to.

Personal

As its name indicates, the Personal section of the System Preferences is where you can customize the way your Mac looks and behaves, suiting it to your tastes. I cover the Language & Text and Security preferences here, because the others are already covered in detail in other chapters of this book. Table 3.3 at the end of this chapter lists the preferences that I discuss in other chapters, gives a very brief description of their functions, and points you to those relevant chapters.

Open the System Preferences before reading any further in this chapter by choosing Apple menu ⇨ System Preferences; you are rewarded with the System Preferences window, as shown in figure 3.1.

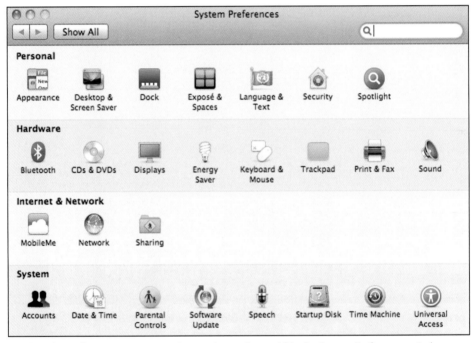

3.1 Click the preference you want to view or change from within the System Preferences window.

Language & Text

Snow Leopard is quite the international sensation and can speak more languages than I ever knew existed! The Language & Text preferences pane helps your Mac flex its multilingual muscles.

Language

The Language tab (see figure 3.2) of the Language & Text preferences pane allows you to decide the order in which languages are used for application menus, for sorting items, and for dialog windows.

3.2 Your Mac can be very cosmopolitan using the Language & Text preferences pane.

Genius

Snow Leopard is fluent in more than 110 languages, so the list of available languages is quite lengthy. To save yourself from having to hunt for the languages you find useful in the future, click Edit List and deselect the languages you don't need.

Text

The Text tab of the Language & Text preferences (see figure 3.3) allows you to customize substitution features, spell-checking, and more text magic. Options available in the Text tab include:

- **Symbol and Text Substitution.** Applications in Snow Leopard can substitute text you don't want for text you do want. For example, if you select the check box next to (c), when you type (c) it will be replaced by the copyright symbol (©). Click the + button in the lower-left corner to add your own custom symbol and text substitutions.

- **Spelling.** Snow Leopard can check spelling for you automatically, and you can use this pop-up to customize languages used.

- **Word Break.** This changes how a word is highlighted when double-clicked. Standard is the typical setting, but those using Japanese as their primary language should select Japanese.

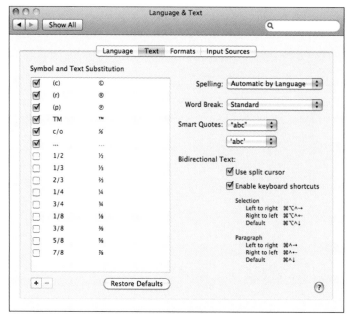

3.3 The Text tab helps customize text substitution and more.

- ● **Smart Quotes.** This modifies how double and single quotes display around your text using the Smart Quotes pop-up menus.

- ● **Bidirectional Text.** The direction of text can vary depending on the language you use. For example, Hebrew text reads right-to-left while English reads left-to-right. The options here let you decide to use keyboard shortcuts to change text direction, and whether to use the split cursor when the cursor is at a boundary between two directional texts.

Formats

You can use the Formats tab to decide how items such as dates, time, monetary increments, and measurements display on your Mac by default. Figure 3.4 shows the options that are available for localizing Snow Leopard.

Click the Customize buttons in the Dates, Times, and Numbers sections to further customize their layouts.

Input Sources

Some languages use more characters than there are keys on your keyboard; in these cases, input methods provide a way for you to access those characters. The Input Sources tab, shown in figure 3.5, allows you to choose from among the multitude of input methods that ship with Snow Leopard.

For more information on this topic, click the Help button (?) in the lower-right corner of this tab.

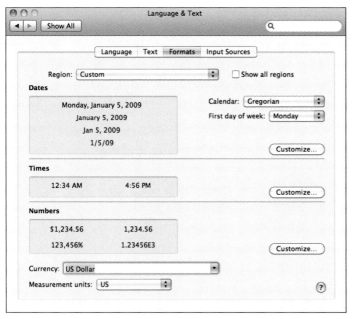

3.4 Choose how best to display regional items with the Formats tab.

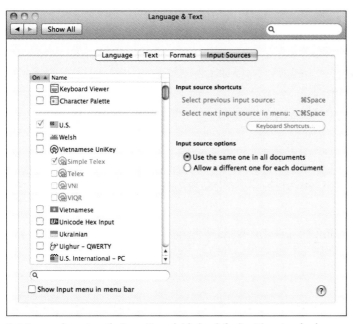

3.5 Access characters that aren't available by default with a standard keyboard using Input Sources.

Security

Even a Mac needs to be secured from outside troublemakers, so Snow Leopard comes packaged with some very nice security features, which you can access through the Security preferences pane in System Preferences.

General

Figure 3.6 shows the options available under the General tab. These are fairly self-explanatory, but some aren't quite as intuitive as others. The General tab options are as follows:

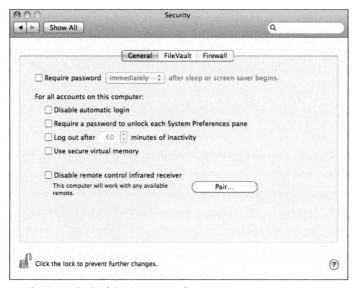

3.6 The General tab of the Security preferences

- **Require password after sleep or screen saver begins.** Select this check box to lock your Mac from any user who doesn't know your account password once it has gone to sleep or a screen saver has been activated. Use the pop-up menu to determine when the password is required.

- **Disable automatic login.** If this checked box is not selected, your Mac simply boots up into the default account without any prompt for a password.

Caution

I highly recommend that you use both the Require password after sleep or screen saver begins and Disable automatic login options. Not selecting these options allows unfettered access to anyone who turns on, restarts, or wakes up your Mac. At this point, the fate of your Mac and all the files it holds is entirely in the hands of the trespasser.

- **Require a password to unlock each System Preferences pane.** There is a lock icon in the bottom-left corner of each preferences pane. If you select this check box, the icon will be in the locked position for every pane in System Preferences and will only unlock with an administrator password.

- **Log out after x minutes of inactivity.** Select this option to have your Mac automatically log out of your account after the specified time of inactivity.

- **Use secure virtual memory.** Your Mac uses portions of your hard drive like RAM (memory) to store information. Select this option to have Snow Leopard erase this information from your hard drive to prevent others from accessing it if they would manage to gain access to your drive.

- **Disable remote control infrared receiver.** Some Macs have infrared receivers that they use to receive commands from an Apple remote control for viewing movies, listening to music, and other activities. Select this check box if you want to disable your infrared receiver so that other Mac owners can't control your Mac using their remote.

FileVault

FileVault lets you enable the Snow Leopard FileVault feature, which I must not recommend unless you are a very savvy and security-minded computer user. FileVault encrypts your entire home folder, which prevents anyone else from seeing its contents. Although this sounds great, the big downfall for someone who is not used to such high security is that if you forget your user account password (or if you don't remember or failed to even set the master password) then the home folder contents are lost. Yikes!

If you want to turn on FileVault protection for your account, click the FileVault tab in the Security preferences pane and click Turn On FileVault in the lower-right corner. Your Mac must have enough space available on its hard drive to store an encrypted version.

Caution If you enable a master password, anyone who knows that password can decrypt the contents of any FileVault-protected accounts on the entire Mac. This endangers every account on the computer, so I highly recommend not setting a master password.

Firewall

A firewall prevents unauthorized users from accessing your Mac through the Internet. These bothersome folks are up to no good, but a firewall may keep them at bay. To select firewall settings, click the Firewall tab in the Security preferences pane. You can select one of these three options:

- **Allow all incoming connections.** Provides no protection at all.

- **Deny incoming connections except for essential services.** According to Apple, essential services are sets of applications that allow your Mac to discover services (such as shared files and printers) provided by other computers on your network. Using this setting keeps services other than these from connecting to your Mac.

- **Set access for specific services and applications.** Select this option to manually pick and choose which applications and services you want to allow access to on your Mac. Click the + button in the lower-left corner of the window to browse your computer for those applications and services; to remove them from the list, click the - button.

Genius

If you are connecting to the Internet through a router, you probably won't need to enable the Snow Leopard firewall because the router will most likely be running one. Check your router's documentation to be certain of its firewall settings.

Hardware

The Hardware section of System Preferences lets Snow Leopard know how you want it to interact with various hardware components of your Mac.

CDs & DVDs

When you insert a CD or DVD into your Mac's disc drive, something's going to happen; however, what happens is up to you entirely. The CDs & DVDs preferences pane lets you tell Snow Leopard how it should behave when you insert a disc, as shown in figure 3.7.

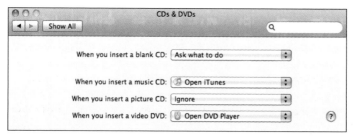

3.7 Tell Snow Leopard how to handle CDs and DVDs from here.

Displays

Displays preferences help you to set the resolution of your Mac's monitor or screen. The options in both tabs of the pane, Display (see figure 3.8) and Color, are standard on any computer.

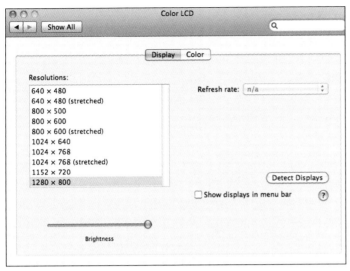

3.8 Adjust monitor settings using the Display pane.

The Display tab allows you to change these settings:

- **Resolutions.** Lets you choose the amount of detail your screen shows. The higher the resolution, the smaller the items are on your screen; the lower the resolution, the larger the items are.

- **Refresh rate.** Determines how often the display is redrawn. If you aren't using a Mac with a built-in display, such as a laptop or an iMac, consult the documentation that came with your monitor for appropriate refresh rates.

- **Detect Displays.** Click this button to have Snow Leopard automatically discover newly connected displays and to choose the settings to use with them.

- **Show displays in menu bar.** Select this check box to place a shortcut to the Displays preferences in the menu bar.

- **Brightness slider.** Drag the slider to increase or decrease the brightness of your display.

The Color tab is where you can set your display to use color profiles so that it can represent colors more accurately. Deselect the Show profiles for this display only check box to see all profiles installed on your Mac.

Genius Sometimes the best color is what suits your eye the best, not what Snow Leopard automatically chooses for your monitor. You can create a custom profile for your monitor to use by clicking the Calibrate button and following the instructions. If color matching is old hat to you, select the Expert Mode check box in the Display Calibrator Assistant's Introduction screen to gain access to a more finely-tuned process.

Energy Saver

Everyone's trying to be a bit greener these days, and Snow Leopard is no exception. The Energy Saver preferences provide settings for your computer, hard drive, and your display to sleep when they are inactive for the period of time that you set by dragging the sliders, as shown in figure 3.9.

Note The Energy Saver preferences differ slightly depending on whether you are on a notebook or desktop. When you're on a notebook, you see Battery and Power Adapter tabs, but on a desktop, you see Sleep and Options tabs.

Click the Power Adapter tab (or the Options tab if you're on a desktop) in the Energy Saver preferences pane to set these options:

- **Put the hard disk(s) to sleep when possible.** Puts the computer's hard drive to sleep whenever it's inactive.

- **Wake for network access.** Lets your Mac wake up when a network administrator is trying to access it through the network.

- **Automatically reduce brightness before display goes to sleep.** The brightness on your display decreases a couple of minutes before it goes to sleep when it is not in use.

- **Start up automatically after a power failure.** If power is interrupted, your Mac automatically restarts itself once the power is restored.

- **Show battery status in the menu bar.** Places a battery icon in the menu bar that allows you to easily monitor the amount of charge still remaining in the battery for a Mac laptop.

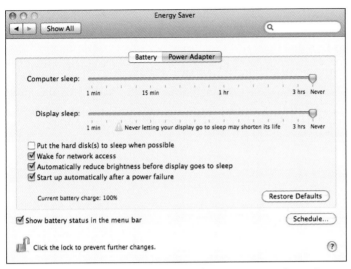

3.9 Save energy by having your display and computer go to sleep when not in use.

Keyboard & Mouse

The Keyboard & Mouse preferences pane gives you the ability to configure how your mouse and keyboard interact with Snow Leopard. You can also set up a wireless mouse and keyboard using Bluetooth, and even create your own keyboard shortcuts.

Click the Keyboard or Mouse tabs to modify their behaviors (you'll only see the Mouse tab when a mouse is attached), such as how quickly the keyboard responds to a key press or how fast your double-click speed is set. The items under each tab are self-explanatory, but if you need further help, click the Help button in the lower-right corner of the window.

The Bluetooth tab is only available on Macs that have Bluetooth installed. Check the battery status of wireless keyboards and mice from here, as well as install new devices by clicking the Set Up New Device button in the lower-right corner.

I love the fact that Apple gives you the opportunity to make your own keyboard shortcuts with the Keyboard Shortcuts tab (shown in figure 3.10). Deselect the shortcuts you want to disable, click the + button in the lower-left corner to create a new shortcut, or highlight a shortcut in the list and click the – button to delete it.

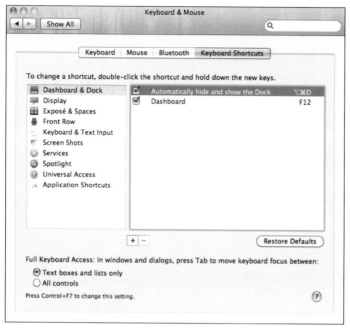

3.10 Create and modify your own keyboard shortcuts.

Genius

I've gotten myself in trouble before by accidentally deleting keyboard shortcuts that I used often. I was able to retrieve those lost shortcuts by clicking Restore Defaults in the lower-right corner, but be warned that if you try this, you lose any custom short-cuts you've created. You can't say I didn't warn you!

Trackpad

The Trackpad preferences pane (shown in figure 3.11) will only appear if you are using a laptop. The multitouch trackpads on Mac laptops provide some pretty cool features, which you can modify to your liking with the options in the Trackpad pane:

- **Adjust tracking, double-click, and scrolling speeds using their respective sliders.**

- **Customize trackpad gestures for scrolling, zooming, and clicking.**

- **Determine if the trackpad should ignore accidental input and whether your Mac should ignore trackpad input altogether whenever a mouse is connected.**

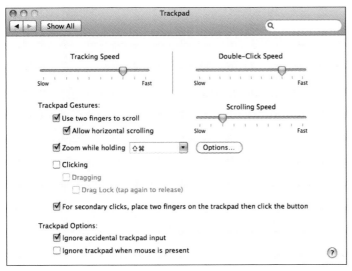

3.11 Tweak your trackpad's settings to reflect the way you work.

Sound

Configure your Mac's sound using the Sound preferences pane, as shown in figure 3.12. Table 3.1 gives a brief overview of each tab in the pane.

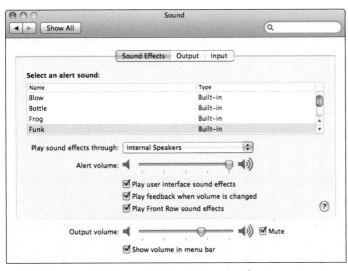

3.12 Change your Mac's sounds using the Sound preferences.

Table 3.1 Sound Preference Pane Options

Tab	Options available
Sound Effects	Select what sounds to use for system alerts, adjust the volume of these alerts, and set the systemwide output volume.
Output	Choose output devices, such as external speakers, to broadcast your Mac's sounds, as well as adjust its sound balance.
Input	Select a sound input device, such as an external microphone. You can adjust devices' input volume and filter unwanted background noise (check the box next to Use ambient noise reduction) as well.

Internet & Network

These preferences are where you tell your Mac how to communicate with the rest of the world through its network connections.

MobileMe

For $99 per year, Apple offers MobileMe, a service that extends your Mac experience to the Internet. The MobileMe service offers the following features:

- **Synchronize calendars, contacts, data, and more.**

- **Access your MobileMe e-mail account through any Web browser on any computer.**

- **Use an iDisk to store files and synchronize folders.**

- **Create your own Web site.**

- **Use Back to My Mac to access your home or office Mac from a remote location using any computer connected to the Internet.**

- **Organize your family's activities, team meetings, church events, and more using Groups.**

- **Share photos and movies with incredible ease using Web Gallery.**

The MobileMe preferences pane is where you can log in to your MobileMe account and set up how your Mac interacts with the MobileMe services. For more information on MobileMe, visit www.apple.com/mobileme/.

Network

The Network preferences pane, shown in figure 3.13, is where you configure settings for your various network connection types.

The list on the left side of the pane shows the network connections that your Mac supports. The contents of this list vary, depending on the network hardware that is available on your Mac.

- **AirPort.** Settings for using your Mac's built-in AirPort card or a third-party wireless adapter to access the network wirelessly.

- **Bluetooth.** Your Mac can use its Bluetooth adapter to share your cellular phone's Internet access, assuming the phone has a Bluetooth adapter as well.

- **Ethernet.** Connection settings for attaching to a network using your Mac's built-in Ethernet port.

- **FireWire.** Snow Leopard also allows you to connect two Macs together with a FireWire cable so that you can share files or Internet connections between them.

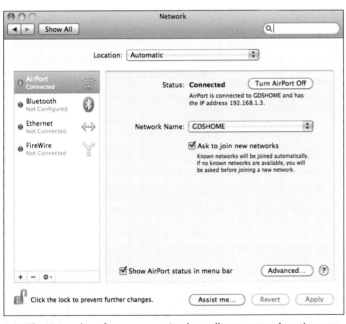

3.13 The Network preferences pane is where all your network settings are configured.

Click one of the network connections to gain access to its innermost workings. The Advanced button in the lower-right corner of each tab's pane is used to inspect or manually set the network connections for that particular connection method, as shown for the AirPort connection type in figure 3.14.

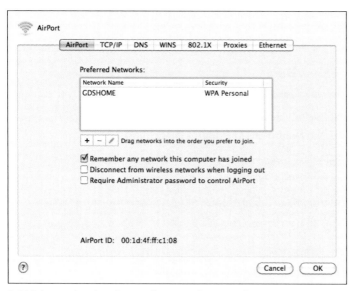

3.14 Advanced settings let you fine-tune the network options.

Detailed information on the options that are available for each of the connection types can be found by clicking the Help button in their respective panes.

System

The System section of the System Preferences contains panes for configuring the accounts on your Mac, updating your Mac's software, choosing a startup disk, and many more systemwide options.

Date & Time

Adjust your Mac's time settings with this preferences pane, shown in figure 3.15. The tabs provide the following options:

- **Date & Time.** Select the Set date & time automatically check box to have your Mac do just that, and then select a time server from the list provided. You can choose to make manual settings by deselecting this option and adjusting the date and time to your preference.

- **Time Zone.** Select the time zone you are in by choosing an area on the map.

- **Clock.** Decide whether and how to display the date and time in the menu bar, and allow your Mac to speak the time to you at the specified intervals.

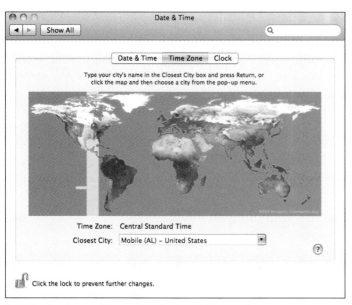

3.15 Set the date and time using the Date & Time preferences pane.

Software Update

Snow Leopard uses the Software Update application to check for updates to the operating system and compatible applications.

The Scheduled Check tab lets you instantly check the Apple servers for new updates by clicking Check Now. You can also schedule update checks by selecting the Check for updates option and selecting how often Software Update should check for updates.

The Installed Updates tab lists all the updates that have been downloaded and installed on your Mac.

Genius

There are several schools of thought when it comes to upgrading to the latest-and-greatest software. In my opinion, if there's an update available for your operating system or an application installed on your system, go ahead and get it. The vast majority of the time, updates don't cause any problems; on the contrary, they usually end up fixing or preventing them.

Speech

Snow Leopard is so intelligent that it can talk to you and even respond to spoken commands! Here are the options that are available.

Speech Recognition

The Settings tab within the Speech Recognition tab, shown in figure 3.16, lets you turn Speakable Items on or off, as well as select the microphone for your Mac to listen to your commands with. You can also select a listening key, which is the key you press to make your Mac listen for your spoken commands.

The Commands tab allows you to customize which spoken commands your Mac responds to. Click the Open Speakable Items Folder button to see a list of the preconfigured commands your Mac understands. Click Helpful Tips to get great advice on how to successfully use the Speakable Items options and commands.

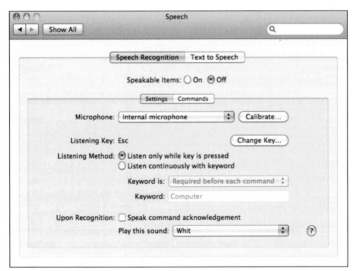

3.16 The options that are available in the Settings tab within the Speech Recognition tab.

Text to Speech

This section of the Speech preferences lets you choose which voice your Mac uses when it speaks to you. Select from several preinstalled voices and modify the rate at which your Mac says the words. You can also have Snow Leopard announce system alerts, announce when an application needs to be looked after, and speak text that you've highlighted in a document.

Startup Disk

This preference pane allows you to choose to start your Mac from any drive that contains a valid Mac OS X installation. When you first open these preferences, you are presented with a list of disks that are considered to be valid startup devices. Select the disk you want to boot up with, and then click Restart.

Universal Access

Snow Leopard implements the Universal Access preferences so that those who may have physical difficulties, such as loss of eyesight, can use a Mac with little to no problem. Table 3.2 lists the tabs and options that are available for each preference.

Table 3.2 Universal Access Preferences

Tab	Options
Seeing	VoiceOver tells your Mac to read all text the mouse moves over.
	Zoom turns on the zoom function, which is activated by the keyboard shortcuts listed in the preferences pane.
	Display provides great options for those Mac users whose eyesight isn't what it once was.
Hearing	These options are for Mac users who have difficulty hearing at normal levels. Adjust the volume from here if you like, and have the Mac flash its screen to alert you to incoming information.
Keyboard	This tab provides options for helping Mac users who may have difficulty using the traditional keyboard.
Mouse & Trackpad	Should you have problems using the mouse, you can use Mouse Keys, which causes the numeric keypad (available on most Mac keyboards) to act as a temporary mouse.

Adding a Disk Images preference pane

Many people use Disk Utility often and need to change its preferences for handling disk images from time to time, depending on the tasks they are trying to perform. It can get old, though, having to open Disk Utility over and over again, and adjust its preferences every time. Apple has a hidden preference pane that you can manually add to your System Preferences window that allows you to change those preferences without having to launch Disk Utility.

1. **Open a new Finder window by pressing ⌘+N from within the Finder.**

2. **Browse to the directory /System/Library/PrivateFrameworks/DiskImages.framework/Versions/A/Resources.**

3. **Double-click the file called DiskImages.prefPane.**

4. **Determine whether to install the Disk Images preference pane only for your user account, or for all user accounts on the computer, and then click Install.**

5. **The Disk Images preference pane, shown in figure 3.17, can be found in the Other section at the bottom of the System Preferences window.**

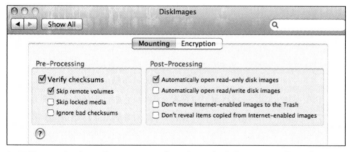

3.17 Determine how Snow Leopard works with disk images when they are presented.

Other System Preferences

Table 3.3 lists the "celebrity" (or important) preferences that I discuss in other chapters of this book.

Table 3.3 More Personal Preferences

Section	Preferences	Functions	Relevant Chapter
Personal	Appearance	Change the overall look of the Snow Leopard menus, scroll bars, and other screen elements.	2
Personal	Desktop & Screen Saver	Select a desktop picture for your user account, as well as a screen saver.	2
Personal	Dock	Make adjustments to your Dock, such as magnification and hiding settings.	2
Personal	Exposé & Spaces	Manipulate how Exposé organizes items, and set up how Spaces works within Snow Leopard.	1
Personal	Spotlight	Choose which categories of files Spotlight will search on your Mac.	1
Hardware	Print & Fax	Install and set up printers.	6
Hardware	Bluetooth	Set up connections with other Bluetooth-enabled devices.	13
Internet & Network	Sharing	Determine how your Mac shares files, drives, and printers with other computers.	13
System	Accounts	Create accounts for multiple users on your Mac.	4
System	Parental Controls	Set Internet and other boundaries for your children or other users.	4
System	Time Machine	Back up your Mac automatically.	14

How Do I Manage User Accounts?

User accounts are the perfect way to make sure that multiple people can use your Mac without the risk of them completely goofing up the whole thing. I show you in this chapter how to create multiple user accounts and what type of accounts you can select. Individual user accounts allow all users to configure their account to their liking, while protecting the other accounts on the Mac. Snow Leopard also provides Parental Controls to help concerned moms and dads keep tabs on their prodigy's computer usage. The Parental Controls in Snow Leopard easily allow parents to configure their child's computing experience to protect both them and their Mac.

Types of Accounts

Let's face it: Some users can be trusted more than others. Factors useful for assessing a user's trustworthiness may be age, maturity, responsibility, or prowess with a computer. Snow Leopard allows you to create user accounts that have nearly complete access to every component of the operating system, those that have strictly limited access, and anything in between.

Administrator

Administrator accounts are the big dogs of the user accounts world. The default account that is created when you first install Snow Leopard is an administrator account. Administrators can handle almost any task on your Mac, including the following:

- **Create and remove (delete) user accounts.**
- **Change settings for other user accounts.**
- **Change all system settings, including those that are locked in System Preferences.**
- **Install software and drivers that any user on the system can utilize (if you allow that, of course).**
- **Decide whether to rule your Mac kingdom with an iron fist or be a benevolent ruler, loved and adored by all of your minions.**

Standard

A standard account is adequate for most users. Standard accounts allow the user enough freedom to customize his or her own account without having the power to alter others. Standard accounts

- **Can install software, but only if they have access to the software**
- **Can customize their working environment with System Preferences; however, they cannot alter System Preferences that are locked**
- **Cannot modify, add, or delete other user accounts**

Managed with Parental Controls

Parental Controls are used to manage, or limit, these accounts and the privileges they have. I discuss Parental Controls in greater detail later in this chapter, so I won't deal with the particulars here.

Sharing Only

A Sharing Only account restricts the user to accessing the computer only through the network, as he would a server. Sharing Only accounts are useful for sharing documents with others in your home or office without giving them access to the rest of your home folder or Mac. The user cannot log on to the Mac with a Sharing Only account name.

Creating New User Accounts

Now that I've covered the different account types, you can start to create some. To make a new user account, follow these steps:

1. **Choose Apple menu ⇨ System Preferences, and click the Accounts icon in the System section to open the Accounts preferences window, as shown in figure 4.1.**

2. **If the lock icon in the bottom-left corner is in the locked position, click the icon to unlock it.** Type an administrator account name and password when prompted.

4.1 The Accounts preferences window is at your disposal.

3. **After you unlock the Accounts preferences, click the + button in the lower-left corner of the Accounts window to add a new account.**

4. **The new accounts window, shown in figure 4.2, helps you to set up the account.**
   Table 4.1 lists the new account fields and options, and explains how to configure them.

5. **When the account settings are in order, click Create Account.**

4.2 The new accounts window is where you type the account's username and password information.

Table 4.1 New Account Settings

Option	Function
New Account	Select the type of account you want to create.
Full Name	Type the name of the user to whom the account belongs.
Account name	Snow Leopard automatically trims the Full Name to provide an Account name, but you can edit it if you prefer.
Password	Create a password to allow access to the account.
Verify	Retype the password you created in the Password field.
Password hint	Type a hint that will help you to remember the password if you are unable to successfully enter it.
Turn on FileVault protection	Select this check box if you want to use FileVault for this account. For more on FileVault, see Chapter 3.

Password assistance

If you have difficulty coming up with a secure password, you can always ask Snow Leopard for a little help. In the new account window, note the icon of the key next to the Password field; click this key icon to open the Password Assistant window, as shown in figure 4.3.

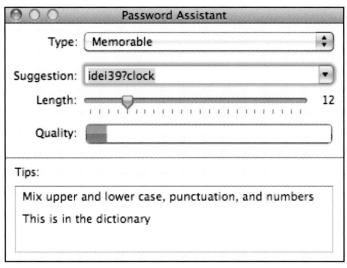

4.3 The Password Assistant can help you out of the password selection rut.

Choose the password type you want to use from these options: Manual, Memorable, Letters & Numbers, Numbers Only, Random, and FIPS-181 compliant. Manual allows you to create your own password, while the other options let Snow Leopard choose a password for you, based on the type you select.

Modify account settings

The new account, named Victoria in this example, is in the account list on the left side of the Accounts window, as shown in figure 4.4.

There are a handful of modifications you can make to the newly created account at this point:

- **Reset Password.** Click this button to reset the account's password. Only an administrator account can perform this action. You would typically only want to use this feature if the user of the account has forgotten his password, but it can obviously be abused by anyone who also has access to an administrator password.

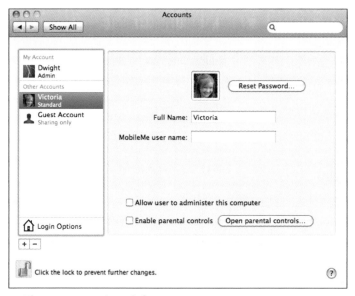

4.4 The new account is ready for use.

- **MobileMe user name.** If the user of the account has a .MobileMe username, type it here.

- **Allow user to administer this computer.** Select this check box if you want to convert a standard account to one with full administrator rights.

- **Enable parental controls.** Change the account so that it is managed with Parental Controls by selecting this check box. See later in this chapter for more on Parental Controls.

- **Delete the account.** You can remove the account completely (if you are an administrator) by clicking the account to highlight it, and then clicking the – button in the bottom-left corner of the Accounts window.

- **Change the user account picture.** Click the user account picture to change it to a different picture. The Edit Picture window opens, as shown in figure 4.5. Select one of the available pictures, or you can select a new picture by clicking Edit Picture and choosing from the Recent Pictures drop-down list or by clicking Choose to browse your Mac for a picture. You can also take a new photo by clicking Take a video snapshot if your Mac has an attached or built-in camera. Drag the slider to alter the picture's size, and click and drag the picture to center it. Click Set when you finish in the Edit Picture window.

4.5 Edit the picture used for the account to match your preferences.

The Root Account

Up until now, you thought that administrator accounts were the ultimate power trip, but now meet the real king of the accounts jungle: the root account! The root account is the only account in a UNIX-based operating system (which includes Mac OS X Snow Leopard) that truly has full access to any and every file, visible or invisible, on the computer. Administrator accounts are limited in their ability to browse folders on other accounts, even though they could delete the other accounts entirely. The root account isn't hindered from doing or accessing anything on the entire system, and that's why it's disabled in Snow Leopard by default. If you are logged in as the root user, one mistake could bring down the entire computer. I don't recommend enabling the root account for any reason; however, if you want to, here's how (consider yourself duly warned):

1. **Choose Go⊅Utilities, and then double-click the Directory Utility icon.**

2. **Click the lock in the lower-left corner of the Directory Utility window, and then type an administrator username and password when prompted.**

3. **Choose Edit⊅Enable Root User from the menu.** The root account is turned on at this point. Enter a password for the root account when prompted to do so. You certainly want to create a password; otherwise, your system will be under an enormous security threat.

Genius

It's easy to change the root account password should the need arise. Choose Edit⊅Change Root Password, type the current password, and then type the new password.

Logging into Accounts

When you first start up your Mac in the morning, or if you have to restart it at some point during the day, you most likely need to log in to the system using your account name and password. You can also log in to other accounts at the same time that yours is logged in without having to restart the Mac or shut down your running applications (now that's cool!).

Login Options

Click the Login Options button in the lower-left corner of the Accounts window to see what options you have (see figure 4.6). Table 4.2 lists and explains each of the available options.

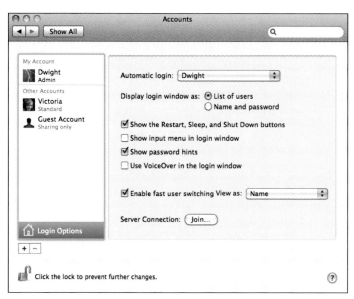

4.6 Login Options allow you to configure how people log in to their accounts on your Mac.

Table 4.2 Login Options

Option	Function
Automatic login	I recommend that you always set this option to Disabled. If you enable this option, your Mac logs in to the default administrator account without prompting you for a password, which is most certainly not a good security decision.
Display login window as	Determine whether the login window at startup should show a list of all the user accounts on the Mac, or whether it should simply prompt for a username and password. Simply prompting for a username and password may be the best idea if security is a concern.
Show the Restart, Sleep, and Shut Down buttons	Select this option to have these buttons appear in the login window.
Show input menu in login window	This option causes the Input menu to be displayed in the upper part of the login window. The Input menu is associated with the Input Sources tab of the Language & Text preferences pane, found in System Preferences. Find out more about Input Sources in Chapter 3.
Show password hints	This option allows the password hints that you entered when creating the account to appear in the login window.
Use VoiceOver in the login window	Select this option to have the contents of the login window spoken to you by the Mac.

continued

Table 4.2 continued

Option	Function
Enable fast user switching	This is the best Login Option of them all. This option allows multiple users to be logged in to the Mac at the same time. Each application that is open in an account remains open, even when someone else is logged in to his or her account. This makes it incredibly convenient for you to allow others temporary access to the Mac while not having to start all of your work over again when they're done. The name of the account that the user is currently logged in to is shown in the upper-right corner of the screen; click that name to access other accounts, and then type the user's name and password to have Snow Leopard switch over to that account.
View as	This drop-down menu determines how the user accounts display in the menu.
Server Connection	Click Join and type the name of a server you want to automatically connect to when you log in to your account.

Genius When utilizing fast user switching, you can quickly access the preferences for your account by clicking the name of the account in the upper-right corner of the screen and selecting Account Preferences from the menu.

Login Items

Login Items are applications or utilities that you have slated to automatically start when you log in to your account. You must be logged in to an account to see its Login Items window, as shown in figure 4.7.

To change the Login Items for an account, follow these steps:

1. **Click the account you want to alter in the accounts list.**

2. **Click the Login Items tab near the top of the Accounts window.**

3. **To add items to the login list, click the + button under the lower-left corner of the list, and then browse your Mac for the items.**

4. **Remove items from the list by highlighting them and clicking the – button under the lower-left corner of the list.**

5. **Select the Hide check box next to any item you want to be automatically hidden after login.** This prevents windows from the open applications cluttering your Finder window when you first log in.

6. **Close System Preferences.**

4.7 You can add or remove Login Items here.

Caution

Some applications or utilities may add items to your Login Items list that they need to be running to perform tasks in the background. Be careful before removing Login Items for antivirus software and other utilities that constantly monitor your Mac's activities.

Setting Up Simple Finder

Simple Finder is a Finder without the frills but with basic functionality for a managed user. Simple Finder only allows the user to access three folders in the Dock: My Applications, Documents, and Shared. Simple Finder doesn't allow access to the remainder of the Mac's hard drive or System Preferences.

To use Simple Finder, follow these steps:

1. **Open the Parental Controls preferences by choosing Apple menu⇨System Preferences, and then clicking the Parental Controls icon in the System section.** Because all actions in the remainder of this chapter are initiated from the Parental Controls preferences window, I won't mention that they need to be open when I give future instructions.

2. **Choose the account you want to modify in the accounts list.**

3. **Select the Use Simple Finder check box in the System tab.** The next time you log in to the account, it will use Simple Finder.

Figure 4.8 shows a typical Simple Finder desktop. The three folders in the Dock give the user access to the applications he or she has permission to use, as well as the Documents folder and the Shared folder.

To use the account with a full Finder, just deselect the Use Simple Finder check box.

4.8 An account running Simple Finder

Changing Finder Preferences in Simple Finder

Simple Finder doesn't allow a user to change many settings. This means that if you do need to change settings, you have to use an administrator account. In previous versions of Mac OS X, you would have to log out of the account using the Simple Finder, log in to an administrator account, disable Simple Finder in the managed account, and finally log back in to the managed account to change Finder settings. Whew! Thankfully, Snow Leopard changes all that. To change Finder settings while in Simple Finder

1. **Choose Finder⇨Run Full Finder, and then type an administrator's username and password.**

2. **Choose Finder⇨Preferences to make the necessary changes.**

3. **Choose Finder⇨Return to Simple Finder when finished.** The Simple Finder window returns to normal.

Limiting Access

Three of the most powerful societal influences on your youngster are the Internet, e-mail, and instant messaging. For all the wonderful content that's available on the Internet, there's an equal amount of horrifying content just waiting to be discovered and devoured by young eyes. The Parental Controls I am about to discuss can help protect our most easily impressionable citizens from some of the worst the world has to offer. Take the time to investigate each of these settings to the fullest extent if you have children who will be using your computer to surf the Internet, receive e-mail, or send instant messages. As a parent, I completely understand the desire to protect your children from things that may be beyond their level of maturity and understanding.

Parental Controls is just as effective with adults as it is with children, so don't be afraid to manage the accounts of those users who aren't very experienced with computers or perhaps haven't quite grown up in other ways. Sometimes you have to do what is best for little Leslie, or even big Bob, whether they like it or not!

Enabling Parental Controls

To use Parental Controls, you must create a Managed by Parental Controls account or enable Parental Controls for an existing account. Follow the instructions in earlier sections of this chapter for creating a new user account or follow these steps to enable Parental Controls on a current account:

1. **Choose Apple menu ⇨ System Preferences and then click the Accounts icon in the System section.**

2. **Click the lock icon in the lower-left corner if it is locked and then type an administrator username and password to unlock the Accounts preferences.**

3. **Select the account you want to enable Parental Controls for in the accounts list.**

4. **Select the Enable Parental Controls check box.**

5. **Click Show All in the upper-left corner of the System Preferences window and then select the Parental Controls icon in the System section.**

6. **Choose the Managed with Parental Controls account in the account list on the left side of the Parental Controls window, as shown in figure 4.9.** The account is ready for you to take control.

4.9 The default Parental Controls window with an account ready to be modified

Application and function restrictions

An alternative to Simple Finder is to run a full Finder but with limitations. Parental Controls lets an administrator choose exactly what applications and utilities the managed account can use and what functions it can perform. To set these kinds of limitations, follow these steps:

1. **In the System tab of the Parental Controls window, select the Only allow selected applications check box.**

2. **In the Select the applications to allow window, browse through the list of available applications and utilities; click the arrows on the left side of the list to expand a category.** When you find an application or utility you want the user of the account to be able to access, select the check box to its immediate left.

3. **At the bottom of the window, select the check box next to the functions you want the user to be able to use, as in figure 4.10.** Table 4.3 further explains each option.

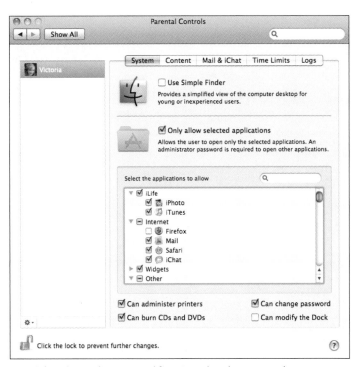

4.10 Select the applications and functions that the managed account can access or use.

Table 4.3 Functional Limitations

Option	Function
Can administer printers	Select this option if you want the user to be able to add or remove printers and to be able to manage jobs in the printer queues.
Can burn CDs and DVDs	This option allows the user to burn music and data to CDs and DVDs.
Can change password	Select this option so that users can change the account password for themselves.
Can modify the Dock	The user can add, remove, and reposition items in the Dock when you select this option.

Web site restrictions

One of the neat features in Parental Controls is the ability to control (for the most part) the Web sites that are accessible while logged into a managed account. To start putting your foot down, click the Content tab in the Parental Controls window and decide whether to allow unfettered access to the Internet, to filter Web sites based on their content, or to restrict access only to certain Web sites.

97

Allow unrestricted access to websites

This works as advertised. If you don't want to restrict the Internet content that can be accessed through this managed account, select this option.

Try to limit access to adult websites automatically

This option enables Web site filtering, which scours the contents of a Web site for buzzwords that might tip the filter off that the site is inappropriate for young and curious eyes. Click Customize to modify how the filter works, as shown in figure 4.11.

4.11 Allow or restrict certain Web sites by customizing the Web site filter.

The Web site filter isn't perfect, so sometimes it may filter content that you consider safe for your children and may let other sites through that you would normally curtail.

Click the + button under the Always allow these websites section to enter the addresses of sites you want the filter to allow through, regardless of whether the site's content conflicts with the filter or not.

Click the + button under the Never allow these websites section to block access to Web sites that the filter might miss and that you do not want your children to have the ability to see.

Profanity in the Dictionary

You're probably wondering why I skipped the first item in the Content pane of the Parental Controls window: Hide profanity in Dictionary. This option obviously has its merit, so please select the check box if you prefer to hide profane words from prying eyes when your youngster uses the Dictionary application that is part of Snow Leopard. This option just seems an odd fit among the Internet filtering and e-mail discussions, so I gave it its own special mention here.

Allow access to only these websites

Select this option to allow access to only the specific sites you enter into the approved list, as shown in figure 4.12.

Click the + button beneath the list of approved sites to add sites (choose the Add bookmark option from the pop-up menu that appears), or highlight sites you don't want on the list and click the − button to remove them.

Mail and iChat limitations

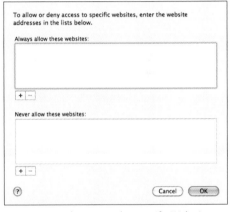

4.12 You can determine the specific Web sites that you want the account user to access.

Just as important as filtering Web site content is the ability to control whom your kids converse with over the Internet. If you choose to allow the user of the managed account access to e-mail and instant messaging, the Mail & iChat tab of the Parental Controls preferences is right where you want to be (figure 4.13).

To place restrictions on e-mail and instant messaging, select the check boxes next to Limit Mail and Limit iChat. Doing so allows you to add contacts to the Only allow emailing and instant messaging with list. Click the + button underneath the list to add new names, or highlight names and then click the − button to remove them from the list.

One of my favorite features in Parental Controls is the ability to have an e-mail sent to the address of your choice that asks for your permission before allowing someone who's not in the approved list to send e-mails or instant messages to the user of the managed account. Select the Send permission requests to option, and then type the preferred e-mail address for these requests to be sent.

4.13 The Mail & iChat tab is where you can control e-mails and instant messages for your managed accounts.

Setting time limits

Another great tool in Parental Controls allows you to set limits on the amount of time the user of the managed account can access the Mac. This is one that kids hate and parents love! Table 4.4 describes the options that are available in the Time Limits tab of the Parental Controls window.

Table 4.4 Time Limit Settings

Setting	Operation
Weekday time limits	Select the Limit computer use to check box, and then drag the slider to set the total amount of time the user of the managed account can be logged in for each weekday (Monday through Friday).
Weekend time limits	Again, select the Limit computer use to check box, and then drag the slider to set the total amount of time the user of the managed account can be logged in for a single weekend day (Saturday and Sunday).
Bedtime	Set the times of day for both school days (Sunday through Thursday) and weekend days (Friday and Saturday) that the user of the managed account cannot have access to it. This prevents them from sneaking around in the middle of the night to check out those Web sites that you may have forgotten to restrict.

Keeping account activity logs

When all is said and done, there is simply no way for you to monitor your kid every second of every day. Apple thought of that when it designed Parental Controls. What better than Snow Leopard to keep track of which Web sites your kids have checked out, which Web sites they are blocked from seeing, the applications they use while logged in, and with whom they are chatting during their session? The Logs tab of Parental Controls, shown in figure 4.14, keeps tabs on all of the account's activity so you will be informed of what happened, even if you weren't there to see it.

Select the amount of time to show account activity in the Show activity for pop-up menu. Determine how the logs should be ordered by choosing either Contact, Website, Application (depending on which collection you highlight in the Log Collections pane), or Date from the Group by pop-up menu. If you find an objectionable site, application, or iChat message, click Restrict at the bottom of the window to block access to it.

Being diligent in browsing these logs will do nothing but further protect your child from things he or she may not be ready to deal with just yet.

4.14 Some may describe these logs as Big Brother gone awry; I call it responsible parenting.

What Can I Do with Applications and Utilities?

Dear Kate,

Here's to the crazy ones. The misfits. The rebels. The troublemakers. The round pegs in the square holes. The ones who see things differently. They're not fond of rules. And they have no respect for the status quo. You can praise them, disagree with them, quote them, disbelieve them, glorify or vilify them. About the only thing you can't do is ignore them. Because they change things.

Take Care,
John Appleseed

Snow Leopard is more than just an operating system; it's also full of applications and utilities designed to make your computing life as productive as possible, while at the same time being simple and fun to use. From word processing to buying music online, from surfing the Web to running connectivity diagnostics on your network, Mac OS X 10.6 comes loaded with all the tools you need. Unlike competitors' operating systems, Mac OS X comes in only one flavor: fully loaded! This chapter introduces you to the myriad programs that come with Snow Leopard so that you know exactly what you can do with this big cat. I also show you how to navigate most Mac applications, as well as how to use common keyboard shortcuts. For good measure, I go in depth with one of Snow Leopard's included applications — Mac OS X's word processing application, TextEdit.

Discovering Applications

Snow Leopard ships with about 25 applications, each of which offers its unique way of handling various tasks. With so many applications, you might be wondering what in the world all these applications can do. I cover the lesser-known or -used applications in short detail in this chapter, going a bit more in depth with Mac's word processor, TextEdit. Because I cover some of the more high-profile applications in other chapters, I only give short introductions for them here (see Table 5.3).

To see all the applications at your disposal, open the Applications folder (shown in figure 5.1). You can do one of the following:

- **Click the Go menu in the Finder and select Applications.**
- **Press ⌘+Shift+A while in the Finder.**

5.1 The Applications folder in all its glory

Let's take a look at some of the hidden gems in Snow Leopard.

Calculator

Calculator, as shown in figure 5.2, is not your run-of-the-mill addition, subtraction, multiplication, and division tool, although it can perform those basic functions with the best of them.

Calculator has three modes: Basic, Scientific, and Programmer. Table 5.1 gives a brief description of each mode.

Table 5.1 Calculator Modes

Mode	Function
Basic	Performs the traditional tasks of addition, multiplication, subtraction, and division.
Scientific	Expands the Basic mode to give you the ability to perform advanced mathematical calculations, such as trigonometric functions, factorial functions, and square roots.
Programmer	Performs calculations that only a true geek could love (or understand, for that matter). Programmers need to perform calculations such as hexadecimal conversion, binary computations, and logical operations. Calculator fits the bill perfectly, as shown in figure 5.2.

If you want to see a printout of your calculations, you can use the Paper Tape function. Choose Window ⇨ Show Paper Tape, or press ⌘+T, to open the Paper Tape window. Choose File ⇨ Print Tape to print your calculations and results.

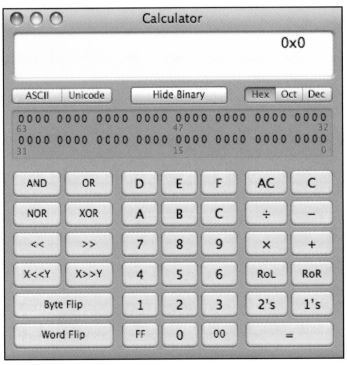

5.2 Calculator can also convert units of measure such as area, currency, speed, and volume.

Chess

You may have noticed that Mac OS X Snow Leopard doesn't come with Minesweeper and Hearts. No, the brainiacs at Apple prefer to include Chess, instead. Chess is one of the world's greatest games, and also one of the most challenging, making it the perfect game to include in such a sophisticated operating system.

To play a game of Chess, simply double-click its icon in the Applications folder. You can play against another person or test your wits against the Mac.

Choose Chess ⇨ Preferences to change things such as the look of the pieces and board, the difficulty level of the computer player, and to allow moves to be spoken aloud. Refer to Chess's Help (choose Help ⇨ Chess Help) for more information about this great version of a classic game.

Genius

If the board position isn't to your liking, click and drag one of the corners of the board in all directions, as shown in figure 5.3, until you get the view you want.

Dwight Spivey – Computer   (White to Move)

5.3 Change the board's position in the window by dragging a corner of the board.

Dictionary

Dictionary, like all the other cool applications in Snow Leopard, does more than just look up defini-
tions to words. Use Dictionary as a standard dictionary (New Oxford American Dictionary, to be
exact), or as a thesaurus (Oxford American Writer's Thesaurus), to find terms in Apple's dictionary,
and to discover articles on Wikipedia.

Simply type a word or topic in the search field in the upper-right corner of the window (next to the
magnifying glass icon), as shown in figure 5.4, to begin a search. Dictionary displays what it finds in
all four sources or only the one you select from the toolbar.

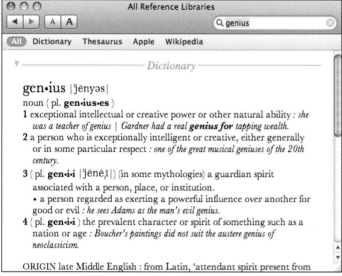

5.4 Dictionary is a great tool for students, writers, business professionals,
and anyone else looking to find the meaning of a word, or articles on it.

DVD Player

DVD Player performs as advertised: It plays DVDs. Clever naming of the application by Apple, if you
ask me.

DVD Player can perform all the basic functions of your regular DVD player. The upside to using this
application instead is that you don't have to leave your Mac's side to catch a flick.

You control the playback of movies with an onscreen remote, as shown in figure 5.5, as opposed to
holding one in your hand.

5.5 DVD Player's onscreen remote control

You can also control playback of your DVDs with your Mac's keyboard, using the keyboard short-cuts listed in Table 5.2.

Table 5.2 DVD Player Keyboard Shortcuts

Function	Keys
Play/Pause	Space bar
Stop	⌘+.
Scan Forward	⌘+Shift+→
Scan Backward	⌘+Shift+←
Volume Up	⌘+↑
Volume Down	⌘+↓
Mute	⌘+Option+↓
Close Control Drawer	⌘+]
Eject DVD	⌘+E

Font Book

Fonts are very important to the look and feel of your Mac, as well as any documents you may cre-ate with its applications. Font Book is a fantastic utility that allows you to manage the fonts you have installed on your Mac.

Font Book, shown in figure 5.6, can install and delete fonts without you having to reboot your Mac. Use it to organize your fonts into collections, enable the fonts you want to use, or disable the fonts you don't want to use, rather than completely deleting them from the system.

Refer to Font Book's Help (choose Help ⇨ Font Book Help) to find out more on using this excep-tional utility.

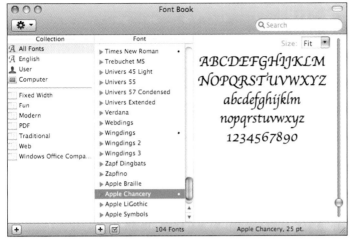

5.6 Font Book helps to organize and manage your Mac's font collections.

Stickies

Stickies is a nifty little application for keeping lists, creating reminders, and quickly entering any information you want. It uses the metaphor of the tiny yellow notes that we all have dangling off our computer monitors, with the exception that these stickies don't fall off and drift under your desk when you're not looking. Stickies automatically saves your notes. Figure 5.7 shows an example of the Stickies version of a virtual sticky note.

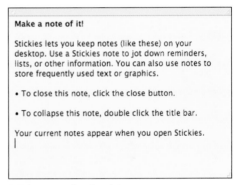

5.7 An example of a sticky note

Additional applications

Table 5.3 lists other applications that come with Snow Leopard and that are mentioned in greater detail in other chapters.

Table 5.3 More Snow Leopard Applications

Application	Primary function
Address Book	Keeps contact information in one handy location. See Chapter 8 for more information.
Automator	Automates the tasks you find repetitive and mundane. Chapter 14 covers Automator in depth.

continued

Table 5.3 continued

Application	Primary function
Dashboard	Organizes tiny applications called widgets. There is much more on Dashboard and widgets in Chapter 2.
Exposé	Helps organize your desktop clutter. Chapter 1 exposes much more of Exposé.
iCal	Lets you create calendars to keep up with your hourly, daily, weekly, monthly, and annual tasks and appointments. Chapter 8 goes into much more detail about iCal.
iChat	Lets you send instant messages to anyone anywhere in the world.
Image Capture	Capture images from your scanners and digital cameras with this handy application. Learn much more in Chapter 12.
iSync	Synchronizes all your contacts and calendars with multiple devices. Chapter 8 goes into more detail.
iTunes	Your Mac's entertainment hub. Chapter 11 gives you the inside scoop.
Mail	Snow Leopard's e-mail application. Discover how to use Mail in Chapter 10.
Photo Booth	Take pictures and videos using your Mac's built-in camera. See more in Chapter 12.
Preview	Capable of opening multiple file types, such as JPEGs, TIFFs, and PDFs. Chapter 7 covers Preview like a blanket.
QuickTime Player	Plays video and sound files in a multitude of formats.
Safari	Mac OS X's standout Web browser. Chapter 9 will have you cruising the Internet jungle in style.
Spaces	Lets you manage your open applications and windows in multiple desktop spaces. Chapter 1 shows you how to utilize this cool feature in Snow Leopard.
System Preferences	The one place where you can make Snow Leopard behave the way you want it to. Make settings for your network, sharing files, changing your Mac's appearance, and much more by checking out Chapter 3.
TextEdit	Snow Leopard's built-in word processor. Begin creating documents by perusing the information about TextEdit later in this chapter.
Time Machine	Back up your Mac's files and folders to keep them safe and to restore them if necessary. Chapter 14 has the lowdown on this very popular feature of Snow Leopard.

Navigating Snow Leopard's applications

Many of the basic functions and menus of Snow Leopard's applications and utilities are accessed in the same way. For example, opening a file from within almost any application is done by choosing File⇨Open. There are also keyboard shortcuts that are universally used among the applications in Snow Leopard.

How to open and close applications

This one is really basic, but still necessary, so I'll keep it short and to the point.

Use one of these methods to open applications:

- **Choose Go ⇨ Applications, or Go ⇨ Utilities, from within the Finder and double-click the application or utility you need.**

- **Click the application's icon in the Dock.**

- **Choose Apple menu ⇨ Recent Items and select a recently used application from the list.**

These techniques close an open application:

- **Choose the application's title menu (immediately to the right of the Apple menu) and select Quit.**

- **Press ⌘+Q.**

- **Click and hold the application's icon in the Dock, and then select Quit from the resulting pop-up menu (see figure 5.8).**

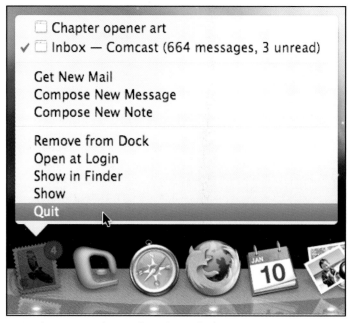

5.8 Easily quit an application from the Dock.

Common commands and keyboard shortcuts

Table 5.4 lists commands that are common among Snow Leopard's applications, as well as the keyboard shortcuts that make issuing those commands even easier.

Genius If you are a Windows user who is converting to the Mac, many of the keyboard short-cuts you are familiar with have Mac equivalents. For example, to print a job in Windows, you would press Ctrl+P, and on the Mac you would press ⌘+P; Ctrl+C copies an item on Windows, while ⌘+C does the same trick on a Mac.

Table 5.4 Commands and Keyboard Shortcuts

Command	Function	Keyboard shortcut
Open	Opens a file or document	⌘+O
Save	Saves the contents of a document	⌘+S
New	Creates a new blank document	⌘+N
Close	Closes the active window	⌘+W
Page Setup	Selects the correct paper size and orientation to print with	⌘+Shift+P
Print	Prints the current document	⌘+P
Copy	Copies highlighted text	⌘+C
Cut	Cuts highlighted text from a document	⌘+X
Paste	Pastes copied or cut text into a document	⌘+V
Select All	Highlights all text in a document	⌘+A
Find	Finds words in the document or window	⌘+F
Find Next	Finds the next instance of a word in a document or window	⌘+G
Find Previous	Finds the previous instance of a word in a document or window	⌘+Shift+G
Force Quit	Forces an application or utility to quit	⌘+Option+Esc
Minimize	Minimizes the active window	⌘+M
Preferences	Opens the application's preferences	⌘+,
Hide	Hides the active application	⌘+H
Quit	Quits the active application	⌘+Q

Easily access applications with a Stack

Snow Leopard has a neat new feature called Stacks that allows you to place folder aliases on the right side of the Dock. You can add a Stack for your Applications folder to the Dock so that you can easily and quickly access all the applications and utilities on your Mac. Follow these steps:

1. **Open your hard drive:**

   - **Double-click your hard drive's icon, or**
   - **Press ⌘+N from within the Finder, and then select the hard drive icon from the Devices section.**

2. **Drag the Applications folder to the right side of the Dock and drop it in.**

3. **Click the Applications folder alias (icon) to open the Stack.**

The Stack can display in either a fan pattern, as in figure 5.9, or in a grid, as in figure 5.10. As you can see, Fan mode doesn't show all the items in the folder if there are a lot in there. Notice at the top of the fan in figure 5.9 that it shows "39 More in Finder" next to the arrow. This means that there are 39 more application icons that can't be shown in the fan due to its configuration; this is where the Grid mode shines. The configuration of the grid allows you to see all of the folder's contents. To select a different view for your stack, simply click and hold the mouse button on the stack's icon, and then select the view you want from the View content as section of the contextual menu.

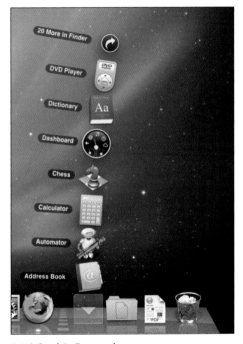

5.9 A Stack in Fan mode

113

5.10 A Stack in Grid mode

Using Utilities

Utilities do a lot of the dirty work for your Mac. They diagnose problems with your network, help you partition your hard drive, format disks, manage color on your screen and in your documents, take screenshots, manage passwords, and much more. Table 5.5 lists the utilities that come with Snow Leopard (as shown in figure 5.11), describes their main functions in life, and lets you know whether more information on the utility can be found elsewhere in this book.

Note All of these utilities have Help systems that will teach you much more about those utilities that interest you the most. To access the Help system for any application, simply click Help in the menu bar.

5.11 Mac OS X Snow Leopard utilities, at your service

Table 5.5 Snow Leopard Utilities

Utility	Primary function
Activity Monitor	Keeps track of all the goings-on in Snow Leopard, such as what applications are running and how much of the processor's capacity is being used.
AirPort Utility	Helps you manage your AirPort Base Station.
AppleScript Editor	A tool to help you write and edit AppleScripts.
Audio MIDI Setup	Helps set up audio and MIDI devices that you connect to your Mac.
Bluetooth File Exchange	Transfers files to and from other devices running the Bluetooth protocol.
Boot Camp Assistant	Creates a separate partition on your Mac's hard drive for installing Microsoft Windows. Chapter 16 gives you the skinny on this awesome addition to Mac OS X.
ColorSync Utility	Manages your Mac's color profiles for devices such as monitors and printers.
Console	Displays messages that are being generated by your Mac or its applications. These messages are generated when an error occurs. This utility is great for tracking down problems with Mac OS X.
DigitalColor Meter	Measures color values on your display so that you can enter the values into other programs, such as graphics applications.
Disk Utility	Formats and manages hard drives, removable media such as CDs and DVDs, and disk images.
Grab	Takes screenshots of items on your Mac. Grab was used extensively in the creation of art files for this book. Grab is covered in Chapter 1.

continued

115

Table 5.5 continued

Utility	Primary function
Grapher	A neat utility that graphs equations, visualizing them in two or three dimensions. You can even animate your graphs with this baby.
Java Preferences	Determine which Java Virtual Machine to use with your browser, Java applications, and Web applications.
Keychain Access	Manages your plethora of passwords in one convenient location.
Migration Assistant	Moves all the user account information from one Mac to another using a FireWire cable. You can bring over your network information, passwords, the contents of your user account's folder, and so on in one fell swoop. Will also help you restore information using a Time Machine backup.
Network Utility	Monitors network traffic and diagnoses any issues that may creep up.
Podcast Capture	Allows you to record and distribute podcasts as long as you have access to a Mac OS X server running Podcast Producer.
RAID Utility	Allows you to configure multiple hard drives to act as one contiguous drive. You must have a RAID (Redundant Array of Inexpensive Disks) card installed on your Mac to use this utility.
Remote Install Mac OS X	Helps install Mac OS X on a MacBook Air, which doesn't have an internal hard drive of its own and relies on drives in other computers or an external drive.
System Profiler	Gives you all the information you could ever want about your Mac's hardware and software.
Terminal	A command-line utility for accessing Snow Leopard's UNIX underpinnings. You play around with this utility quite a bit in Chapter 15.
VoiceOver Utility	Allows your Mac to describe your screen's contents verbally. Your Mac literally speaks to you and reads the contents of your open documents and windows. This is obviously a fantastic utility for anyone who has difficulty seeing what is on the Mac's screen.
X11	Lets you run UNIX applications alongside your Mac OS X applications. This is an optional utility that you can install, either during installation or later, from your Mac OS X Snow Leopard installation disc.

Working with Documents in TextEdit

TextEdit is Snow Leopard's built-in word processing application, and it can handle a good deal of your basic document-writing needs. TextEdit is one of those names that advertises just what the application does: It edits text. TextEdit's interface is simplicity itself, as are the functions it provides. Although you don't get all the frills of a full-fledged word processor like Microsoft Word, Apple's Pages, or OpenOffice, TextEdit is surprisingly more capable than it appears at first glance (it can even open documents created by the aforementioned big boys).

Setting TextEdit Preferences

I am a big fan of making things work the way you want them to on your computer, not the way Apple or anyone else says you have to. The way I work may do wonders for my production, but may cause you to groan with frustration or yawn in tedium. Most applications allow you to change their default behaviors to match your style of working (or playing, as the case may be), and TextEdit is thankfully no exception.

To alter TextEdit's default behaviors, choose TextEdit ➪ Preferences from the menu, or press ⌘+,. The Preferences window opens and permits access to two tabs: New Document, and Open and Save. Tables 5.6 and 5.7, in conjunction with figures 5.12 and 5.13, respectively, let you see what these two tabs offer in the way of customizing your TextEdit experience.

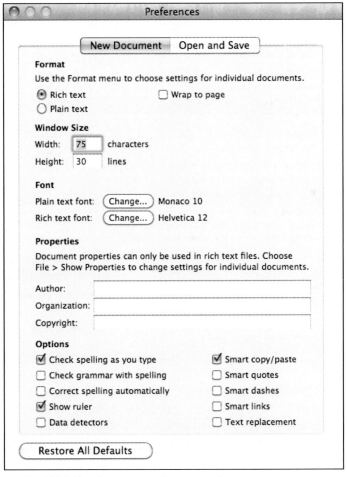

5.12 TextEdit's New Document preferences options

Table 5.6 The New Document Preferences

Preferences	Functions
Format	Lets you select Rich text (RTF) or Plain text (txt) as your default format for new documents.
Wrap to page	Causes text to wrap to document margins instead of window margins.
Window Size	Sets the default window size for new documents.
Font	Lets you choose the default font to use for new plain text or rich text documents.
Properties (RTF only)	Enter information you want to include with each document you create, such as your name, the company you work for, and any copyright information that may be legally necessary for the document.
Check spelling as you type/Check grammar with spelling	Activates the spelling and grammar checkers.
Show ruler	Displays a ruler at the top of each window.
Smart copy/paste	Automatically adds any necessary spaces when text is added or deleted.
Smart quotes	Uses curly quote marks instead of straight ones.
Smart links	Automatically turns Internet addresses into links that open to the appropriate Web site when clicked in the document.
Restore All Defaults	Reverts back to TextEdit's original default preferences.

Table 5.7 Open and Save Preferences

Preferences	Functions
Ignore rich text commands in HTML/RTF files	Opens HTML and RTF files automatically as plain text, retaining no formatting at all. This is beneficial to Web developers who need to edit their code.
Delete the automatic backup file	TextEdit saves a backup of your file as it is saving it. Select this option to delete that backup once the save is complete.
Add ".txt" extension to plain text files	Automatically tags plain text files with the .txt extension at the end of their filenames.
Autosaving	Lets you select the time increments for automatically saving documents that you modify.
Plain Text File Encoding	Lets you decide which text encoding to use by default when opening and saving plain text files. I suggest sticking with Automatic unless you really know what you are doing with these settings.

Preferences	Functions
HTML Saving Options	Lets you choose the default document type, styling, and encoding to use when saving documents as HTML files.
Preserve white space	Preserves blank areas that are already in your document so that they aren't lost during formatting.
Restore All Defaults	Reverts back to TextEdit's original New Document and Open and Save default settings.

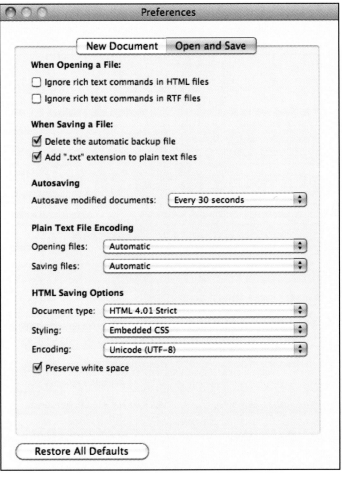

5.13 The Open and Save preferences options for TextEdit

Creating and saving your document

Open TextEdit by choosing Go from within the Finder, selecting Applications, and double-clicking the TextEdit icon. TextEdit opens a new document automatically when you first start it up, as shown in figure 5.14.

Creating a new document doesn't get much easier, but what if TextEdit is already open? Simply do one of the following:

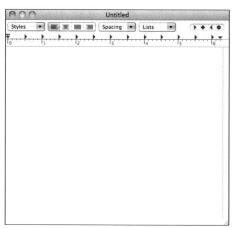

- **Choose File ⇨ New.**

- **Press ⌘+N.**

5.14 TextEdit waiting patiently for your input

A shiny new document opens, ready for you to type your information. To get started with your document, just begin typing!

After you create a document, you typically want to save it so that you can refer to it again sometime in the future.

To save a document, do the following:

1. **Choose File ⇨ Save, or press ⌘+S, to open the Save dialog.**
2. **Type a name for your document in the Save As field.**
3. **Navigate to the location on your Mac where you want to save the document.**
4. **Click Save.**

Opening an existing document

To open a document from within TextEdit, do the following:

1. **Choose File ⇨ Open to display the Open dialog.**
2. **Navigate your Mac's hard drive until you are in the folder of the file you want to open.**
3. **Select the name of the file to open, and click Open to display the document in TextEdit.**

You can now view, print, or edit your document as needed.

A word about file formats

You may notice that at the bottom of TextEdit's Save As dialog (see figure 5.15) is a File Format menu. TextEdit's default file format is RTF, which stands for Rich Text Format. Most word processors on any computing platform (including Mac, Windows, and Linux) can open RTF documents, so you don't have to worry much about whether other computer users can view or edit your TextEdit documents. RTF allows you to make formatting changes to your document, such as adding some punch to your fonts by changing their size and color.

If you click the File Format pop-up menu, you see the other formats that TextEdit can save your document in (see figure 5.15). Table 5.8 describes the file formats so that you can decide whether something other than RTF is right for you. What is the coolest thing about the availability of these formats? Not only can TextEdit save your documents in them, but it can also open any document that uses them; this gives you extreme flexibility when it comes to opening and saving files that originate with users of other operating systems and word processors.

5.15 Choose any of these formats to save your TextEdit documents.

Genius

There is one more file format not listed in figure 5.15 or Table 5.7: plain text (.txt). Plain text doesn't allow you to format your documents with fancy fonts or pictures, however. So what's the appeal of plain text? First, most programming is done in the plain text format. Second, plain text is a format that all word processors, even those that run in command-line operating systems like DOS and UNIX, can open, read, and edit. To create a plain text file, choose Format ⇨ Make Plain Text from the menu.

Table 5.8 TextEdit File Formats

Format	Uses
Rich Text Format with Attachments (RTFD)	This is essentially RTF with graphics included, such as pictures.
Web Page (.html)	HTML stands for HyperText Markup Language, which is a programming language used to create Web pages. It allows you to edit Web pages or quickly create new ones.
Web Archive	This is used primarily as a format in which Safari saves Web pages. TextEdit can open, edit, and save these files.
OpenDocument Text (.odt)	OpenDocument is a relatively new standard for word processor files that is native to the OpenOffice.org office suite.
Word 2007 Format (.docx)	Microsoft made a break from Word's traditional file format with Office 2007.
Word 2003 Format (.xml)	Open, edit, and save files that were created from Word 2003 using XML (Extensible Markup Language), another programming language used extensively on the Web.
Word 97 Format (.doc)	This format should be very familiar to anyone who's used Microsoft Word in the past. It is one of the most widely used formats on the planet.

Formatting Your TextEdit Documents

Sometimes simply typing text into your documents may be good enough for the task at hand, but other situations may call for something nicer, neater, and more polished. Because TextEdit uses RTF, formatting elements of your documents, such as manipulating fonts and adding pictures, is almost too easy. The look and feel of a document can be very important, even more so to the reader than the writer, and something as simple as a font choice can affect how the reader responds to the text.

Using fonts

Mac OS X Snow Leopard comes with a wide variety of built-in fonts to spice up your life in the world of word processing. To manipulate fonts in a document, do the following:

1. **Open an existing file, or create a new one, in TextEdit by doing one of the following:**

   - **Choose File ➪ Open or File ➪ New.**

   - **Press ⌘+O or ⌘+N.**

2. **Highlight the text you want to change by clicking and dragging the mouse over it.** You can highlight all the text in the document by pressing ⌘+A, or choosing Edit ➪ Select All.

3. **Choose Format ➪ Font to change the fonts used in your document.** You can change the font size, make the letters bold, underline words, change the color of the text, and much more. See the upcoming section for information on the Fonts window.

4. **Choose Format ➪ Text to manipulate text on the page.** Move the alignment of the text to the left, right, or center. You can also change the spacing widths between lines, change the direction of your writing from right to left (necessary for text in some languages, such as Hebrew), create tables from existing text, and even more.

Using the Fonts window

The Fonts window, as shown in Figure 5.16, gives you a central location in TextEdit where you can choose and stylize fonts. Open the Fonts window by choosing Format ➪ Font ➪ Show Fonts.

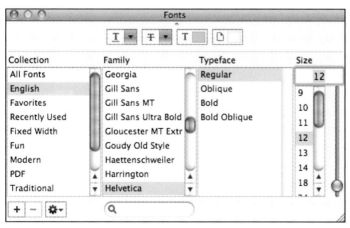

5.16 The Fonts window in TextEdit makes it easy to change the look of your document's text.

The toolbar at the top of the window allows you to make changes to the appearance of the text, such as the following:

- **Text Underline and Text Strikethrough.** Decide whether to use a single or double line for the underline or strikethrough, as well as what color the line should be.

- **Change the color of the text.**

- **Add a drop shadow to the text.** You can also change the way the drop shadow is displayed, by changing the shadow's opacity, blur, offset, and angle.

Select the fonts to use in your document by browsing the list in the Fonts window. You can change the size of the font, as well as change its typeface characteristics (such as making it bold or italic).

Checking spelling and grammar

No matter who you are or how well educated you may be, at some point, someone will catch you in a spelling or grammatical error. Thankfully, writers have brilliant editors who come behind us and clean up our frequent messes, but most folks aren't so blessed. It is to those unlucky enough not to have editors that I dedicate this section of the chapter.

TextEdit may be a simple program, but it's quite a smart one, too. Do you have a problem spelling words like "millennium" or "weird?" Does "I am doing well" come out as "I is doing well?" If so, TextEdit has your back.

To check spelling and grammar in your documents, do the following:

1. **Choose Edit ⇨ Spelling and Grammar ⇨ Show Spelling and Grammar to open the Spelling and Grammar dialog, as shown in figure 5.17.**

2. **Click Find Next, and TextEdit goes one-by-one through each spelling or grammar violation.** It even makes suggestions for rectifying the problems.

3. **Click Change if you agree to the suggested changes, click Ignore to skip and move to the next violation, or click Learn to teach TextEdit the spelling of a word that may not be in its vocabulary.**

4. **Close the Spelling and Grammar window by clicking the red dot in the upper-left corner when finished.**

Genius

TextEdit can check your spelling and grammar on the fly, too. Choose Edit ⇨ Spelling and Grammar, and click Check Spelling While Typing to have TextEdit check each word as you type it. Choose Edit ⇨ Spelling and Grammar, and click Check Grammar With Spelling so that TextEdit checks your grammar along with the spelling of your words. To have TextEdit look over your document at any time, press ⌘+;.

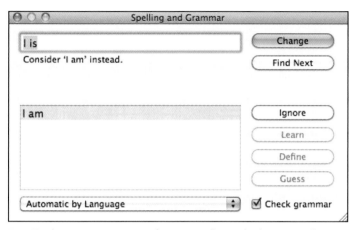

5.17 You have no more excuses for poor spelling or bad grammar if you use TextEdit.

How Can I Print with Snow Leopard?

Like surfing the Web and accessing e-mail, printing is one of the basic functions of life for your Mac. The Mac OS has always been known for its printing prowess, but Snow Leopard ups the ante quite a bit from previous versions of Mac OS X in terms of ease of installation and managing jobs. Because the Mac has been the publishing industry's best buddy for more than two decades, Apple has made sure that printing a document from Mac OS X is just what it should be — simple and intuitive — which is exactly how I like it, thank you very much.

Set Up a Printer

Installing a printer in Mac OS X is a snap, provided that everything the Mac needs to communicate with the printer is installed (software and drivers) and the necessary hardware (devices and cables) is functioning up to par.

Caution

Before you purchase a printer, make absolutely certain that the printer is Mac compatible (most are compatible with your Mac, but it's best to be sure). Don't just trust the well-meaning employees at the electronics superstore; check it out for yourself by going to the printer manufacturer's Web page and checking the specifications for the printer, or look for familiar Mac logos on the printer's box. Logos to look for would be the large X logo with the "Made for Mac OS X" tagline, and the happy Mac, which is the same as the Finder icon on the left side of your Dock (see figure 6.1). If you buy your printer directly from Apple it's a safe bet the printer is Mac compatible.

There are three main steps that you must take before you can use your printer with your Mac:

1. **Install the software that came with your printer.**

2. **Connect your printer to your Mac or your network.**

   - **If your printer has a USB connection, connect one end of the USB cable to the printer and the other end to your Mac.**

   - **If your printer has a network, or Ethernet interface, use an Ethernet (or RJ-45) cable to connect it to your network's router or switch.**

Mac logo

6.1 This is one of the familiar Mac logos to look for on the box of the printer you want to purchase.

3. **Use the Print & Fax System Preferences pane to create a print queue for the printer (in other words, install the printer).**

Installing your printer's software

Mac OS X needs special software, called a driver, to be able to communicate effectively with your printer, just as it does to speak to any other device you may connect to it, such as a scanner or input device (such as a mouse or trackball). Mac OS X comes preloaded with tons of printer drivers from several of the most popular printer manufacturers, and so chances are pretty good that you won't need to install any additional software. However, the safest way to go is to install the software the manufacturer provides in the box, typically on a CD; if no CD is in the box, you can download the latest software from the manufacturer's support Web site.

Note I think it's always a good idea to just go to the manufacturer's Web site and download the drivers right from the beginning. This ensures that you have the latest and greatest software for your printer.

Caution Be sure the driver files you download are for the version of Mac OS X you are using; if you're reading this book, the automatic assumption is that you're running Snow Leopard or Mac OS X 10.6.

Unfortunately, there's not one right way to install drivers. Printer manufacturers provide drivers and software in a number of ways using different installer applications, so the way you installed your HP printer's software may be different than it was when you installed your Konica Minolta, Brother, Xerox, or Epson software.

Some printer manufacturers may install other software in addition to the printer driver, such as utilities that allow you to monitor the printer's consumables (such as toners, ink cartridges, and drums), perform maintenance tasks, and run diagnostics for troubleshooting. These utilities are typically installed in the Hard Drive ⇨ Applications folder. Consult your printer manufacturer if you're not sure about what software should be installed to maximize your use of the printer (other than the driver, of course).

Generally, you should follow the installation instructions included in the printer box, but here is the typical process used to install printer drivers and software:

1. **Insert the CD that came with your printer, or download the software from the printer manufacturer's Web site.**
2. **Double-click the CD's icon to open a window to see its contents (if one doesn't open automatically), and then double-click the software installer icon.** Safari automatically opens and mounts the disk image, and displays a window showing the disk image's contents. Double-click the installer icon in the disk image's window.
3. **Type your user account login password when prompted during installation.**

4. **When the software installation is complete, you see a prompt similar to figure 6.2.**
Click Close to complete the process.

6.2 Click Close to finish the driver software installation process.

Your Mac should now have the necessary drivers and utilities to communicate with your printer. You can now move on to the second major step in your printer setup, connecting your printer.

Connecting your printer

How you connect your printer is just as important as having the correct driver software installed. Some printers come with only one connection type, which is usually USB, but others may have multiple connection options, the most common being an Ethernet interface for directly connecting the printer to your network.

On-demand Print Drivers

The Mac OS X installer application no longer installs several gigabytes of printer drivers by default; instead, it installs drivers as needed when a printer is detected. For example, if you have a printer connected to your Mac or network during installation of Mac OS X Snow Leopard, the installer detects it and installs the drivers needed by the printer. This process only works with printers by manufacturers that have supplied drivers to Apple. Software Update finds new drivers as they become available.

USB

Connecting with USB is certainly the easiest way for your Mac to get its print on, and USB is reasonably fast for most printing needs. There's not much to it, really. Follow these steps:

1. **Connect one end of the USB cable to the printer.**

2. **Connect the other end of the USB cable to the Mac.**

Voilá! The printer is connected!

Genius

Most printers don't ship with a USB cable in the box, so be sure to pick one up before you leave the store where you purchase it. If the store employees don't know what kind of cable you need, tell them it is a USB device cable. A USB device cable has a standard A plug on one end (the flat, rectangular USB connector most of us are familiar with), and a standard B plug on the other end (a smaller, almost completely square connector). The standard B plug is the end that you connect to your printer.

Network

Connect your printer to your network if you want multiple Macs to be able to print to it. Typically, connecting to a network involves hooking up your printer to a router or network switch through an Ethernet cable. There are other methods of using your printer with a network, such as sharing the printer from a Mac, using print servers (devices designed to connect a printer that doesn't have an Ethernet port to an Ethernet router), or using a wireless network adapter. Sharing a printer is covered later in this chapter and also in Chapter 13.

Using print servers and wireless network adapters to connect your printer to a network achieves the same goals as using an Ethernet cable, which is to assign a network or IP (Internet Protocol) address to the printer. Because Ethernet cable is the most common method, I will stick with it as the default network connection to concentrate on.

Here are general instructions for connecting your printer to a network:

1. **With the printer off, insert one end of the Ethernet cable into the Ethernet port on your printer.**

2. **Insert the other end of the Ethernet cable into an available Ethernet port on your network router or switch.**

3. **Turn on the printer.** Consult your printer's documentation to find out how to determine what IP address is assigned to your printer by your network router.

Which Network Protocol Should I Use?

Network printers can communicate with your Mac using one of three protocols: AppleTalk, Bonjour (known as Rendezvous in an earlier incarnation), and IP Printing.

- **AppleTalk**. This is an older protocol developed by Apple in the late 1980s and early 1990s, and some newer printers are no longer using it. As a matter of fact, Apple has been trying to steer Mac users away from it since Mac OS X 10.2. However, it requires no configuration at all; your Mac just sees it on the network when you are creating a print queue, and you can easily install it.

- **Bonjour**. This is the newest no-configuration-needed protocol from Apple. Like AppleTalk before it, your Mac simply sees a printer running the Bonjour protocol, and printer queue installation is a snap. Older printers most likely won't have Bonjour, so AppleTalk will have to suffice.

- **IP (Internet Protocol) Printing**. This is the most difficult to set up because you must know the IP address of the printer being installed. I say it's the most difficult, but the only real difficulty with IP Printing is that it is more time consuming to set up than the other two competing protocols.

If you're on a small network, AppleTalk or Bonjour are the best bet because of their extreme simplicity. Consult with your IT administrator if you are on a larger corporate network to find out how he or she prefers you to install the printer. I would only use IP Printing if your IT department prefers it.

Create a print queue

The next step on your printer installation odyssey is to create a print queue. Creating a print queue allows you to print to the printer from your Mac, as well as manage print jobs. I'm going to show you how to set up a print queue for your printer, regardless of the connection type it uses.

Note

If you connect with USB after installing the printer's software, your Mac sometimes automatically creates a print queue; you don't have to lift a finger! To see whether this is the case, choose Apple menu ⇨ System Preferences ⇨ Print & Fax. If a print queue has been created you will see it in the Printers list on the left side of the window. Now, get to printing!

Now that you have the printer connected, let's get your printer rolling. Follow these steps:

1. **Choose Apple menu ➪ System Preferences, or click the System Preferences icon in the Dock.**

2. **Click the Print & Fax icon in the Hardware section of the System Preferences to open the Print & Fax preferences pane (see figure 6.3).**

3. **Click the + button in the lower-left corner of the pane (see figure 6.4) to add a printer to the list.** In order to delete a printer from the printer list, you would highlight the printer in the list and click the – button.

6.3 Click the Print & Fax icon to open its preferences pane.

4. **When the Add Printer window opens, use one of the following methods to create a print queue for your printer:**

    ● **If you are installing the printer through USB, AppleTalk, or Bonjour, do the following:**

    1. **Click the Default button in the upper-left corner of the window's toolbar.**

    2. **Click the name of the printer in the window.**

    3. **The Print Using pop-up menu should automatically show the name of the printer you are setting up.** If not, click the pop-up menu, choose the Select a driver to use option, browse the list of installed printer drivers, and select the one you need, and then click Add in the bottom-right corner.

133

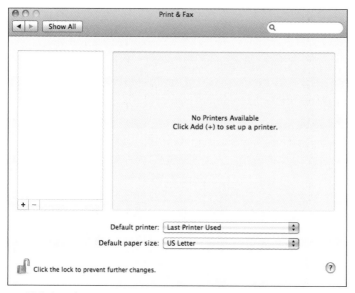

6.4 Click the + button to open the Add Printer window.

- **If you are using IP Printing as your protocol, do the following:**

1. **Click the IP button in the toolbar.**

2. **Select the correct protocol from the Protocol pop-up menu.** Consult your printer manufacturer's documentation, Web site, or technical support department for more information on which protocol to choose.

3. **Type the printer's IP address into the Address field.**

4. **Type the printer's queue name into the Queue field.** Again, consult your printer manufacturer's documentation for the proper setting.

5. **Edit the Name and Location fields to your liking.**

6. **The Print Using pop-up menu may show the name of the printer you are setting up.** If not, click the pop-up menu, choose the Select a driver to use option, browse the list of installed printer drivers, and select the one you need, and then click Add in the bottom-right corner (see figure 6.5).

Your newly installed printer queue is now visible in the printer list of the Print & Fax window, similar to the one shown in figure 6.6.

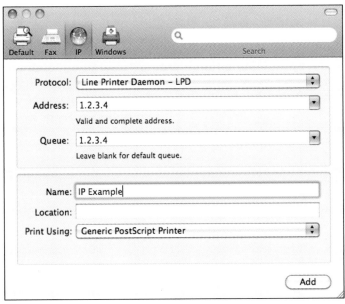

6.5 Be sure to type the correct Address and Queue information when using IP Printing.

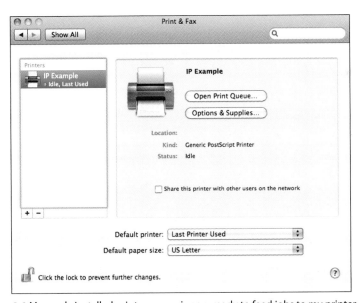

6.6 My newly installed printer queue is now ready to feed jobs to my printer.

CUPS

At some point during your printing experience with Snow Leopard, you may run across the term *CUPS*. CUPS is an acronym that stands for Common UNIX Printing System, which is the print system utilized by Mac OS X. It has no relation to the containers that hold our liquid refreshment, nor is it referring to protective athletic wear. CUPS controls all aspects of printing in Mac OS X, such as creating print queues, creating print jobs using the information provided to it by the printer's driver software, and managing jobs in the print queue.

To make certain you can now enjoy the fruits of your labor, you need to try a test print. Follow these steps to do so:

1. **Highlight the printer in the printer list by clicking its name.**

2. **Click Open Print Queue.**

3. **In the print queue's menu (upper-left corner of your screen, next to the Apple menu), choose Printer ⇨ Print Test Page, as shown in figure 6.7.**

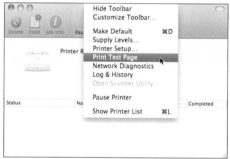

6.7 Print a test page to make sure everything is working properly with your printer.

Print Documents

Now that you have a printer installed, you can get busy printing those pressing sales figures, your family's vacation photos, or that map showing how to get to Aunt Linda's house.

TextEdit is the application I will use to show you how to print documents in Snow Leopard. From the Finder, choose Go ⇨ Applications (or ⌘+Shift+A), and then double-click the TextEdit icon.

TextEdit automatically opens a new blank document when it first starts up. Type something interesting in the document, and let's print it out.

To print from just about any application in Mac OS X, do the following:

1. **Choose File ⇨ Page Setup:**

    a. **Select the printer you will be printing to in the Format For pop-up menu (see figure 6.8).**

b. **Choose the paper size you want to print on in the Paper Size pop-up menu (also figure 6.8).**

c. **Make adjustments to the Orientation and Scale as you see fit.**

d. **Click OK.**

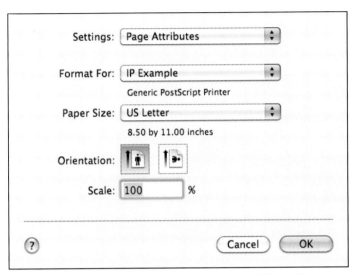

6.8 The standard Page Setup dialog used in most Mac OS X applications

2. **Choose File ⇨ Print, or press ⌘+P:**

a. **The standard Print dialog is now open, as shown in figure 6.9.**

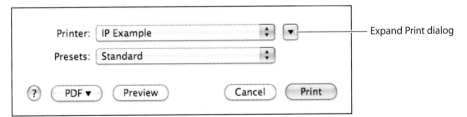

6.9 This is the standard Mac OS X Print dialog used by most applications.

b. **Click the blue box containing the down arrow that's just to the right of the printer name to expand the Print dialog (figure 6.10).**

c. **Change any print options, if necessary.** See the next section for a description of the print options that are available.

d. **Click Print to send your print job to the printer queue, where it is passed on to the printer.**

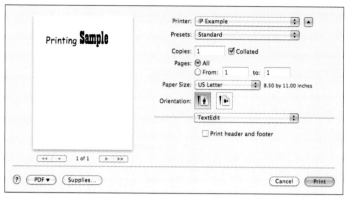

6.10 The expanded Print dialog gives you access to the printer's features.

Genius

Some printers (typically PostScript-capable laser printers) are able to directly print documents such as PDFs, or images such as JPEGs and TIFFs, by simply dragging and dropping the file into the print queue for the printer; you don't even have to open the file in an application. Check with your printer manufacturer to see whether your printer can handle such a cool task.

Discover Snow Leopard's print options

Snow Leopard has many built-in print options that allow you to configure your print jobs in so many ways that your head will spin. I cover the most often-used options in this section.

Caution

Some applications, such as QuarkXPress and Adobe InDesign, use their own print dialogs, which can really throw you for a loop if you're used to the standard Mac OS X way of doing things. Peruse the application's documentation to learn how to navigate the myriad options they provide.

The main sheet of the standard Print dialog offers some bare-bones basics, as well as application-specific print settings. Figure 6.10 illustrates the main sheet of the standard Print dialog when using TextEdit, and Table 6.1 breaks down the basic print options.

To access the other printing options that Mac OS X Snow Leopard provides, click the options pop-up menu, as shown in figure 6.11. Tables 6.2 to 6.7 list the other printing options and their functions.

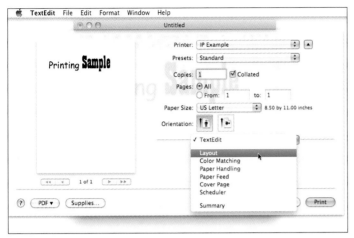

6.11 Choose from several option sheets to customize your Snow Leopard printing experience to the max.

Table 6.1 Basic Print Options

Option	Function
Printer	Select a printer from the pop-up menu.
Presets	Choose a preconfigured set of options.
Copies	Enter the number of copies you want to print.
Collated	Select this check box to print all pages of the document sequentially before printing the next copy.
Pages	Specify the page range you want to print.
Paper Size	Select the size of the media you are printing on.
Orientation	You can select Portrait or Landscape.
Options menu	This is a pop-up menu that allows you to select from several option sheets (see figure 6.11). This menu is typically set to the application-specific settings in the main sheet of the Print dialog. For example, figure 6.10 shows TextEdit.

Table 6.2 Layout Options

Option	Function
Pages per Sheet	Use this option to print multiple pages of your document on a single side of your paper.
Layout Direction	Choose how the pages are laid out on the page when printing multiple pages per sheet.
Border	Place a border around the individual pages when printing multiple pages per sheet.

continued

Table 6.2 continued

Option	Function
Two-Sided	This option is only available if your printer supports a duplexer option, which allows the printer to print on both sides of the sheet.
Reverse Page Orientation	This option causes the job to print out upside down. This is useful if you have media, such as letterhead that needs to be printed in a certain direction but you can't place it in the printer in that direction.
Flip horizontally	Anything on the page will flip and print as if being viewed in a mirror.

Table 6.3 Color Matching Options

Option	Function
ColorSync/In Printer	Choosing ColorSync allows Snow Leopard to handle color matching, while choosing In Printer lets the printer do all the grunt work.
Profile	This option allows you to associate a color profile with this print job.

Table 6.4 Paper Handling Options

Option	Function
Pages to Print	Print all pages, or just the odd- or even-numbered pages.
Destination Paper Size	Allows the document to be printed on a different paper size than specified in the Page Setup dialog. This option is only available if the Scale to fit paper size check box is selected.
Scale to fit paper size	Select this check box to scale the page's contents to fit the size selected in the Destination Paper Size pop-up menu.
Scale down only	Select this check box to prevent the items on the page from being scaled larger than they presently are.
Page Order	Choose from Automatic, Normal, or Reverse page order.

Table 6.5 Paper Feed Options

Option	Function
All pages from	Select a paper tray to print the job from. This option is only useful if your printer supports multiple paper trays.
First page from	Print the first page of a document using a particular paper tray. For example, use this option if you want to print the first page of a job on your company's letterhead, which is in one tray on your printer.
Remaining from	Print the remainder of the print job from the paper tray you select. This option is only available when selecting the First page from option. Continuing the example from the First page from option, select the paper tray on your printer that contains plain paper to finish the rest of your job, as opposed to wasting letterhead.

Table 6.6 Cover Page Options

Option	Function
Print Cover Page	Select either Before document or After document if you want to print a cover page that differentiates your jobs from those of other people using the printer.
Cover Page Type	Select the type of cover page to print. This option is only available if Before document or After document is selected in the Print Cover Page options.
Billing Info	This information is used to identify you if you are being billed for each job you print.

Table 6.7 Scheduler Options

Option	Function
Print Document	Specify a time for Snow Leopard to send this document from the printer's queue to the printer.
Priority	Set the level of this document's priority so that it prints ahead of or behind other jobs as necessary.

Creating your own PDFs

PDF files have become a standard document format that almost anyone who has used a computer has seen at some point. Most documents on the Internet are PDF files. All computer users can open PDFs, whether they are running Mac OS X, Windows, or Linux, as long as they have a PDF reader application installed, such as Preview or Adobe Reader.

Once upon a time, PDFs could only be generated by expensive software. Mac OS X has changed that due to its extensive use of the PDF file format throughout the operating system. Snow Leopard affords you the ability to create PDFs from any document you want for free!

Let's use the trusty TextEdit document you created earlier in this chapter to illustrate creating a PDF.

To create a PDF using Snow Leopard, do the following:

1. **Open a document in an application. In this case, the TextEdit document you created earlier.**

2. **Choose File ⇨ Print.**

3. **Click PDF in the lower-left corner of the window (see figure 6.12) to see the PDF options you have at your beck and call.**

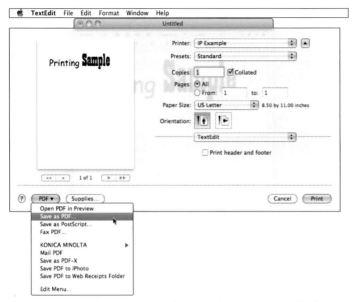

6.12 Snow Leopard gives you several options for creating PDF files from any document you want.

4. **Select Save As PDF from the menu to open the Save dialog, as shown in figure 6.13.**

5. **Give the PDF an appropriate name, decide where on your Mac to save it (it defaults to your user account's Documents folder), and click Save.** I describe the Security Options button in the next section.

6.13 There are a lot of options available in the PDF Save dialog.

Security options

The ability to create PDFs with any document on your Mac without expensive third-party software is a huge boon, no doubt about it. However, that third-party software (specifically Adobe Acrobat) has always had the ability to make PDF files secure from prying eyes that shouldn't be seeing their contents. This is a great feature and is required in some corporations when disseminating sensitive information. Previous versions of Mac OS X were lacking in this department, but Snow Leopard has come to the rescue of the security-obsessed among us.

6.14 Secure your PDFs from anyone not authorized to view them.

To secure your PDFs, look back at step 5 of the previous section, prior to clicking Save. Click Security Options to see the PDF Security Options dialog (see figure 6.14). Table 6.8 spells out the available options. Click OK to assign the security options you have selected for this file.

Table 6.8 PDF Security Options

Option	Function
Require password to open document	Select this check box to enable the password feature. Type a secure password in the Password field, and then retype it in the Verify field.
Require password to copy text, images and other content	Select this check box to prevent someone from copying elements of the PDF and pasting them into an unsecured document without knowing the password to do so. Type a secure password in the Password field, and then retype it in the Verify field.
Require password to print document	If this check box is selected a user must know the password in order to print this document. Type a secure password in the Password field, and then retype it in the Verify field.

Why and how to create PostScript files

When you first click Print in the Print dialog, Snow Leopard immediately creates PDF information for the print job. Sometimes you may need to generate a PostScript file for a certain job, especially if you work in the publishing industry and outsource your printing, or to troubleshoot a printer or printing issue. Because PDF uses a subset of the PostScript language it's relatively easy for Mac OS X to convert the PDF data generated when you first click Print into a PostScript file. To create a Postscript file, follow these steps:

1. **Choose File ⇨ Print in your application's menu.**
2. **Click PDF in the lower-left corner of the Print dialog.**
3. **Select Save as PostScript from the pop-up menu.**
4. **Give the document a name, select a location to save it to, and click Save to generate a PostScript file.**

Assigning ICC profiles to a printer

Having spent many a year in the printing industry myself, a frequently asked question is how to use ICC profiles with a printer. An ICC profile is a data file that characterizes how a device handles color. ICC profiles may be generic, or they may be specific to a particular device, such as a monitor or printer. Consult the manufacturer of your device to inquire about its support of ICC profiles. These profiles can be assigned to single print jobs using the application that designed the document, and they can be assigned to printers on an individual basis. Consult your application's documentation to find out how to use ICC profiles with them, but I've taken the liberty of showing you how to use the ColorSync Utility to assign profiles to individual printers. Follow these steps:

1. **From the Finder, press ⌘+Shift+U to open the Utilities folder.**
2. **Double-click the ColorSync Utility icon.**
3. **Select Devices from the toolbar at the top of the window.**
4. **Click the arrow next to Printers to expand the list.**
5. **Highlight the printer to which you want to assign the profile (figure 6.15).**

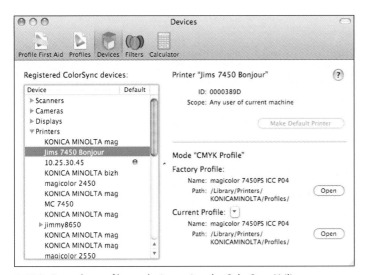

6.15 Assign color profiles to devices using the ColorSync Utility.

6. **Click the arrow button just to the right of Current Profile and select Other.**

7. **Browse your Mac for the ICC profile you want to use with the device, select it, and click Open to assign the profile.**

8. **When you print using the printer to which you assigned the profile, turn off any color-matching options provided by the manufacturer in the Print dialog to force the printer to use the profile.**

How Do I Work with PDFs and Images?

PDFs, or Portable Document Format files, are the de facto standard for dissemi-

nating documents over the Internet and throughout many corporations due

largely to their portability across multiple operating systems, their relatively

small file sizes, and availability of security options for sensitive information.

Snow Leopard includes an application built right into it called Preview that has

the ability to open, edit, and save PDFs, because most of the graphics that you

see on your screen are created by virtue of PDF technology anyway. I'll show

you how to work with PDF files using Preview in this chapter. Preview isn't lim-

ted to handling just PDFs, however; it's also quite a handy way to open, and

even edit, image (picture) files. Apple does provide a fantastic program called

Photo for editing and organizing pictures, but it's part of its iLife suite of appli-

cations, not Snow Leopard. Because not every person who buys Snow Leopard

has iLife, I'll concentrate on using Preview for your digital picture needs.

File Types Supported by Preview

Preview is sort of a Swiss army knife application, meaning that it can handle many different file types and various tasks. Table 7.1 lists the file types supported by Preview.

Table 7.1 File Types Supported by Preview

File extension	File type/Description
PDF	Portable Document Format. A widely used cross-platform document format.
JPG	Joint Photographic Experts Group. A popular image file format used by most digital cameras. Also known as JPEG.
GIF	Graphics Interchange Format. An image file format mainly used on the Internet for small animations.
HDR	High Dynamic Range. An image file format associated with high-end digital cameras.
TIFF	Tagged Image File Format. A popular image file format used primarily by graphic artists.
PSD	Photoshop Document. Adobe Photoshop's default image file format.
PNG	Portable Network Graphics. An image file format.
BMP	Bitmap. An image file format.
RAW	A file format for an image that has not been processed in any way. This format is mostly used by digital cameras and scanners.
SGI	Silicon Graphics Image. The native raster graphics file format of Silicon Graphics workstations.

Open and Save Files in Preview

Preview can open any of the file types mentioned in Table 7.1. To open a file in Preview, do the following:

1. **From within Finder, choose Go ⇨ Applications, and then double-click the Preview icon to open the application.**

2. **Choose File ⇨ Open, or press ⌘+O, to display the Open dialog.**

3. **Browse your Mac for the file you want to open, click the file's icon to highlight it, and then click Open, as shown in figure 7.1.**

If Preview's icon is in your Dock, whether due to it already being open or because you keep an alias for it there, you can simply drag and drop a file onto the Preview icon in the Dock to open it.

7.1 Choose the file you want to open in Preview.

If you make changes to a file you've opened in Preview, and you want to save those changes, press ⌘+S; you can also choose File ➪ Save. If you make changes to a file but you want to save the changed file under a different name, press ⌘+Shift+S to open the Save As dialog, as shown in figure 7.2. Type a new name for the file, choose a location to save the file on your Mac, and then click Save.

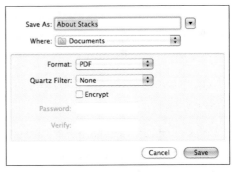

7.2 Name your file, choose a location to save it to, and then click Save.

Note If you can't seem to find the location you want to save your file to, click the blue square containing the black arrow. This expands your Save As window, allowing you to browse your entire hard drive.

Link File Types to Applications

If you've ever double-clicked a file to open it, only to have it open in an application you didn't expect, you'll love this little nugget. To make a certain file type open in only the application you designate for it, do the following:

1. **Click the file one time to highlight it, and then press ⌘+I to open the file's Info window, as shown in figure 7.3.** You can also Ctrl+click or right-click the file and select Get Info from the pop-up list to open the Info window.

2. **If the gray triangle to the left of the Open with section is pointing to the right, click it to expand the section.**

3. **Click the pop-up menu to choose the application you want to set as the default for opening this file.**

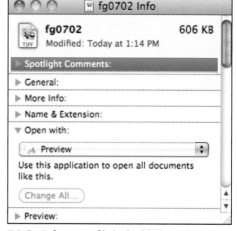

7.3 Get Info on any file by highlighting it and pressing ⌘+I.

4. **To make the selected application the systemwide default for opening all files of this type, click Change All.**

5. **Close the Info window by clicking the red button in the upper-left corner.**

Set Preview's Preferences

The way you set the preferences for Preview affects how you use the application. I'm a big advocate for making Snow Leopard and all of its applications work the way you want them to. It's very important to set any application's preferences to fit your work style.

Preview's preferences are divided into four categories: General, Images, PDF, and Bookmarks.

Open Preview, and then press ⌘+; to open the Preview Preferences window.

General

Table 7.2 breaks down the settings in the General tab of Preview's Preferences window.

Table 7.2 General Preferences

Preference	Function
When opening files	Determine how you want Preview to open multiple files: Open all files in one window, open groups of files in the same window, or open each file in its own separate window.
Window background	Change the default background color of the windows you open in Preview by clicking the color box and then choosing a new color from the color palette window.

Images

Table 7.3 explains the options that are available in the Images tab of the Preview Preferences window.

Table 7.3 Image Preferences

Preference	Function
Initial image scale	Opens images at their actual size or scales them to fit your window.
Define 100% scale as	Determine whether 100% scale of an image is based on screen pixels or actual printout.

PDF

The PDF tab's options, seen in figure 7.4, are explained in Table 7.4.

Table 7.4 PDF Preferences

Preference	Function
Initial document scale	Allows Preview to automatically scale the PDF or set it to open at the scale you desire.
Define 100% scale as	Determine whether 100% scale of a PDF is based on screen pixels or actual printout.
On opening documents	Select the first check box to open the window's sidebar only when a PDF contains a table of contents, and select the second check box to begin viewing a PDF from the last page you viewed the previous time it was open.

continued

151

Table 7.4 continued

Preference	Function
Viewing documents	Select these check boxes to smooth lines in text and line art and to use logical page numbers when viewing PDFs.
Annotations	Select this check box to assign a name to annotations you make in a PDF, and type the name in the Name field.

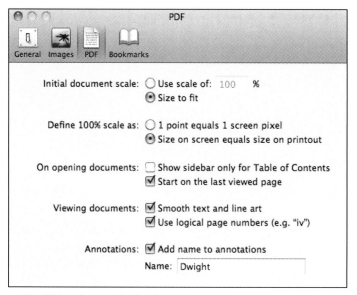

7.4 The PDF preferences for Preview

Bookmarks

Preview allows you to bookmark images and PDFs so that you can zip right to them when needed; this is very much like using bookmarks in a Web browser. To add a bookmark, open the file you want and press ⌘+D, or choose Bookmarks ⇨ Add Bookmark from the menu.

The Bookmarks tab lists all the bookmarks you've created. You can rename them or delete them from the list by clicking the Remove button.

View and Edit PDFs

Snow Leopard is a whiz at opening, viewing, editing, and creating PDF files. I've already covered opening files; I'll concentrate on viewing and editing them in this section, while Chapter 6 expounds on the creation of PDFs.

To get started, you need to open a PDF, as described earlier in this chapter.

Mark up and annotate PDFs

To *mark up* a PDF is to highlight, strike through, or underline text that needs to be edited or removed; to *annotate* means to add notes or links, or to spotlight an area of the page with an oval or rectangle. Figure 7.5 shows an example of markups and annotations.

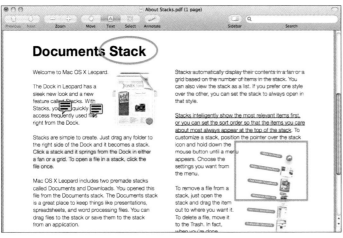

7.5 Mark up and annotate PDFs with Preview.

To mark up a PDF, do the following:

1. **Click and drag the mouse cursor over the text you want to mark up to highlight it.**

2. **Choose Tools ➪ Mark Up.**

3. **Select which type of markup to use:**

   - Highlight Text (⌘+Ctrl+H)

   - Strike Through Text (⌘+Ctrl+S)

   - Underline Text (⌘+Ctrl+U)

To make annotations, do the following:

1. **Choose Tools ⇨ Annotate.**

2. **Select which type of annotation you want to use:**

   - Add Oval (⌘+Ctrl+O)

   - Add Rectangle (⌘+Ctrl+R)

   - Add Note (⌘+Ctrl+N)

   - Add Link (⌘+Ctrl+L)

Genius

If marking up and annotating PDFs is something you do often, memorize the keyboard shortcuts for them. Keyboard shortcuts can save you much more time than you may realize. It's well worth taking the time to learn them if you work in a fast-paced environment.

Delete pages from a PDF

Just a couple of years ago, the only way to delete or rearrange PDF pages was to pay through the nose for a third-party program that could accomplish these tasks. Thanks to Apple, Preview now has that ability, providing a professional level of service without having to shell out a professional level of money.

To delete a page from a multipage document, do the following:

1. **If the sidebar is not visible on the right side of the window, choose View ⇨ Sidebar, or press ⌘+Shift+D.**

2. **Find the page you want to delete in the sidebar and click to select it.** The sidebar must be displaying thumbnails, not Table of Contents or Annotations. To set the sidebar to display thumbnails, click the pop-up menu at the bottom of the sidebar and choose Thumbnails.

3. **Choose Edit ⇨ Delete Selected Page (⌘+Delete) to remove the page from your PDF.** Preview automatically renumbers your pages for you.

4. **Save your PDF (⌘+S) to keep the changes, or press ⌘+Z to undo a change.**

Rearrange pages in a PDF

As mentioned in the previous section, rearranging pages in a PDF is a treat for anyone who doesn't have an expensive third-party application. To shuffle your PDF's pages, do the following:

1. **Make the sidebar visible by pressing ⌘+Shift+D.**

2. **Search the sidebar for the page you want to move.** The sidebar must be displaying thumbnails, not Table of Contents or Annotations. To set the sidebar to display thumbnails, click the pop-up menu at the bottom of the sidebar and choose Thumbnails.

3. **Click and drag the page to the location in the sidebar you prefer, and then drop it in place (figure 7.6).**

4. **Save the changes by pressing ⌘+S, or undo them by pressing ⌘+Z.**

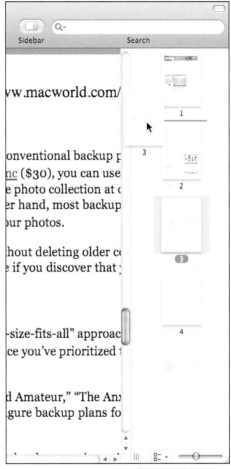

7.6 Move the page to its new home and drop it in.

View and Edit Images

Preview is more than happy to fill the role of basic image editor if you don't already have one with more frills, like iPhoto or Adobe Photoshop. While not able to manipulate photos and add effects to them like the two applications I just mentioned, it can handle standard resizing, rotating, and a few other nifty tricks.

Open an image in Preview, and we'll get started.

Get the Inside Scoop on Images

Most people simply want to open, view, and perhaps minimally edit their pictures, but others (and you know who you are!) want the lowdown on every element of the picture. You like to know information such as the camera used to take the image, the compression type, the aperture, the Photometric Interpretation (a fancy name for color model), and other geeky information that only a professional photographer could appreciate.

Preview can get all that stuff for you if you simply choose Tools⇨Inspector or press ⌘+I when your image is open. The Inspector lays it all out for you, as you can see in figure 7.7.

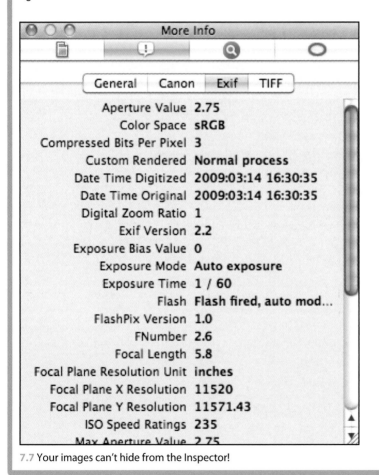

7.7 Your images can't hide from the Inspector!

Resizing and rotating images

If a photo or image is just too big dimensionally, Preview can easily squeeze it until it fits the spot where you want to place it.

To adjust the size of your image, choose Tools ➪ Adjust Size. You are presented with the dialog shown in figure 7.8.

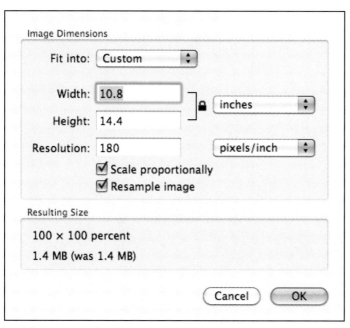

7.8 Adjust an image's size in Preview.

Make changes to these settings if you need to adjust your image, and click OK when you are finished. Table 7.5 explains the options and how they affect the image.

Table 7.5 Size Adjustments

Option	Function
Fit into	Lets you choose automatic size settings from the pop-up menu. Use Other to make a custom size.
Width and Height	Changes the physical size of the image.
Resolution	Changes the quality of the image. Increasing this number may have adverse affects on the image.
Scale proportionally	Keeps the dimensions of the image intact when selected. For example, if you change the width, the height changes proportionally.
Resample image	Deselect this check box if you want to reduce the dimensions of a file without losing image details.

Preview also lets you rotate images to change their orientation. If you have a picture that was taken by holding the camera sideways (to take a full-length shot of someone) you can rotate that image so that the subject is standing upright instead of on his or her side when you open the image in Preview.

To rotate an image to the left, press ⌘+L; to rotate it to the right, press ⌘+R.

You can also flip an image to make the subject face a different direction, as I've done in figure 7.9. I flipped my image both vertically and horizontally to give you a better idea of what these functions do.

To flip your image horizontally, choose Tools ⇨ Flip Horizontal; to go vertical, choose Tools ⇨ Flip Vertical.

7.9 My son is flipping out in this picture!

Genius

You can also crop an image in Preview. Notice that the mouse cursor changes to a crosshair when you move it over your image; use this crosshair to select an area on your image that you want to crop, or extract, from the rest of the image. Place the crosshair underneath or over the area you want to crop, and then click and drag to draw a box around the area. Once the area is selected, press ⌘+K, and then save your new image (⌘+S).

Adjusting color in images

Sometimes the colors in your pictures just don't look quite right. What is someone who isn't a color specialist to do? Preview has the answers! Preview can handle basic color adjustments very well, indeed.

To make color corrections in Preview, choose Tools ⇨ Adjust Color, or press ⌘+Option+C. The color adjustment sliders in the Adjust Color window, shown in figure 7.10, can work wonders on your images.

When you move the sliders, your image is automatically updated to reflect the adjustments that you made.

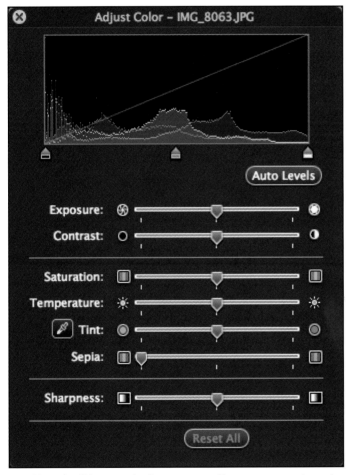

7.10 Move the sliders to make the necessary adjustments to your image's colors.

How Do I Organize My Life with iCal and Address Book?

If your life is anything like mine, you need as much organization as you can get, and iCal and Address Book will come to your rescue. iCal helps you create calendars for different subjects, such as Family or Work, and Address Book can keep all your contacts in a central location. You can create events in iCal so that you can schedule all your important dates and organize your time throughout the day, week, month, and year; Address Book allows you to access your contacts through any application programmed to use it, like Mail or iChat. iCal can also remind you of your scheduled events, so for those of you guys reading this, you don't have any more excuses for forgetting your anniversary! In this chapter, I show you how to make iCal and Address Book essential to your Snow Leopard experience.

Creating Calendars

Open iCal to get started; choose Go ⇨ Applications in the menu and double-click the iCal icon.

You can create calendars that reflect the different areas of your everyday life, such as a calendar for your work schedule, another for bill due dates, and one for school events. Having a separate calendar for each area of your life will make it easy to organize your time.

There are three ways to create a new calendar:

- **Choose File ⇨ New Calendar.**
- **Press ⌘+Option+N.**
- **Click the + button in the bottom-left corner of the iCal window.**

Performing one of these three actions creates a new calendar in the Calendars list on the left side of the window. Name the calendar by simply typing its name. Continue to create as many calendars as you need before proceeding.

Your calendars are now ready to be put to work. There are a number of ways in which to manage the calendars themselves:

- **Arrange calendars in the list by simply clicking and dragging them into the order you prefer, as shown in figure 8.1.**
- **Rename a calendar by right-clicking, or Ctrl+clicking, it in the Calendars list and selecting Get Info from the pop-up menu.** Type a new name for the calendar in the Name field.
- **The events you enter in your calendars (more on that just a bit later in this chapter) are represented using the color of their respective calendars.** You can change the color of a calendar by right-clicking or Ctrl+clicking it in the Calendars list and then selecting Get Info. Click the color button in the upper-right corner of the window and select a color from the list.
- **Notice the check box that's just to the left of each calendar you create.** That check box indicates whether the events are displayed for the calendar in question. Deselecting some of these check boxes can help make sense out of a particularly busy schedule.
- **Create groups to arrange similar calendars together in the calendar list.** Choose File ⇨ New Calendar Group or press ⌘+Shift+N, and then give the new group a descriptive name. Arrange calendars into groups by simply dragging and dropping them underneath the desired group.

8.1 Click and drag calendars into the order you prefer.

Genius

You can change the way your calendars are displayed in the iCal window by clicking the Day, Week, and Month tabs at the top of the window. Click the right or left arrows on either side of those tabs to scroll to the previous or next day, week, or month. If you choose to use Day or Week view, you can always see a miniature monthly calendar in the window by clicking the View or Hide Mini-Month button in the bottom-left corner of the window.

Adding events to calendars

A calendar without an event is about as useful as a car without tires, and it probably won't even get you as far. Events are the items that you add to your calendars to make them come alive; they are your life, only organized.

To create a new event

1. **Select the day the event begins.**

2. **Press ⌘+N to create a new event for that day.**

3. **Type a descriptive name for the event.**

You now have your first event, but you will most likely want to edit the contents of the event before considering it a done deal, so continue on.

Editing calendar events

After you create the event, some tweaking may be in order. To edit your event, follow these steps:

1. **Open the event information window by double-clicking the event or by clicking the event to highlight it and then pressing ⌘+E.** If this is not a new event, but a previously created event that you need to edit, simply double-clicking the event only displays its basic information; click the Edit button to gain access to its details, which are shown in figure 8.2.

2. **Click to the right of each item in the event information window to edit it. Table 8.1 lists the available items and their functions.**

3. **Click Done.**

Table 8.1 Event Information

Item	Function
location	Where the event is to be held.
all-day	Select this check box if this event will take up a day, as opposed to an hour or two.
from and to	Select the beginning and end dates and times for your event.
repeat	Click the options menu next to this item if you want the event to be repeated, such as a reoccurring event like a birthday or weekly meeting.
calendar	Choose which calendar in your calendar list this event belongs to.
alarm	Select from several alarm types, such as e-mail, onscreen messages, and sound. You can set multiple alarms for each event.
attendees	Invite others to add this event to their calendar.
attachments	You can attach documents and other files to your events. For example, you could attach a grocery list to a scheduled shopping trip.
url	Place a relevant Web site address or shared calendar address.
note	Type any additional information you may need for the task.

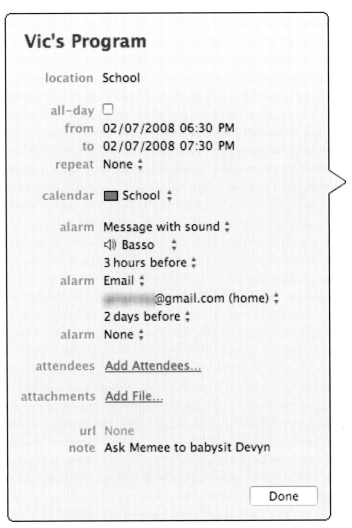

Vic's Program

location	School
all-day	☐
from	02/07/2008 06:30 PM
to	02/07/2008 07:30 PM
repeat	None ⬍
calendar	▪ School ⬍
alarm	Message with sound ⬍
	◁)) Basso ⬍
	3 hours before ⬍
alarm	Email ⬍
	▮▮▮@gmail.com (home) ⬍
	2 days before ⬍
alarm	None ⬍
attendees	Add Attendees...
attachments	Add File...
url	None
note	Ask Memee to babysit Devyn

Done

8.2 Your event is ready for all the editing you need to do.

Setting iCal Preferences

You can change the iCal preferences to customize how iCal works. Choose iCal ➪ Preferences to see what options are available to you (see figure 8.3).

The General tab allows you to make the most basic of setting adjustments; those settings are listed in Table 8.2.

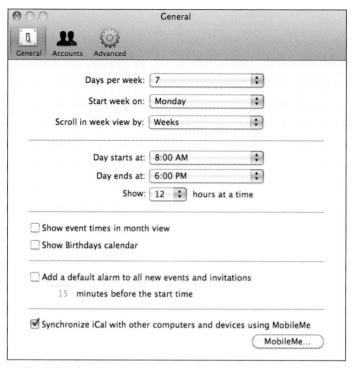

8.3 The iCal preferences window

Table 8.2 The iCal General Preferences Tab

Setting	Function
Days per week	Set the number of days for your normal week. You might change this setting to 5 to reflect a 5-day workweek.
Start week on	Choose which day to start your week.
Scroll in week view by	Select to view either weeks or days when in week view.
Day starts at	Decide what time your typical day begins.
Day ends at	Set what time your typical day is over.
Show x hours at a time	For use in Day viewing mode.
Show event times in month view	Select this option to show appointment times when in Month view. These are hidden by default due to space restrictions.
Show Birthdays calendar	Select this option to display a calendar that lists birthdays from your Address Book.
Add a default alarm to all new events and invitations	Every new event or invitation will be assigned an alarm that will go off in the time you specify when you select this option.
Synchronize iCal with other computers and devices using MobileMe	If you have a MobileMe account, you can synchronize your calendars.

The Accounts tab allows you to subscribe to CalDAV and Exchange servers, which some companies and organizations use to share calendars among several users. To subscribe to your company's or organization's CalDAV server, click the + button in the lower-left corner, and type the server's information (contact your IT department for this information, if needed).

The Advanced tab, shown in figure 8.4, helps you set preferences for time zone support, to-do's, events, alarms, and invitations.

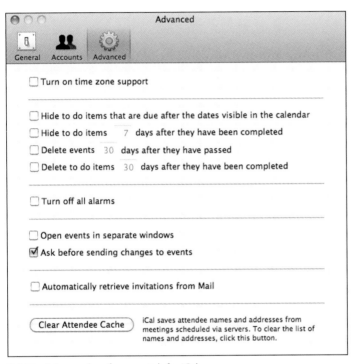

8.4 The Advanced preferences tab for iCal

Table 8.3 lists the Advanced preferences available for iCal.

Table 8.3 The iCal Advanced Preferences Tab

Setting	Function
Turn on time zone support	Allows you to view your schedule as it would be in a time zone other than your default. When you select this check box, a time zone pop-up menu appears in the upper-right corner of the iCal window; select the appropriate time zone from this menu.
Hide to do items that are due after the dates visible in the calendar	To do items that you create won't appear in the to do list (displayed by pressing ⌘+Option+T) if their dates are after the current view being used for your calendar.

continued

Table 8.3 continued

Setting	Function
Hide to do items x days after they have been completed	Select the number of days it will take for a to do item to be hidden from view after it has been completed.
Delete events x days after they have passed	Automatically removes events from your calendars after the number of days you specify past their completion.
Delete to do items x days after they have been completed	Automatically removes to do items from the to do list after the number of days you specify past their completion.
Turn off all alarms	Prevents any alarms from occurring.
Open events in separate windows	Causes events to open in a separate window when double-clicked.
Ask before sending changes to events	Check this box to have iCal alert you to make certain you want to send changes you've made to events.
Automatically retrieve invitations from Mail	Select this check box to have event invitations show in iCal instead of just Mail.
Clear Attendee Cache	Empties the names and addresses of attendees to whom you've sent invitations in the past.

Sharing Calendars

Life is much easier when everyone is on the same page, be it your company or your family. iCal offers two ways to share your calendars with others: publishing your calendar and exporting your calendar.

Publishing a calendar

When you publish a calendar, you place a copy of it on the Internet or a local WebDAV server. Other users can then access it through iCal, another third-party calendar application, or a standard Web browser using any computing platform. To publish a calendar

1. **Click the calendar or calendar group you want to publish in the calendar list.**

2. **Choose Calendar ⇨ Publish from the menu; the Publish calendar menu appears (shown in figure 8.5).**

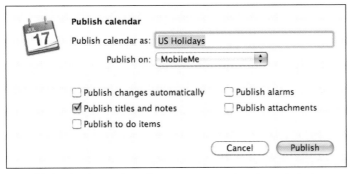

8.5 Publish calendars to share them over a network or through the Internet.

3. **When the menu opens, type in a name for your calendar if you don't want to use the default.**

4. **Select where to publish your calendar (your MobileMe account or a private server) using the Publish on pop-up menu.** If you select Private Server, enter the server information, along with a login name and password to gain access to it.

5. **When the options are set to your liking, click Publish.**

Exporting a calendar

Exporting a calendar is a good way to move calendars from one computer to another. You can also edit calendars that you've exported, although you cannot edit calendars that you've published from another computer.

To export a calendar

1. **Click to select the calendar or calendar group you want to export from the calendar list.**

2. **Choose iCal ⇨ Export to open the Save As window, as shown in figure 8.6.**

3. **Give a descriptive name to the file, choose a location to save it, and then click Export.**

4. **Share the exported calendar by e-mailing it to others, placing it on a server that can be accessed by other users, or any other way you can think of.**

Genius

The default format of exported calendars in iCal is ICS. ICS files can be imported into almost any third-party calendar application, so you don't have to worry about your Windows or Linux pals not being able to view your calendar; likewise, you can use their calendars in iCal if they export them from their application using the ICS format.

8.6 Export calendars from iCal and import them on other computers.

Subscribing to calendars

It stands to reason that if some people are publishing their calendars, then there must be others subscribing to them. Following are two ways to subscribe to calendars. This is the easy way:

1. **Choose Calendar ⇨ Subscribe from the menu.**

2. **Type the URL (the Web address) of the calendar you want to subscribe to in the Calendar URL field.**

3. **Click the Subscribe button to see the information window for the calendar, as shown in figure 8.7.**

4. **Decide whether to remove Alarms, Attachments, and To Do items (which I recommend if you don't know the person who created the calendar), and how often to have the calendar automatically refresh in case there are any changes made to it by its creator.**

Find Calendars on the Web

Can't find calendars to subscribe to? Try one of these links to find tons of calendars just begging for your subscription:

- **www.apple.com/downloads/macosx/calendars/**
- **http://icalshare.com/**

5. **Click OK to complete the subscription process.**

```
"Celtics" Info

    JUL
    17          Name:  Celtics

          Description:  Boston Celtics



       Subscribed to:  webcal://ical.mac.com/ical/Celtics.ics
             Remove:  ☑ Alarms
                      ☑ Attachments
                      ☑ To Do items
        Last updated:  Sunday, March 22, 2009 5:10:13 PM CT
        Auto-refresh:  No

                                     Cancel      OK
```

8.7 Subscribing to calendars is a snap with iCal.

This is even easier:

1. **If someone sends you the link to his or her calendar in an e-mail, or if you click the link to a calendar from a Web page, iCal automatically begins the subscription process.**

2. **You can pick it up from step 3 in the previous steps to finish the subscription.**

Printing Calendars

If you're like me, you understand that, while the concept of a paperless office sounded pretty cool in the 1980s, it most certainly — and to some degree, thankfully — hasn't come to fruition. Sometimes I just like to have a printed page in hand, as opposed to being tied to my desk or lugging around a laptop. I love my Mac but we're not permanently attached at the hip. iCal can provide you with great printed calendars to use for yourself or that you can print and give to others. This is a great tool for offices and schools or any other organization or team, for that matter. Another plus to printed calendars is that you will have a much easier time hanging them on your fridge than you would hanging your computer's screen.

To print your calendars, follow these steps:

1. **Choose File ➪ Print.**

2. **Select from among the myriad options shown in figure 8.8, and then click Continue.** Table 8.4 lists the printing options and gives brief explanations of them.

3. **Click Print in the Print window to send the job to your printer.**

8.8 The iCal printing options

Table 8.4 The iCal Printing Options

Option	Function
View	Choose what view to use for your printed calendar from the pop-up menu.
Paper	Select a paper size to print your calendar on.
Time range	Decide when the printed calendar or calendars should begin and end using the Starts and Ends pop-up menus.
Calendars	Select the check boxes next to the calendars whose events you want to include.
Options	Determine whether to print all-day events, timed events, minicalendars, calendar keys, or if you want to print in black and white only, instead of color.
Text size	Choose what size font to use when printing your calendar's text.
Zoom	Drag the slider to enlarge the preview image.

Working with Contacts in Address Book

Have you ever needed to find that elusive phone number or address for a prospective client and had to thumb through ten devices and books to find it? Apple created Address Book just for you. Creating contacts in Address Book can sure make rounding up all those Christmas card addresses a lot easier.

Contacts are files that contain information for people in your life, such as street addresses, e-mail addresses, birthdays, and even their pictures. To get started, open Address Book:

1. **Click Go ➪ Applications.**

2. **Double-click the Address Book icon to open Address Book.**

Address Book is fairly useless without contacts, so let's start adding a few.

New cards

A card contains all of the contact's information, and so you need to create a new one to get started. There are a few ways to begin creating a new card:

1. **Choose File ➪ New Card from the menu.**

2. **Press ⌘+N.**

3. **Click the + button underneath the Name column in the Address Book window.**

Any of these actions creates a new blank card that's waiting for input from you, as shown in figure 8.9.

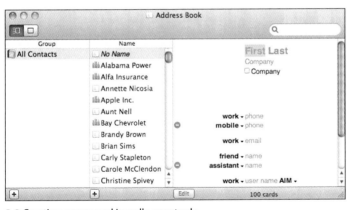

8.9 Creating a new card is really easy to do.

Begin typing information into the card, using the Tab button on your keyboard to move to the next available field. If there is a field that you don't want to use, simply leave it blank and it won't appear on the card once you've saved it. To add new fields, choose Card ➪ Add Field and select one from the list.

When you finish adding information to the card, press ⌘+S or click Edit below the card's window to save it. You can always edit the information in the card by clicking to highlight it in the Name column of the Address Book window, and then clicking Edit beneath the card's window. The Edit button turns blue when in editing mode.

Genius You can also add new cards quite easily when you receive a vCard in an e-mail. A vCard is sort of like a digital business card that someone may attach to e-mails so that others, such as you, can easily save the contact information. Using Mail, simply double-click the vCard in the e-mail to create a new card in Address Book.

New groups

A great feature that I use quite a bit in Address Book is groups. Using groups, you can create different categories of contacts, such as Family, Work, and Church. As with cards, you have several techniques you can use to create new groups:

1. **Press ⌘+Shift+N.**
2. **Choose File ➪ New Group from the menu.**
3. **Click the + button underneath the Group column in the main Address Book window.**

Be sure to give your group a descriptive name of the items it will contain. To add cards to the groups, just drag and drop the desired card from the Name column onto the preferred group in the Group column, as shown in figure 8.10. This action doesn't remove the card from the Name column; it just places a copy of the card in the group.

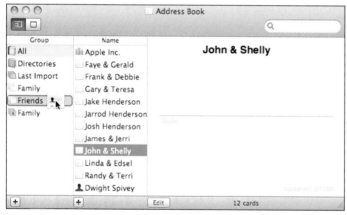

8.10 Drag and drop names onto the group you want them to be listed under.

Genius There's an even faster way to create a group. Select multiple cards from the Name column by holding the ⌘ key while you click the names, and then choose File ➪ New Group from Selection.

How to Use Smart Groups

Smart Groups are groups that cards are automatically added to if they meet certain criteria that you have already specified. For example, if you create a Smart Group that looks for cards that have certain last names, when a new card is created using that last name, it is immediately added to the Smart Group. To create a Smart Group, follow these steps:

1. **Press ⌘+Option+N, or choose File⇨New Smart Group from the menu.**

2. **Give the Smart Group a descriptive name.**

3. **Decide whether the Smart Group will contain cards that match any or all of the conditions you are about to set.**

4. **Add or remove conditions by clicking the + or – buttons to the right of the first and subsequent conditions.**

5. **Check the Highlight group when updated check box to have Address Book notify you when a card has been added to the Smart Group.**

6. **Click OK to save the new Smart Group, or click Cancel to get rid of it.**

You can change a Smart Group's criteria at any time, as shown in Figure 8.11, by Ctrl+clicking its name in the Group column and selecting Edit Smart Group.

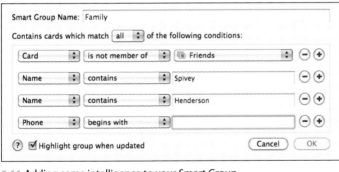

8.11 Adding some intelligence to your Smart Group.

Importing contacts

Address Book can import files from other applications when created in the following formats:

- **vCard**

- **LDIF**

○ **Tab-delimited**

○ **Comma-separated (CSV), which is usually the most compatible with other applications.**

Consult the other application to find out how to export contacts from it in one of these formats.

To import contacts, follow these steps:

1. **Choose File ⇨ Import, and then select the format of the file you will be importing.**

2. **Browse your Mac for the file you want to import, click to highlight the file, and then click Open in the bottom-right corner.**

   ○ **If importing a tab-delimited or comma-separated file, choose the Text File format.**

   ○ **If importing a vCard that contains contacts you already have in Address Book, you must choose how to handle the conflict.** As shown in figure 8.12, you can choose to update the old card with the new information, keep the old card, keep only the new card, or keep both cards.

8.12 Decide the ultimate fate of your new vCards.

Exporting contacts

The file format preferred by Address Book for exporting contacts is vCard. vCard is a standard format that's common to most applications that have functionality similar to Address Book.

To export vCards from Address Book follow these steps:

1. **Select the contacts you want to export from either the Group or the Name column.**

2. **Choose File ⇨ Export, and then select vCard as the format.**

3. **Give the exported vCard a name, browse to the destination on your Mac's hard drive you want to save the exported file to, and then click Save.**

Genius

I'm sure you noticed in the File ⇨ Export menu that there is another selection called Address Book Archive. Choose this format when you want to make a complete backup file of your Address Book database. I highly recommend performing this kind of export after you import a large number of files to make sure you don't lose all the work you've just put in. At the very least, make one of these backups once a month.

Setting Address Book Preferences

As with most other applications, Address Book has many preferences to help you customize your experience. Open the preferences by either choosing Address Book ⇨ Preferences from the menu, or pressing ⌘+,.

General

The General preferences allow you to make several basic appearance and behavior modifications, as shown in figure 8.13.

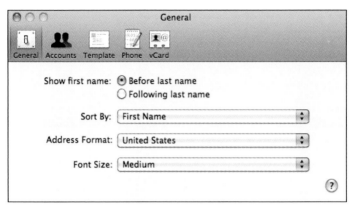

8.13 The General preferences, at your disposal

While these options are fairly self-explanatory, Table 8.5 gives a brief description of each.

Table 8.5 General Preferences Options

Option	Function
Show first name	Display a contact's first name before or after the last name.
Sort By	Decide to sort contacts by first name or last name.
Address Format	Select the country that uses the address format you want to use.
Font Size	Choose a default font size for Address Book.

Accounts

The Accounts preferences (shown in figure 8.14) allow you to synchronize contacts with other accounts you may have, such as MobileMe, and also helps you share your Address Book with others.

- **Select a check box next to the type of account you want to synchronize your contacts with.**

- **Click the Sharing tab and then select the Share your address book check box to share your Address Book with other computers on your network.**

Template

Use the Template preferences, shown in figure 8.15, to modify what fields are automatically displayed when creating new cards. Remove fields by clicking the – buttons to the left of them, and add fields by clicking the + button or by choosing a field type from the Add Field pop-up menu.

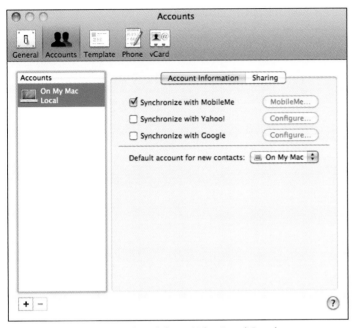

8.14 Sync your contacts with MobileMe, Yahoo!, and Google.

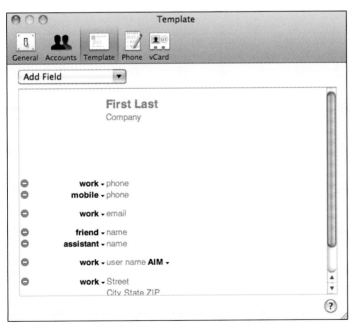

8.15 I love the Template preferences for allowing customization of the new card fields!

Phone

Phone simply allows you to modify the format in which Address Book displays phone numbers. You may want to change this to reflect the country that you or your contact are in. Choose the preferred format from the Formats pop-up menu, or create your own format by clicking the blue triangle next to the Formats pop-up menu, and then clicking the + button in the bottom-left corner of the window.

vCard

The vCard options allow you to change the default vCard format version in Address Book, and to specify just how much information you want to share with others when sending them your vCards. Table 8.6 explains the vCard options shown in figure 8.16.

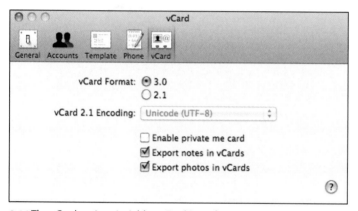

8.16 The vCard options in Address Book's preferences

Table 8.6 vCard Options for Address Book

Option	Function
vCard Format	Choose between versions 3.0 and 2.1. Version 3.0 is the default; choose 2.1 if others have problems importing your vCards.
vCard 2.1 Encoding	Select the appropriate encoding for your language. English speakers generally want to stick with Western (Mac OS Roman). This is only available if you select 2.1 for the vCard format.
Enable private me card	Lets you choose which items in your personal vCard to share with those you are sending the vCard to. For example, you may not want them to know your personal e-mail or your home address, but you may want them to see other fields in your card. When this check box is selected you can edit your personal vCard and deselect the items you don't want to be exported with your contact information.

Option	Function
Export notes in vCards	Select this check box to include notes you have typed in your contacts' vCards information.
Export photos in vCards	Selecting this check box will include any photos that you associate in vCards with the card or cards being exported.

Getting Detailed Maps of Addresses

A great feature included in Address Book is the ability to see maps of the addresses in your cards. This functionality really shines when you need to get to a client's location but aren't sure where to go. Here's how to use this cool feature:

1. **Click the card you need in the Name column so that you can see the contact information.**

2. **Ctrl+click (or right-click if you have a two-button mouse) the address in the contact information window, and then choose Show Map, as shown in figure 8.17.**

8.17 Choose Show Map from this contextual menu to get a detailed map.

3. **Safari automatically opens to the Google Maps page, displaying a map of the address's location.** From here you can even get directions from your current location to the address. Address Book and Google Maps work well together to give you accurate information; this feature is a pleasure to use.

Syncing Contacts and Calendars with Handheld Devices

Snow Leopard is quite a friendly operating system, connecting and interacting with tons of different devices right out of the box. You won't even need to download drivers to connect to most devices, such as PDAs and cell phones. Snow Leopard can connect to and synchronize information with these kinds of devices, making it very easy to keep contact information and calendar data consistent across multiple devices. iSync is the synchronization tool of choice for most handheld devices and Snow Leopard, and is simplicity incarnate. iPhone and iPod touch owners use iTunes to synchronize their devices.

Connecting a device to your Mac

In order for your Mac to synchronize with a device, it must first be able to converse with it. This means the device must be supported in Snow Leopard. Then you need to connect it to your Mac. Typically, devices connect through a wireless Bluetooth connection or a USB cable.

Supported devices

Snow Leopard has built-in support for so many devices, it's mind numbing. PDAs using the Palm OS, cell phones from all major brands, and Pocket PCs are all supported for use with iSync. To see a list of approved devices, visit www.apple.com/macosx/features/isync/index.html.

Bluetooth

The most common method of connecting a device with iSync is through Bluetooth. Bluetooth is a wireless connection protocol used mainly for small device-to-device connections.

Before you can synchronize your Bluetooth device, make sure that Bluetooth is enabled on both the device and your Mac. If your Mac is an older model, you may need to connect a USB Bluetooth adapter in order to use the Bluetooth protocol. Open System Preferences by choosing Apple menu ⇨ System Preferences; if you see a Bluetooth logo in the Hardware section, your Mac is Bluetooth capable.

Consult your device's documentation for help in enabling Bluetooth on your device.

To enable Bluetooth on your Mac, follow these steps:

1. **Choose Apple menu ⇨ System Preferences.**
2. **Click the Bluetooth icon in the Hardware section.**

3. **Select the check boxes next to On and Discoverable, as shown in figure 8.18, to turn on Bluetooth and to make your Mac visible to other devices running Bluetooth.** Don't close the Bluetooth System Preferences yet!

8.18 The Bluetooth System Preferences window, with no devices configured for Bluetooth communication

Genius

Make sure that your Bluetooth-enabled device is also set to be discoverable. This allows your Mac to see the Bluetooth device.

Next, configure your Bluetooth device to communicate with Snow Leopard:

1. **If there are no devices set up for Bluetooth communication with your Mac, click Set Up New Device.** Otherwise, click the + button in the bottom-left corner of the Bluetooth preferences window.

2. **In the Bluetooth Setup Assistant Introduction window, click Continue.**

3. **Select the type of device you're configuring from the list, and click Continue again.**

4. **Highlight the device's name and click Continue.** Bluetooth Setup Assistant gathers information about your device at this point.

5. **When it is finished, click Continue.** Next, your Mac and device will pair up. Bluetooth Setup Assistant generates a passcode that you must enter on your device to complete the process. Once the pairing process is complete, Bluetooth Setup Assistant asks which services you want to use with your device.

6. **The only option necessary for our purposes in this chapter is Set up iSync to transfer contacts and events.** Make sure that its check box is selected, and then click Continue.

7. **Click Quit on the next screen to complete the device setup procedures.** You are now ready to use your device with iSync. In some cases, iSync automatically opens and your device is listed in its window. If that's not the case for you, I explain how to add a device to iSync in just a bit.

USB

iSync is also able to communicate with devices that connect with USB. To connect a USB device, follow these steps:

1. **With iSync closed, turn on the device.**

2. **Attach one end of the USB cable to the device and the other to your Mac.**

3. **Open iSync and follow the instructions in the next section of this chapter.**

Caution Apple highly recommends that you only synchronize your device with one computer. This is to avoid the possibility of synchronization problems. Possible issues could be the loss of data, receiving duplicate information, or simply synchronizing the wrong information.

Syncing with iSync

It's syncing time. Open iSync to get started:

1. **Choose Go ➪ Applications.**

2. **Double-click the iSync icon to open the application.** The iSync window is quite sparse until you add devices for it to synchronize with, as shown in figure 8.19.

8.19 The iSync main window is a barren landscape when it's without a device to synchronize with.

Add a device to iSync

iSync is now ready to add a new device to its repertoire. To add a new device, follow these steps:

1. **Press ⌘+N, or choose Devices ⇨ Add Device from the menu. iSync should find any Bluetooth-enabled devices you've set up for use with your Mac, or any USB devices that are attached to your Mac and turned on.**

2. **Double-click your device, and it is added to iSync, as shown in figure 8.20.** The iSync synchronization options shown are defined in Table 8.7.

3. **Close the Add Device window.**

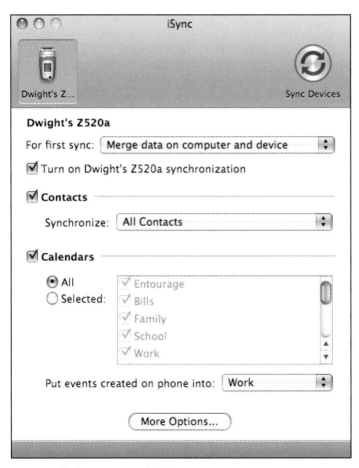

8.20 My cell phone is now added to iSync.

Sync devices with your Mac

Before you actually begin the synchronization of your device with iSync, make sure that all the synchronization options are set to your satisfaction. Table 8.7 lists the available options.

185

Table 8.7 iSync Synchronization Options

Option	Function
For first sync	This option is only visible prior to the first synchronization of the device. Decide whether to merge information from the device and your Mac or to erase the data on your device before syncing.
Turn on *device* synchronization	Select this check box to allow your Mac to synchronize with the particular device.
Contacts	Select this check box to allow iSync to synchronize contact information between the Mac and your device. Choose which contacts to synchronize from the Synchronize pop-up menu.
Calendars	Select this option to allow calendar events to be synchronized between the Mac and your device. Decide which calendars in iCal to synchronize with your device.
Put events created on phone into	Decide which calendar in iCal will store the calendar events you create on your device.
More Options	Click this button to make extra synchronization options available for this device. These extras include synchronizing only contacts that have phone numbers associated with them, synchronizing alarms, synchronizing all-day events, and deciding whether to synchronize events prior to or after a specified period of time.

When the synchronization preferences are set, click the Sync Devices button in the upper-right corner of the iSync window. iSync shows a progress bar of the synchronization process, as shown in figure 8.21.

If you change your mind, stop the synchronization process by clicking the Cancel Sync button on the right side of the iSync window.

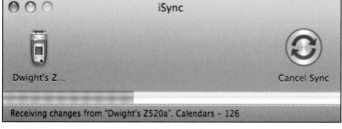

8.21 iSync is working to get your device and your Mac in concert with one another.

When synchronization is complete, iSync lets you know. Your contacts and calendar events are now synchronized between your Mac and the device.

Sync alert

You will be alerted during the synchronization process when the amount of information that is going to be changed on your Mac and the device it's synchronizing with reaches a certain percentage, which is set by you in the iSync preferences (see the next section), as shown in Figure 8.22. This is simply to inform you what items will be changed or added so that you can decide whether or not to continue with the synchronization.

8.22 The Sync Alert window lets you know when a lot of data is about to change on your Mac and the device you're synchronizing it with.

Syncing a Palm OS Device

Synchronizing information with a Palm OS device requires a bit more than synchronizing with a cell phone. You must have the Palm Desktop software installed on your Mac and have synchronized your Palm device with the HotSync Manager before using iSync. Consult the iSync Help section for much more information on using your Palm OS device; choose Help ⇨ iSync Help from the menu, and search for Palm OS to find all the relevant topics on setting up the Palm OS device.

iSync preferences

Figure 8.23 shows the iSync Preferences window. You can modify these settings to make iSync work the way you want it to, and to allow your Mac to synchronize with other devices.

Table 8.8 lists the preferences that are available for iSync.

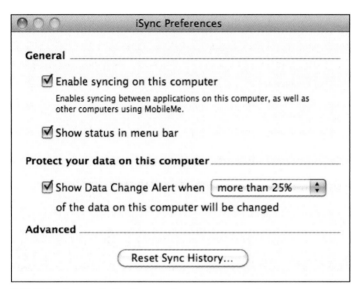

8.23 Make changes to the iSync preferences as needed.

Table 8.8 iSync Preferences Explained

Option	Function
Enable syncing on this computer	This option is pretty much a necessity if you want to synchronize any device with your Mac. The only good reason I've ever encountered for disabling synchronization is if you're running memory-intensive applications and need to temporarily keep your Mac from using up its memory resources unnecessarily.
Show status in menu bar	Selecting this option displays an iSync icon in the menu bar so that you can easily monitor or initialize synchronization.
Show Data Change Alert when x percentage of the data on this computer will be changed	Set a percentage to decide at what point iSync will display the Sync Alert.
Reset Sync History	Clicking this button completely restores the synchronization settings for every application your Mac uses to sync information with, such as Mail, iCal, iSync, and even .Mac. Perform this reset if you are having problems synchronizing with a device.

Caution

When you reset your synchronization history, all the default synchronization settings in Snow Leopard and its applications are restored to their defaults. If you change any of the synchronization settings prior to resetting the synchronization history, those changes need to be made again.

Syncing an iPhone or iPod touch with iTunes

There are a couple of handheld devices (very popular ones, I might add) that won't work with iSync: Apple's iPhone and iPod touch. If you're an owner of one of these devices you have nothing to fear; iTunes is here to save the day and synchronize your calendars and contacts. Follow these steps:

1. **Connect your device to your Mac.**
2. **Open iTunes.**
3. **Click your device's name in the source list under Devices to highlight it.**
4. **Click the Info tab to see the sync settings for Contacts and Calendars (shown in figure 8.24).**

8.24 iTunes keeps your iPhone and iPod touch in sync with your contacts and calendars.

5. **Select the check boxes next to Sync Address Book contacts and Sync iCal calendars.**
6. **Click Apply in the lower-right corner (you may need to scroll down to see it), and then click Sync.**

iTunes will inform you when the synchronization process is complete.

How Do I Master the Web with Safari?

Since the advent of television, nothing has impacted the way humans con-
duct their daily activities quite like the Internet. For many people, checking
e-mail and surfing the Web are as routine as waking up in the morning. Snow
Leopard comes loaded with the third version of the Web's best surfboard:
Safari. Safari is a lightning-fast and standards-compliant Web browser that
will have even the most demanding of browser critics smiling. Because most
computer users are quite familiar with the bare basics of Web browsing, we'll
jump right into the meat and potatoes of using and customizing Safari.

Setting Safari Preferences

At the heart of Safari's great features are its preferences. They tell Safari how you want it to behave in both everyday browsing and special circumstances. In this section of the chapter, I discuss the preferences in some detail so that you can take maximum advantage of them to streamline and customize your surfing experience.

General

Table 9.1 gives the scoop on the options available in the General pane of Safari's preferences, which is shown in figure 9.1.

Table 9.1 General Preferences

Option	Description
Default web browser	Choose which Web browser will be the default for your Mac, if you've indeed installed browsers other than Safari, such as Firefox or Opera. Thankfully, there's no longer an Internet Explorer for Mac, so that's one more pat on the back for Snow Leopard!
New windows open with	Select whether new windows should open with your home page, a blank page, your bookmarks, or the same page as the previous window.
New tabs open with	Choose to open new tabs in Top Sites (more on Top Sites later in this chapter), your home page, an empty page, the same page as the current tab, or display your bookmarks.
Home page	Type the URL (address) of the Internet site you want to be your home page. Click Set to Current Page to make the Web site you are currently viewing your home page.
Remove history items	Delete items from your browsing history after the pre-scribed length of time.
Save downloaded files to	Select which folder your downloaded files will be saved in.
Remove download list items	Safari keeps a history of files you've downloaded. This option lets you choose how often items on that list should be purged.
Open "safe" files after downloading	Select this option to have Safari automatically open certain types of files, such as disk images and zipped archives, when they finish downloading.
Open links from applications	Choose to open links from other applications, such as your e-mail program, in either a new window or a new tab in the current window.

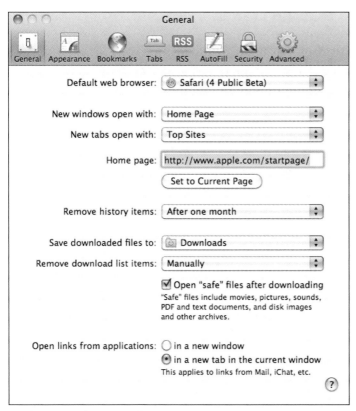

9.1 These are Safari's General options.

Appearance

The Appearance pane, seen in figure 9.2, lets you choose the fonts that Safari uses to display text in a window. Click the Select buttons to choose a font if the default Times and Courier aren't to your liking.

If you are a speed freak (or conversely, are using a dial-up connection) and don't care about the pictures and graphics that adorn most of today's Web sites, deselect the Display images when the page opens check box; pages will zip open, displaying their text but no images.

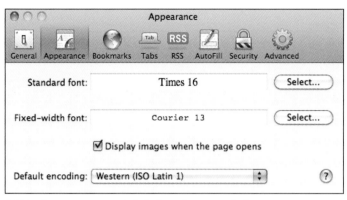

9.2 The Appearance pane in Safari's preferences window.

Bookmarks

The selections in the Bookmarks pane (see figure 9.3) allow you to include links that are in Top Sites, your Address Book, and home pages of devices running the Bonjour network protocol in your Bookmarks bar, Bookmarks menu, or your Collections.

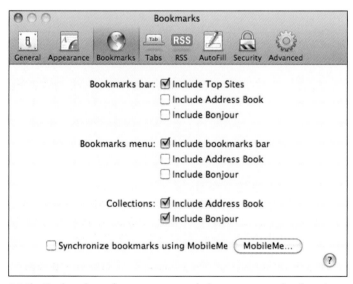

9.3 The Bookmarks preferences pane can help manage your bookmarks.

If you have multiple Macs and a MobileMe account, you can synchronize your Safari bookmarks by selecting the Synchronize bookmarks using the MobileMe check box.

Tabs

The Tabs pane (see figure 9.4) lets you tell Safari how it should handle new tabs when they are opened, as well as whether it can close multiple tabs at once without prompting you.

There are also keyboard shortcuts listed to help you easily open and navigate to new tabs and windows.

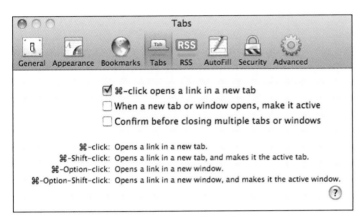

9.4 Tell Safari how to utilize tabs in the Tabs preferences pane.

RSS

Figure 9.5 shows the options that are available to you in the RSS preferences pane; Table 9.2 describes them for you.

Table 9.2 RSS Feed Preferences Options

Option	Description
Default RSS reader	If you've downloaded other RSS readers, you can designate one of them to be the default reader for your Mac using this drop-down menu.
Automatically update articles in	Safari can let you know when a site has updated its contents by displaying the number of new articles in the Bookmarks bar, Bookmarks menu, or both.
Check for updates	Determine how often Safari should check your subscribed RSS feeds for updates to their content.
Mark articles as read	Choose whether to mark articles as having been read after you view the page or click its link. The Highlight unread articles option causes unread feeds to be more visible.
Remove articles	Decide how often to delete old articles. Click Remove Now to instantly clear out all of the articles.

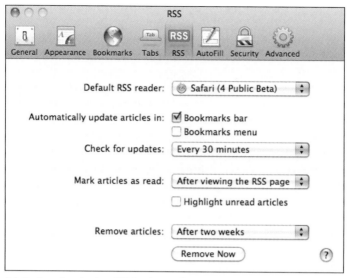

9.5 Options for viewing RSS feeds in Safari

AutoFill

Safari uses AutoFill to remember the information you type into forms on Web sites so that it can automatically enter that information for you in the future. The options available, shown in figure 9.6, are

- **Using info from my Address Book card.** This option lets Safari use the information you've entered about yourself in the Address Book application. Click Edit to open Address Book and change your information.

- **User names and passwords.** Select this option to have Safari save the usernames and passwords that you use to log on to secure Web sites. I do not recommend this option if security is of any importance to you. Click Edit to see a list of Web sites and the usernames used for them.

- **Other forms.** Safari remembers the information you type into fields of Web sites, such as online application forms or addresses for driving directions. Clicking Edit allows you to see all the sites in which you've entered information in the past.

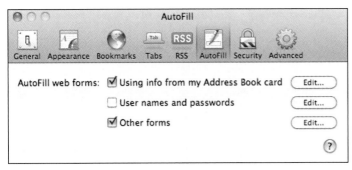

9.6 AutoFill helps you quickly enter information for Web pages containing fields.

Security

Table 9.3 lists the options available in the Security pane, as shown in figure 9.7.

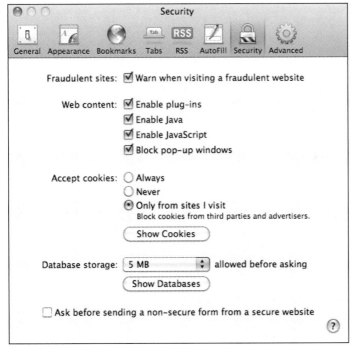

9.7 Choose how to best secure your browsing expeditions.

Note

One of my few gripes with Safari is the inability to allow some Web sites to open pop-up windows while blocking others. With Safari, it's all or nothing: You either enable pop-up blocking, or you don't. Because some sites have legitimate uses for pop-ups (some folks would argue that all pop-ups are legitimate, but that's not for us to debate here), you have to temporarily turn off pop-up blocking when visiting those sites and turn it back on immediately after leaving them.

Table 9.3 Security Options for Safari

Option	Description
Fraudulent sites	Select the check box to have Safari warn you when you visit a site that may be fraudulent.
Web content	Plug-ins help Safari view or play certain types of content on Web sites, such as movies and sound files. Java and JavaScript are also used for interactive elements on many Web pages. Select the check boxes next to these options to enable Safari to use them to enrich your browsing. Select the Block pop-up windows option to avoid those pesky ads that infest some Web sites.
Accept cookies	Cookies are text files that some sites use to authenticate you or to track your browsing habits. It's best to select the Only from sites I visit option. Click Show Cookies to view the cookies that Safari is currently storing.
Database storage	Some sites allow you to create and edit documents online, and they use space on your hard drive to store those documents. Use this drop-down menu to allocate the amount of hard drive space you want available for such tasks. Click Show Databases to see a list of databases stored by Safari.
Ask before sending a non-secure form from a secure website	When you select this check box, Safari prompts you if you are about to send sensitive information in a form that has little or no security from what is supposed to be a secure site.

Advanced

The Universal Access options in the Advanced pane (see figure 9.8) allow users to make small text display with a larger font for easier reading, and let them use the Tab key to navigate items on a Web page without using a mouse.

The Style sheet drop-down menu lets you choose a Cascading Style Sheet of your own to use when browsing the Web.

Click Change Settings next to the Proxies option to allow your Mac to access the Internet when using a firewall. You may want to ask your IT department what proxy settings to use if you are on a corporate network.

Selecting the Show Develop menu in menu bar option displays the Develop menu, which is used mainly by programmers for testing their Web pages.

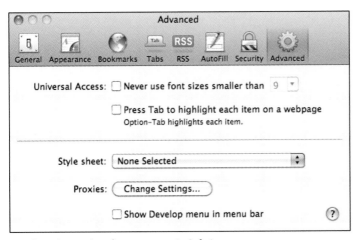

9.8 The Advanced preferences pane in Safari

This Web Site Won't Open in Safari!

Sometimes Web developers put (usually) superficial limitations on which browsers can access their Web sites; for example, if the developer harbors a personal preference for Internet Explorer. Thankfully, this practice is beginning to rapidly decline with the increased use of browsers such as Safari and Firefox, so hopefully you won't often run into this problem. You can bypass their contrived limitations, however:

1. **Enable the Develop menu by selecting the Show Develop menu option in the Advanced Preferences pane of Safari.**

2. **Choose Develop ⇨ User Agent.**

3. **Select the browser version you want Safari to emulate from the list.** Safari can even pretend it's a browser on a Microsoft Windows PC.

4. **Refresh the offending Web page, and usually you will bypass the bogus limitation.**

199

Using Bookmarks

Bookmarks are links that you create for your favorite Web sites so that you can easily and quickly visit them. To bookmark a Web site, follow these steps:

1. **Choose Bookmarks ⇨ Add Bookmark, or press ⌘+D.**

2. **Give the bookmark an appropriate name.**

3. **Select a location for the bookmark to reside.**

4. **Click Add, as shown in figure 9.9, to create the bookmark.**

Type a name for the bookmark, and choose where to keep it.

Apple - Start

📖 Bookmarks Bar

Cancel   Add

Organizing bookmarks

9.9 Create bookmarks so that you can quickly access your favorite locations on the Web.

Like toys in a child's room, bookmarks can get quickly out of hand if they aren't organized. To open the Bookmarks window, as shown in figure 9.10, choose Bookmarks ⇨ Show All Bookmarks, press ⌘+Option+B, or simply click the icon in the Bookmarks bar that looks like an opened book.

The bookmarks list is on the left side of the window (under Bookmarks Bar), and houses your bookmark collections. Each collection can contain subfolders as well as bookmarks.

You can organize bookmarks in the Bookmarks window by doing the following:

- **Arrange bookmarks in a collection.** Select the collection you want to organize, and arrange the bookmarks in the order you want them to appear by dragging and dropping them into their preferred position in the list.

- **Arrange bookmark folders in the order you want them to be listed.** Click and drag the bookmark folder you want to move to its new position in the bookmarks list.

- **Create new collections.** Click the + button under the left column to create a new bookmark collection, and then give the collection a descriptive name.

- **Create subfolders in collections.** Select the collection you want to add a subfolder to. Click the + button under the right column and give the subfolder a descriptive name.

⊙ **Change the name or address of a bookmark.** Select the collection that contains the bookmark you want to change. Right-click or Ctrl+click the bookmark, and select either Edit Name or Edit Address to make your changes.

⊙ **Delete a bookmark or collection.** Right-click or Ctrl+click the item you want to remove, and select Delete from the list.

Genius

Safari has an even easier way to create a bookmark. Simply click and drag the address of the page in the Address field to the Bookmarks bar, give it a name, and then click OK.

9.10 Bookmarks waiting to be whipped into shape

Genius

You can keep bookmark folders in the Bookmarks bar to provide fast access to multiple sites. Apple has already provided a News folder and a Popular folder in the Bookmarks bar; you can experiment with them to see how beneficial this functionality is.

Importing and exporting bookmarks

Most browsers can export a list of their bookmarks so that you can easily back them up or use them in another browser. To import bookmarks into Safari, follow these steps:

1. **Choose File ⇨ Import Bookmarks.**
2. **Browse your Mac using the Import Bookmarks window, and find the bookmarks file you want to import.**
3. **Highlight the file and click Import.** The Bookmarks window automatically opens and reveals the list of imported bookmarks so that you can organize them.

To export bookmarks from Safari, follow these steps:

1. **Choose File ⇨ Export Bookmarks.**
2. **Name your bookmarks file in the Export Bookmarks window.**
3. **Browse your Mac for a location to save the bookmarks and click Save.**

Customizing Safari's Main Window

You can personalize your browsing experience by making some custom changes to Safari's main window. There are several options for making Safari more efficient for you:

⦿ **Hide or show the status bar at the bottom of Safari's window, which displays information about a links address (see figure 9.11), how many elements of a page have been loaded, and more.** Click the View menu and choose either Hide Status Bar or Show Status Bar (depending on its current state).

9.11 Viewing the URL for a link using the status bar at the bottom of Safari's window

⦿ **You can choose whether to display the Bookmarks bar by clicking the View menu and selecting either Hide Bookmarks Bar or Show Bookmarks Bar.**

● **If you're tired of that URL field cluttering up your browser window click the View menu and select Hide Toolbar.** Resurrect the toolbar by clicking View and choosing Show Toolbar.

● **Add items to or remove items from the toolbar by clicking View and selecting Customize Toolbar.** In the resulting dialog (see figure 9.12), click and drag items you want to add from the window to the toolbar and drop them in place. To remove items from the toolbar, simply drag them out of the toolbar and drop them outside of the Safari window where they disappear in a puff of smoke.

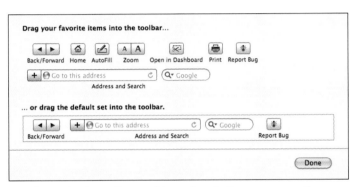

9.12 Customize the toolbar to add your favorite items or remove those that are simply in your way.

Genius

You can rearrange the items in your toolbar with Mac OS X's typical ease. Hold down the ⌘ key and then click and drag an item in the toolbar to move it to a better location. Other items in the toolbar shift around automatically to accommodate the item being moved.

Viewing Your Favorite Pages with Top Sites

Top Sites is a new feature to Safari (as of version 4) that shows you a preview of the Web sites you frequent most often, and it works in typical Apple fashion: really cool and really easy. To view your Top Sites, as I'm doing in figure 9.13, click the Top Sites button on the left side of the Bookmarks bar. Simply click a sites page in the Top Sites window to visit the site.

Top Sites

9.13 Top Sites displays your favorite Web sites in a neat three-dimensional grid.

Here are a few tips to maximize your Top Sites experience:

- **Get a really cool look at a history of the sites you've seen recently by clicking Search History.**

    - **Safari displays sites you've recently viewed using Cover Flow (see figure 9.14).** Click and drag the slider to fly through your history.

    - **Type part of a site's name in the Search field to instantly find it.**

    - **Click Clear History to erase the list of sites you've previously visited.**

9.14 Cover Flow helps you see the sites you've visited recently.

● **Click Edit to organize sites on the Top Sites page, as illustrated in figure 9.15.**

   ● **Click the X in the upper-left corner of a page to remove it from Top Sites.**

   ● **Select the pin to keep a site on the Top Sites page permanently.**

   ● **Determine a size for the sites by clicking the Small, Medium, or Large button on the lower-right side of the window.**

   ● **Rearrange the placement of sites on the Top Sites page by dragging and dropping a page into a new position.**

   ● **Click Done when you finish organizing your Top Sites page.**

9.15 It's really easy to organize the sites in your Top Sites page using the Edit button.

Private Browsing

Are you the type who doesn't like the world knowing your business? Do you value your privacy when surfing the Web? Are you a super spy who doesn't want your evil arch nemesis to know what Web sites you've been visiting? You are in luck if you use Safari! Private Browsing is a feature of Safari that prevents anyone else using your Mac from ever knowing what pages you've viewed during your browsing session. To enable Private Browsing, follow these steps:

1. **Choose Safari ⇨ Private Browsing.**

2. **Click OK to enable Private Browsing, as shown in figure 9.16.**

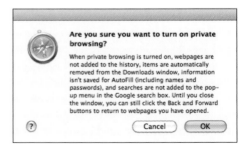

Are you sure you want to turn on private browsing?

When private browsing is turned on, webpages are not added to the history, items are automatically removed from the Downloads window, information isn't saved for AutoFill (including names and passwords), and searches are not added to the pop-up menu in the Google search box. Until you close the window, you can still click the Back and Forward buttons to return to webpages you have opened.

Cancel OK

9.16 Enable Private Browsing for added privacy.

Note To quit Private Browsing choose it from the Safari menu again, and make sure you close any windows you had open(not tabs, but the actual window). If you don't close the window, someone else could use the Forward and Back buttons to view the sites you were visiting.

Viewing RSS Feeds

Many sites that change their contents frequently offer an alternative method for viewing their content: RSS. RSS (Really Simple Syndication) pages simply show you the titles of the most recent articles on the site, along with some of the first few lines in the article to give you a good idea of what the article is about. Clicking the title should open the site containing the complete article if you are interested.

Whenever Safari detects a site that uses RSS it displays a blue RSS icon on the right side of the address bar. Click the RSS icon to view the RSS page for the site, as shown in figure 9.17.

RSS icon

9.17 RSS is a good way to get a quick overview of the latest happenings on your favorite sites.

Viewing Windows Media Files

Watching videos on the Web is becoming more and more common, and two of the most popular formats for viewing video are QuickTime and Windows Media. Snow Leopard has QuickTime built right in, but it has no way for you to view Windows Media files out of the box. Don't worry: The Windows Media Components for QuickTime, by Flip4Mac, make this a nonissue. To get the WMV (Windows Media) components, follow these steps:

1. **Go to www.microsoft.com/mac/products/flip4mac.mspx, and click the appropriate links to download the WMV Components disk image.** Safari automatically opens the installer program, as shown in figure 9.18.

2. **Click Continue and accept the license agreements.**

3. **Select your Mac's hard drive as the drive to install the necessary files on, and then click Continue.**

4. **Click Install, and type the username and password of an Administrator account to begin the installation.** When you see the Install Succeeded prompt, you are finished and can now view Windows Media files on your Mac.

9.18 You are just a few steps away from viewing Windows Media files in Snow Leopard.

Note

The WMV components will work with any browser on your Mac, not just Safari. Nothing further needs to be done in your other browsers to view Windows Media files.

Finding Text on a Web Site

Sometimes you may be only looking for a word or a phrase on a Web page, but it's so packed with information that it would take you half the day to find it. Safari provides a great mechanism for finding text on a Web page that can quickly point you to what you need. To search for text on a Web page, follow these steps:

1. **Press ⌘+F to open the Find field near the upper-right corner of the window.**

2. **Type the search term or phrase in the Find field (in our example, Apple), and Safari immediately begins searching as you type, as shown in figure 9.19.**

3. **Safari displays the number of matches it has found for your search terms to the left of the Find field.** The page is grayed out and the instances of the search term are highlighted.

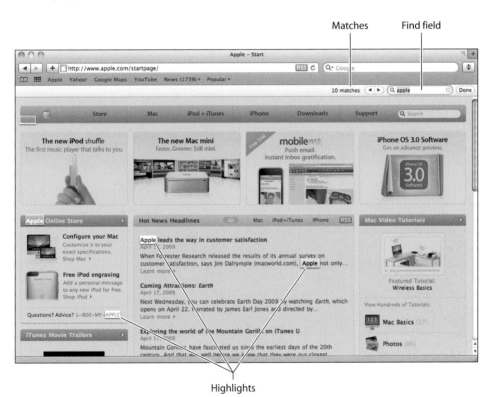

Matches   Find field

Highlights

9.19 Safari grays out the page and highlights found instances of my search terms — in this case, the word Apple.

209

4. **Click the left- and right-arrow buttons to cycle through the matches.**

5. **Click the Done button next to the Find field when you finish.**

Troubleshooting Safari

Safari can make your Web surfing life a joy, but no life is perfect. Just like anything else, Safari can have moments when it doesn't behave up to par, even if some of those times aren't its fault. Let's take a quick look at some of the most common problems experienced when surfing the Web with Safari, see what could cause them, and how to hopefully rectify the situation.

A Web page won't open

There could be a lot of reasons why a Web page won't open:

- **The page may be temporarily down.** If so, try accessing it later.

- **You may not have an Internet connection.** Even if you were cruising the Web just seconds before, something could have happened to make you lose connectivity.

- **The cached site is corrupt.** If this is the case, your browser keeps trying to open the corrupt cache site instead of refreshing it. To fix this, try emptying the cache and reloading the Web site. Choose Safari ⇨ Empty Cache from the menu, and then select Empty.

- **Be sure that you are entering the correct address for the Web site.** This one has bitten me more than once!

Unable to download files

Sometimes when you click a link on a site, the linked file may simply appear not to download (for example, you can't find it on your Mac) or it may indeed not be downloading at all. You can view the files being downloaded, or files that have previously been downloaded, by choosing Window ⇨ Downloads. The Downloads window displays a list of downloaded files, as seen in figure 9.20. Here's a few things to check when this problem occurs:

- **From the Downloads window, see if the file download is in the list to find out if Safari has tried to download but failed.**

- **If you see the file in the Downloads window, but can't find it on your Mac, click the magnifying glass to the right of the file's name.**

- **Should a link simply not download the promised file, contact the proprietors of the site.** Perhaps there is a missing or broken link to the file.

Downloaded files won't open

Sometimes that file you're downloading just won't cooperate and open. What to do? Here are a few suggestions:

- **Is the file completely downloaded?** If not, resume the download or start it over.

9.20 A list of my most recently downloaded files

- **Try downloading the file again just in case it was corrupted during the download process.**

- **Some files you download may be a file type not natively supported by Mac OS X.** Find out what type of file it is (the extension on the end of the file is a dead giveaway) and search Google for software that will open that type of file on a Mac.

The AutoFill feature isn't working

I think AutoFill is pretty convenient, and when it's not working, I'm not a happy camper.

- **Be sure that AutoFill is turned on by choosing Safari ⇨ Preferences and clicking the AutoFill tab.** Select the check box next to each of the options you want to use.

- **The information needed may not have been entered before.** If that's the case, type the info again.

Images aren't displaying correctly

There you are surfing along, and all of a sudden the page that should be chock-full of images has none. In some cases this may not be a big deal, but in others it may be huge (how can you properly shop for a new Mac if you can't see what it looks like?). Here are a couple of ideas:

- **Perhaps Safari doesn't know it should be displaying images.** Choose Safari ⇨ Preferences and click the Appearance tab. Select the Display images when the page opens check box.

- **The links to the images on the site may be missing or broken.** Contact the Webmaster of the site.

How Do I Stay Connected with Mail?

Mail is Snow Leopard's easy-to-use e-mail application that is head and shoulders above most e-mail programs that I've used. Mail was already a great e-mail client in its previous incarnation, but with Snow Leopard, it took a big leap forward. The inclusion of Microsoft Exchange Server support right out of the box makes the newest version of Mail an instant hit.

Getting Around in Mail

Mail is a very straightforward application, and most of its tools are in plain view for easy clicking capability. Figure 10.1 shows Mail's main window so that you can get familiar with its features.

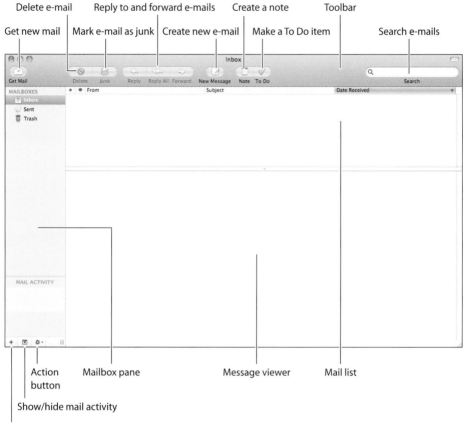

10.1 Mail's main window in its default layout

Table 10.1 explains a few of the features that are available in the main window. All others are discussed in further detail throughout this chapter.

Table 10.1 Mail's Main Window Features

Feature	Description
Junk	If you use e-mail at all, at some point you will get junk e-mail. Junk e-mail is anything that you simply don't want, whether it is unsolicited advertising or messages from your long-lost cousin who just found out you won the lottery. Highlight the offending message in the Mail list and click the Junk button to permanently mark an e-mail as junk, and to filter future e-mails like it automatically into the Junk folder.
Search	Type a search term into the Search field, and Mail finds all e-mails that contain the term.
Mailbox pane	Lists all the mailboxes you have created in Mail. Click a mailbox to display its contents.
Add button (the plus symbol)	Click to quickly create a new mailbox or a new Smart Mailbox, or to add an RSS feed.
Show or hide	Click to show or hide the Mail activity window, which displays a progress mail activity bar when sending or receiving mail.
Action button	Select a mailbox from the Mailbox pane, and then click the Action button (looks like a small gear) to perform the actions in its pop-up list for that mailbox. The Action button also works with RSS feeds.
Mail list	Displays all the e-mails currently in the mailbox that you have selected in the Mailbox pane.
Message viewer	Shows the contents of the e-mail you have selected in the Mail list.

Customizing the Toolbar

The toolbar is where Mail's controls reside, but you aren't limited to just the default set of controls. You can modify the controls to your liking quite easily:

1. **Choose View ⇨ Customize Toolbar.**

2. **From the huge list of available controls (shown in figure 10.2), select the ones you want to add to the toolbar.**

3. **Click and drag the controls you want to add into the toolbar and drop them into the position you want.** You may also want to rearrange the controls using the same drag-and-drop technique. The neat thing is how the other controls move out of the way of the one you are moving.

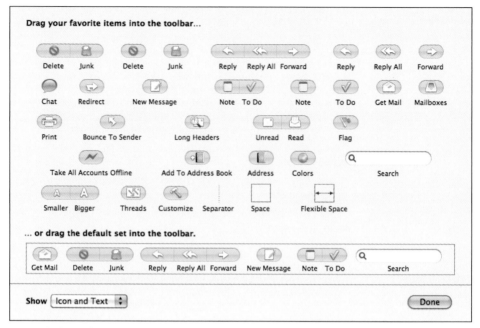

10.2 A plethora of tools for you to use

4. **Delete controls from the toolbar by clicking and dragging them out of the window and dropping them.** They disappear from the toolbar with a puff of smoke!

5. **Click Done when you finish customizing.**

Managing E-mail Accounts

Mail won't do much more than take up space on your hard drive if you don't have an e-mail account. When you sign on with an Internet service provider (ISP) it should provide you with all the information you need to add an e-mail account to Mail. Be sure to get all the e-mail information from it before you begin to use Mail.

Automatic setup

The first time you start Mail, in the Welcome to Mail screen you are asked to set up an account, as shown in figure 10.3.

Welcome to Mail

Welcome to Mail

You'll be guided through the steps to set up your mail account.

To get started, provide the following information:

Full Name: Genius

Email Address: mosxslpg@gmail.com

Password: ••••••••

(?)   (Cancel)   (Go Back) (Create)

10.3 The Welcome to Mail screen

To set up the account, follow these steps:

1. **Type a name for the account.**

2. **Type the e-mail address you will use for the account.**

3. **Type the password for your e-mail account.**

4. **Click Create and Mail does the rest of the work for you!**

You can also set up additional accounts automatically. Follow these steps:

1. **Choose Mail ⇨ Preferences, or press ⌘+,.**

2. **Click the Accounts button in the Preferences window to open the Accounts pane (see figure 10.4).**

3. **Click the + button in the lower-left corner to add an account.**

4. **Type the required information in the Add Account window, select the Automatically set up account check box, and click Create.**

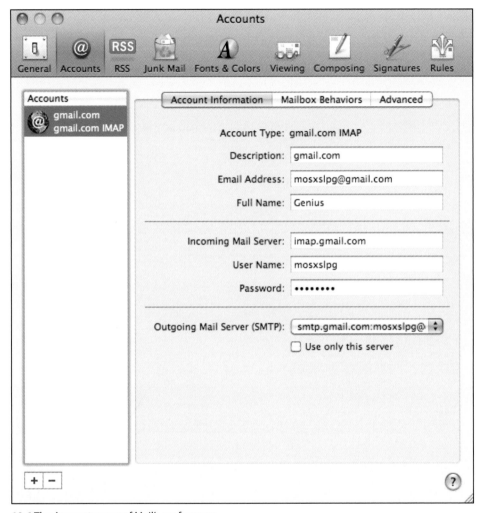

10.4 The Accounts pane of Mail's preferences

Manual setup

Mail supports POP, IMAP, and Exchange e-mail accounts, and you can add any of these types manually if you prefer this to an automatic setup. Ask your ISP or network administrator what type of account you have and what settings you need to know when setting up your account.

To manually create a new account, follow these steps:

1. **Choose Mail ⇨ Preferences, or press ⌘+,.**

2. **Click the Accounts button in the Preferences window to open the Accounts pane.**

3. **Click the + button in the lower-left corner to add an account.**

4. **Type the required information in the Add Account window, deselect the Automatically set up account check box, and click Continue.**

5. **In the Incoming Mail Server window (see figure 10.5), choose your Account Type (in my case, IMAP), and type the required information as provided by your ISP or network administrator.** Click Continue.

10.5 This information is required to receive e-mail.

6. **In the Outgoing Mail Server window, type a Description for your SMTP server and choose an Outgoing Mail Server (see figure 10.6), which is required for you to send e-mail to other people.** Check the Use Authentication box if a username and password are required by your e-mail provider, and type the information in the appropriate fields. Click Continue to proceed.

10.6 Type this information, and you're almost done configuring the account.

7. **Select the Take account online check box to instantly begin using your account, and then click Create.**

Composing E-mail

Composing your own e-mail and sending it to your intended recipient is a snap with Mail. To begin sending that world-changing memorandum, do the following:

1. **Click the New Message button in the toolbar.**

2. **In the New Message window, type the e-mail address of the person you want to receive your message in the To field, as shown in figure 10.7.** To send a copy of the e-mail to other folks, type their addresses in the Cc field.

3. **Type the topic of your e-mail in the Subject field.**

4. **Click the Customize button on the left, and choose whether any other fields, such as Priority, should appear in the New Message window.**

Customize button

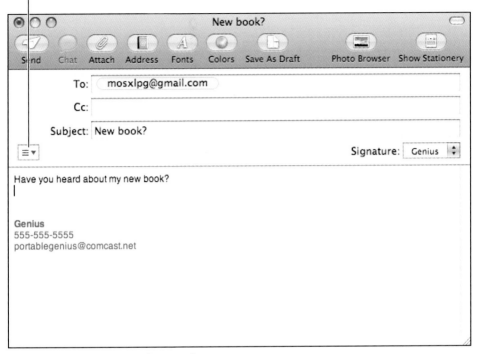

10.7 Putting together that perfect e-mail

5. **Type the content of your e-mail and click the Send button in the upper-left corner.**

6. **Congratulate yourself for being a full-blown member of Internet society.**

Genius Just like the toolbar in the main Mail window, the toolbar in the New Message window can be modified to suit your style. With a New Message window open, choose View ⇨ Customize Toolbar to arrange, remove, and add items to enhance your productivity.

Using Stationery

One of the coolest features in Mail for Snow Leopard is the ability to customize e-mails with Stationery. Stationery is preformatted e-mails that Apple provides with Mail, and this feature can transform an ordinary e-mail into a stunning creation. To use Stationery, follow these steps:

1. **Open a New Message window.**

2. **Click the Show Stationery button in the toolbar.**

3. **Browse the topics listed on the left of the Stationery field (underneath the Subject field and immediately above the e-mail content window), and select the Stationery that is appropriate for your message.**

4. **Customize the contents of your e-mail by dragging and dropping your own images into the image placeholders (if any), and type your own text in the preformatted text fields.**

Adding attachments

Sometimes you want to e-mail a picture or send along an accompanying document with your message; these additions are called attachments. To add an attachment to your e-mail, follow these steps:

1. **Open a New Message window and type the addresses of your recipients.**

2. **Click the Attachment button in the toolbar.**

3. **Browse your trusty Mac for the file you want to attach, select it, and then click the Choose File button.** If you are sending a picture from your iPhoto or Photo Booth libraries, click the Photo Browser button in the toolbar, click and drag a picture from the Photo Browser window, and drop it into the body of the e-mail, as shown in figure 10.8.

4. **Send your e-mail on its merry way by clicking the Send button in the toolbar.**

10.8 Drag and drop your picture into the e-mail.

Keep Your Recipients Anonymous

Sometimes when sending an e-mail to multiple recipients you may need to keep the names and e-mail addresses of your recipients secret. This technique is called Blind Carbon Copy, or Bcc for short, and Mail makes it a snap to do:

1. **Open a new message window.**
2. **Click the Customize button and select Bcc Address Field.**
3. **Enter the addresses of recipients in the Bcc field and this will conceal the identities of those you sent the e-mail to when the e-mail is read.**

Formatting content

Add a little pizzazz to your message by customizing its fonts and their colors. To format the e-mail, follow these steps:

1. **Open a New Message window.**
2. **Type the text of your e-mail.**
3. **Highlight the text you want to format.**
4. **Click the Fonts button in the toolbar, and then select the font you want to use.** You can alter the font's typeface and size, underline the text, change the font's color, add a shadow to the text and modify it, and even rotate the text.

Receiving, Replying to, and Forwarding E-mail

Your Inbox typically attempts to receive e-mails automatically every few minutes, but you can also have Mail check the server for new e-mails manually in one of the following ways:

● **Click the Get Mail button in the toolbar.**

Note You don't have to be working in Mail to see when new e-mail arrives, but Mail does have to be running, of course. The Mail icon in the Dock displays a red circle containing the number of unread e-mails so that you can easily tell when you have new mail waiting to be read.

- **Press ⌘+Shift+N.**

- **Choose Mailbox ⇨ Get New Mail, and then select the account you want to check.**

When someone sends you an e-mail, it shows up in your Inbox for the account the e-mail was sent to. It appears in the Mail list in bold letters and has a blue dot to the left of the From field. The Inbox also displays a light-blue oval with the number of unread e-mails it contains. Simply click the e-mail in the Mail list to read it in the Message Viewer.

To reply to or forward an e-mail you've received, follow these steps:

1. **Highlight the e-mail you want to respond to in the Mail list.**

2. **Click the Reply button to respond to the person who sent the e-mail to you, the Reply All button to send a message to all recipients of the e-mail, or the Forward button to send the e-mail to other parties.**

3. **Type text or add attachments to your message.**

4. **Click the Send button in the toolbar.**

Organizing Mailboxes

In this section, I show you how to use Mailboxes to keep your e-mail organized, Notes to keep your thoughts straight, and To Dos to keep that list of tasks in tip-top shape.

Mailboxes

Mailboxes keep your e-mail organized, and each account can have several mailboxes. Table 10.2 lists some of the types of mailboxes that accounts can have.

Table 10.2 Functions of Standard Mailboxes

Mailbox	Description
Inbox	Incoming messages to your e-mail account are stored here.
Drafts	Sometimes you may want to save an e-mail you've typed so that you can send it at a later time. The Drafts folder is where those saved e-mails reside until you are ready to send them.
Sent	Copies of messages you have sent to people are kept here.
Trash	This is where your deleted messages reside until you are ready to completely erase them from your Mac.
Junk	Messages that are flagged as junk mail are deposited into this mailbox. This way, they don't intrude with your normal activities but can be sifted through later at your convenience.

Back Up Those Mailboxes!

It is always a great idea to keep a backup of your e-mails in case something happens to Mail, Snow Leopard, or worse, your Mac. You can restore your lost e-mails to their proper places if you've been making consistent backups of your mailboxes.

To back up a mailbox

1. **Select the mailbox you want to archive.**

2. **Choose Mailbox⇨Archive Mailbox.**

3. **Select the folder in which you want to save the mailbox archive, and click the Choose button.**

4. **An archive of the mailbox is created in the appropriate folder using the MBOX format.**

To restore a mailbox, follow these steps:

1. **Choose File⇨Import Mailboxes.**

2. **Select the radio button next to Mail for Mac OS X and click Continue.**

3. **Browse your Mac to find the archived mailbox you want to restore, select it, and then click Choose.**

Creating custom and Smart Mailboxes

Mail lets you create your own mailboxes to suit your individual needs. You can make custom mailboxes that are named for different items or topics (such as "Bills"), or you can use Smart Mailboxes. A Smart Mailbox allows you to create rules that the Smart Mailbox follows. For example, you could set up a Smart Mailbox that automatically moves any e-mail that comes from a particular person to itself.

To create a new custom mailbox, follow these steps:

1. **Click the + button in the bottom-left corner of the Mail window, and select New Mailbox.**

2. **In the New Mailbox dialog, as shown in figure 10.9, select a location for the new mailbox to be saved.**

3. **Give the new mailbox a descriptive name and then click OK.** The new mailbox appears in the Mailbox pane on the left side of the Mail window.

New Mailbox

Enter name for new local mailbox to be created at the top level of the "On My Mac" section.

Location: 🖥 On My Mac

Name: Stuff

(?)   (Cancel)   (OK)

10.9 Creating a new mailbox

To set up a Smart Mailbox (I love these things), follow these steps:

1. **Click the + button in the lower-left corner of the Mail window, and select New Smart Mailbox.**

2. **In the sheet that appears (see figure 10.10), give the mailbox a descriptive name.**

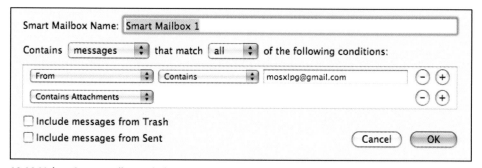

10.10 Make a Smart Mailbox to help you organize and save time finding e-mails.

3. **Select what the mailbox will contain and how the items in it should match the criteria you are about to define.**

4. **Define the criteria for items that the mailbox should or should not contain.** Click the + button to the right to add a new criterion or the – button to remove it.

5. **Decide whether to include messages that are in the Trash or Sent mailboxes, and select or deselect the check boxes as appropriate.**

6. **Click OK to create the new Smart Mailbox.**

Notes and To Dos

Mail provides the convenience of letting you create Notes, which are ways to jot down ideas when you have them, and save them in Mail or send them to someone via e-mail.

To take a note, follow these steps:

1. **Click the Note button in the toolbar.**

2. **Type the contents of the note in the New Note window.**

3. **Click Done to save the note, click Send to e-mail the note, click Attach to add an item to it (just like with an e-mail), click Fonts or Colors to format the text, or click To Do to make the note a To Do item.**

To Dos are simply tasks that you need to accomplish. You can keep track of your To Do items with Mail. There are a couple of ways to create a To Do item:

- **Click the To Do button in the toolbar and type the necessary information, such as the title of the item and the due date.**

- **Highlight text in any message or note that you want to keep track of, such as a part number for an item you need to order or a meeting you need to attend, and click the To Do button in the toolbar.**

Notes and To Dos can easily be accessed in the Mailboxes pane under Reminders, as shown in figure 10.11.

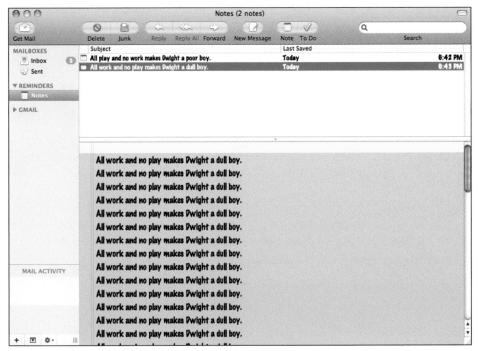

10.11 Click Notes or To Dos to see a list of each.

Using RSS Feeds

RSS (Really Simple Syndication) is used by Web sites that update their information on a frequent basis, such as news sites. The site uses an RSS feed to broadcast when updates to the Web site have been posted. Mail in Snow Leopard can act as an RSS reader, meaning that you can use it to track when new articles are posted to your favorite sites. I love this feature, and use it instead of third-party RSS reader applications because I can have one less application open while retaining the functionality.

To use RSS feeds in Mail, follow these steps:

1. **Find out the address of the RSS page for the site you want to track.** When using Safari for your Web browser, it's very easy to detect whether a Web site uses an RSS feed: You see the letters RSS to the right of the address in Safari's Address field.

2. **Click the + button in the lower-left corner of Mail's window, and select Add RSS Feeds.**

3. **Select the Specify a custom feed URL radio button, as shown in figure 10.12.**

4. **Type the address of the feed (or copy and paste its address from a Web browser Address field) into the text field.**

○ Browse feeds in Safari Bookmarks
◉ Specify a custom feed URL

feed://www.christianpost.com/rss/feed.xml?category=index

☐ Show in Inbox   Cancel   Add

10.12 Adding an RSS feed to Mail

5. **Click Add.** The feed appears under the RSS heading in the Mailboxes pane.

6. **Click the feed in the Mailboxes pane to see its latest postings.**

7. **If the article snippet intrigues you, click the Read More link to open the full article in Safari.**

Troubleshooting Mail

Occasionally you may find yourself having trouble. The most common problem with Mail is the inability to send or to receive e-mails. The final two topics in this chapter attempt to help resolve the problems.

Unable to send messages

Sometimes you may find that you can't send messages. The reason may be that the Send button is grayed out, or you might receive an error message stating that you cannot connect to the SMTP server for your ISP. Here are a few things for you to try when facing this daunting situation:

- **If you have an Internet connection, open Safari and see if you can load a Web page.** If not, choose Apple menu ➪ System Preferences ➪ Network and make sure you have a connection.
- **Check the SMTP settings for your account.**
  1. **Choose Mail ➪ Preferences.**
  2. **Click the Accounts button and click the account you are having trouble with.**
  3. **Be sure the Outgoing Mail Server (SMTP) option is set correctly.**
  4. **If your SMTP server isn't set up at all, check with your ISP for the proper settings.**
- **Make sure you have the latest software updates for Snow Leopard.** Choose Apple menu ➪ Software Update and install any updates available.

Unable to receive messages

Starting to feel lonely? Maybe it's because you haven't received an e-mail from your friends and family lately. Well, don't feel too unloved yet; check to see if Mail is able to receive e-mail.

- **Is your account offline?** If so, that prevents you from being notified of any new messages. You can tell that an account is offline because it has a small lightning bolt icon to the right of it in the sidebar, as shown in figure 10.13. To put it back online, click the lightning bolt icon and select the Take All Accounts Online option.

- **Are you currently connected to the Internet?** If not, then be sure to connect.

- **Send a message to yourself to test your connection settings.** Check with your e-mail provider to make sure you are using the correct settings for your account.

- **Is the name of your mailbox grayed out?** If so, choose Window ⇨ Connection Doctor and follow any instructions that may be given for any accounts that are having difficulty connecting to your ISP.

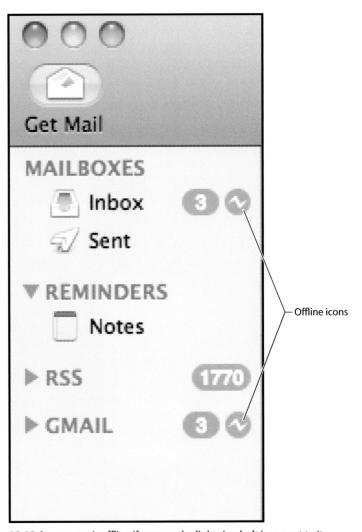

Offline icons

10.13 An account is offline if you see the lightning bolt icon next to it.

What Are iTunes' Coolest Features?

Gotta have that music! And those movies. Don't forget about the television shows and podcasts, too! In today's world, we want our entertainment now, we want it affordable, portable, and we prefer it digital. Snow Leopard can meet all those needs with a nifty little tool called iTunes. Since its introduction in 2001, iTunes has become an integral part of our entertainment arsenal. When you throw an iPod or iPhone into the mix, iTunes becomes an absolute necessity. Thankfully, it's just as intuitive and easy to use as everything else Mac; you'll be addicted to its charms before you know it!

Getting Around in iTunes

iTunes can handle most of your digital entertainment needs, but you need to know how to use its menus, buttons, and features before you can get much use out of it. This section on finding where everything is located, and the next section that describes the iTunes preferences, will make you a near-expert iTunes user in little time at all.

Understanding the iTunes window layout

Figure 11.1 shows the iTunes default interface, and points out the multitude of buttons and menus. Table 11.1 describes what many of these buttons and menus can help you do in iTunes.

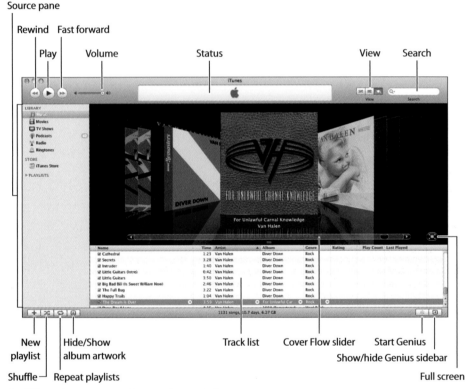

11.1 iTunes is your personal entertainment hub.

Table 11.1 iTunes Functionality

Item	Description
Library	Lists all of the items available for you to use in iTunes.
Store	Click to access the iTunes Store.

Item	Description
Playlists	Lists the playlists and Smart Playlists that you have created.
Album artwork/ Video viewer	See the album artwork for the song you are listening to, or watch videos.
Cover Flow slider	Drag to fly through the album covers when in Cover Flow view.
Start Genius	Click to start the Genius playlist.
Show/hide Genius sidebar	Hides or shows the Genius sidebar on the right side of the iTunes window.
Full screen	Puts iTunes into Full Screen mode.
Search	Type text to help you find items in your iTunes Library, such as the name of a song or the artist who sings it.
View	Choose to view items in a list, grouped together by their albums or using Cover Flow.
Status	Shows the status of songs currently being played, CDs being burned, and items being copied.

Full Screen mode

I'm a creature of habit so I still prefer the standard view in iTunes, but I'm beginning to understand why others tend to like Full Screen mode even better. Full Screen mode lets iTunes take over your entire screen, but with a bare minimum of controls at your disposal, as shown in figure 11.2.

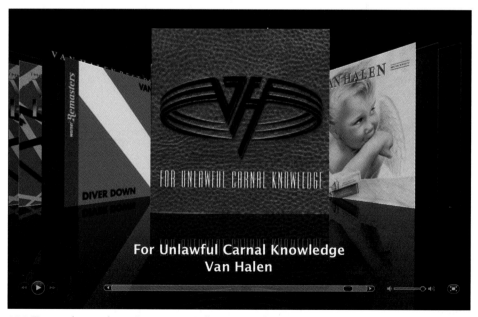

11.2 iTunes takes up the entire screen in Full Screen mode.

Note
iTunes can also be used in a third mode called MiniPlayer, which is a miniature version of the iTunes window. To enable the MiniPlayer, click the green zoom button in the upper-left corner of the iTunes window. Click the green zoom button again to access the full iTunes interface.

Setting iTunes Preferences

iTunes preferences are where you tell iTunes how to interact with you, as well as with items such as iPods, iPhones, and Apple TV. Let's explore these preferences because they determine how iTunes functions to best suit your needs. Choose iTunes ➪ Preferences to get started.

General

The General tab lets you choose what items are shown in the Source pane, how iTunes should react when a CD is inserted in your Mac, and whether or not to automatically check for updates.

Playback

The Playback preferences, shown in figure 11.3, determine how iTunes plays your music and videos.

Genius
Selecting the Sound Check option is a good idea. This prevents you from listening to one song that may have a lower volume level and then having your eardrums blown out by another song whose volume level is much higher. Sound Check evens all the volume levels of items in your Library so that there are no surprise attacks like the one I described.

Sharing

The Sharing preferences determine whether you can see other shared iTunes libraries from users on your network and how you share your libraries with other users, if at all. You can share your iTunes library with up to five other computers on your network as long as they are in the same network subnet as your Mac. While you can listen to music and watch video shared by other computers on your network, you cannot add them to your iTunes library.

Store

You can decide how iTunes handles your purchases. You can choose to download items on the fly with the 1-Click feature, or purchase them the more traditional way using the shopping cart method.

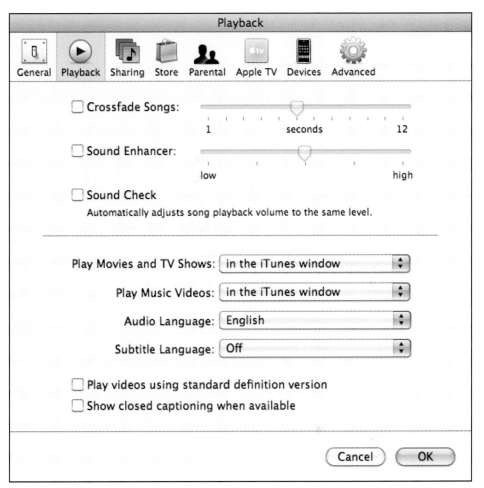

11.3 The Playback preferences allow you to listen to music and watch movies and television shows the way you want.

Parental

Most parents don't like to think of their kids having unfettered access to any and everything on the Internet, so why should items in iTunes be any different? The Parental preferences let Mom and Dad decide what limits to place on iTunes content for their children.

Apple TV

The Apple TV preferences simply help you synchronize with an Apple TV appliance. You can set iTunes to automatically look for Apple TVs when it opens.

Devices

The Devices preferences pane simply displays a list of iPods or iPhones that are backed up on your Mac. Select the Disable automatic syncing for all iPhones and iPods check box to prevent your Mac from trying to sync automatically every time one of these devices is connected.

Consult your iPhone or iPod documentation for synchronizing with iTunes and using iTunes to change their settings.

Advanced

The Advanced preferences are where you make the most useful settings in iTunes, as shown in figure 11.4. Table 11.2 breaks down some of the major features under each tab.

Table 11.2 Major Functions Available in Advanced Preferences

Option	Description
iTunes Music folder location	Lets you choose to keep your imported music in a location other than the default, which is in the Music folder of your user account.
Keep iTunes Music folder organized	I highly recommend selecting this check box, which allows iTunes to organize its Music folder, as opposed to just throwing in tracks in a willy-nilly fashion.
Copy files to iTunes Music folder when adding to library	Makes a copy of a music file in your iTunes Music folder when adding the track to your library. You can deselect this option if you don't want to have multiple copies of the same file strewn throughout your system, but I personally prefer to make the copy in my iTunes folder and delete the original. It's just easier for me to keep organized that way.
Streaming Buffer Size	Set this option to Large if you experience stops in the playback of movies or music you are streaming from the Internet.
Use iTunes for Internet playback	Click Set if you want iTunes to be the default player for audio and video tracks from the Internet.
Reset all dialog warnings	Clicking this button reactivates warnings that iTunes gives you. For example, if you've told iTunes to stop asking you if you're certain you want to make a purchase, clicking Reset causes iTunes to begin asking about purchases again.
Keep MiniPlayer on top of all other windows	Select this check box to keep the MiniPlayer from being hidden under other open windows.
Keep movie window on top of all other windows	Select this option to keep movies playing over other open windows.
Display visualizer full screen	Sets the default size of your Visualizer to full screen, which rocks!
Group compilations when browsing	Selecting this option causes tracks that are part of a compilation to be grouped together instead of by the individual artists who created them.

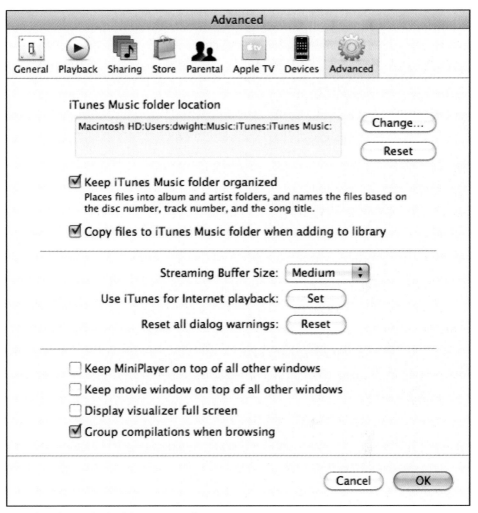

11.4 The Advanced tab of the iTunes preferences

Organizing and Playing Media

iTunes is a pretty useless application without content. It's also a master at helping you organize that content. This section quickly teaches you how to import your own music from CDs or files and how to use the iTunes Store to find and add new content to your collection.

Importing music

Bringing your music into iTunes is the first order of business. Apple makes it ridiculously easy to import your CD collection and music files that you have stored on other computers or discs.

Automatically importing from CDs

When you insert a CD into your Mac, you're asked if you want to import its contents into iTunes, as shown in figure 11.5. Click Yes to automatically import all the content on your CD into iTunes.

Your newly imported content now appears in your Library.

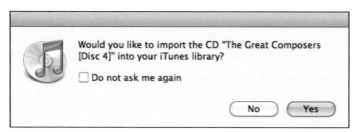

Would you like to import the CD "The Great Composers [Disc 4]" into your iTunes library?

☐ Do not ask me again

No   Yes

11.5 A confirmation dialog appears when you insert a music CD.

Importing individual music files

iTunes lets you import music files that exist on other media as well, such as a folder on your hard drive or another computer on your network. To import music files

1. **Press ⌘+O.**

2. **Browse your Mac or your network for the music file or files you want to import from within the Add to Library window.**

3. **Highlight the music files and click Open.**

The new music is now available in your Library.

Creating playlists

You can create playlists using the songs in your Library. Playlists are collections of songs that you arrange in the order that you want them to play. Here's how to make a playlist:

1. **Press ⌘+N. A playlist called Untitled appears in the Playlists section of the Source pane.**

2. **Type a name for your new playlist.** I'm creating a playlist for a compilation of songs by U2.

3. **Find the items you want to add to your playlist in your Library, and drag and drop them onto the name of the new playlist, as shown in figure 11.6.**

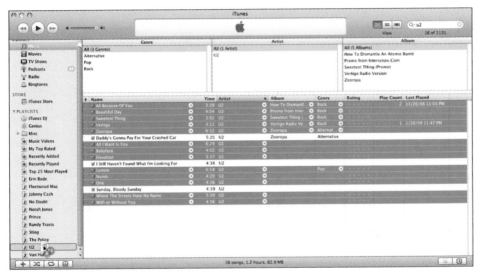

11.6 Adding songs to my new playlist

Setting up Genius playlists

iTunes can create a playlist of songs that go well together using the songs already in your Library. This Genius playlist uses anonymous information from your Library to create the playlist. iTunes also uses your Genius playlist to suggest similar songs in the iTunes Store. Follow these steps:

1. **Open the Genius sidebar, as shown in figure 11.7, by clicking the Show/hide Genius sidebar button in the bottom-right corner of the iTunes window.**

2. **Click Turn On Genius to start the feature.** You will need to sign in using your iTunes Store account.

3. **Select a song from your iTunes Library.**

4. **Click the Genius button in the lower-right corner (shown in figure 11.7) to create a playlist based on the song you selected.** View the playlist by clicking Genius under the Playlists heading on the left side of the iTunes window.

Genius button

Show/hide Genius sidebar button

11.7 The Genius sidebar explains what Genius playlists are, allows you to enable the feature, and view suggested songs from the iTunes Store.

Using Smart Playlists

Smart Playlists automatically add songs to themselves based on criteria that you set for them. iTunes already comes with a few Smart Playlists, such as Recently Played and Recently Added. To create a new Smart Playlist, follow these steps:

1. **Press ⌘+Option+N.**
2. **Enter the criteria the Smart Playlist should use when adding songs.** In figure 11.8, I'm creating a new Smart Playlist that adds any songs to it that are by Randy Travis (yes, you could say my taste in music is fairly eclectic).

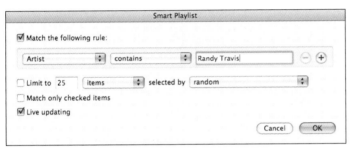

11.8 Creating a new Smart Playlist

3. **Add more criteria by clicking the + button on the right side of the window or remove criteria by clicking the – button. Select the Live updating option to have the Smart Playlist check every time you add an item to your Library to see if it meets the criteria you assigned.**

4. **Check the Match only checked items box to have iTunes include only songs that have a check mark next to them in the Library.**

5. **Click OK when you are finished. Your Smart Playlist automatically populates itself based on the criteria you entered.**

Burning CDs

I enjoy a variety of music, and I love having the ability to create my own albums and burn them to CDs. There's nothing to it:

1. **Create a playlist and add the music you want to burn to a CD.**
2. **Right-click, or Ctrl+click, the playlist you want to burn, and select Burn Playlist to Disc, as shown in figure 11.9.**
3. **Insert a blank CD into your Mac, and iTunes takes care of the rest!**

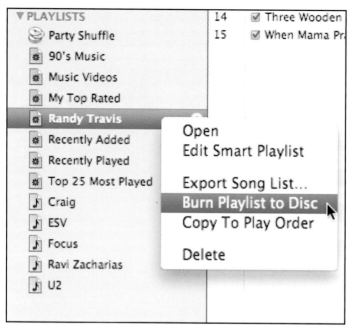

11.9 Burning a playlist to a CD

Print Your Music

The old days of handwriting the names of your songs onto those boring blank CD labels are over! iTunes lets you create custom CD jewel case inserts, song lists, and album lists in a snap. Follow these steps:

1. **Highlight the playlist, artist, or album you want to print information about.**

2. **Press ⌘+P to open a print window.**

3. **Choose whether to print a jewel case insert, a song list, or an album list.**

4. **Select from one of the available themes.**

5. **Click the Print button in the lower-right corner.**

6. **Choose the printer you want to send the job to, and click the Print button.**

Managing audio file information

iTunes allows you to manage the information contained in your tracks, which helps you to organize your Library and find tracks faster and easier. The Info, Video, Sorting, Options, Lyrics, and Artwork tabs in the information window let you specify items such as the composer of the track, the album it belongs to, the year it was composed, and more, including letting you add lyrics and album artwork to the track.

1. **Select an audio track in your Library.**

2. **Press ⌘+I to open the information window, as illustrated in figure 11.10.**

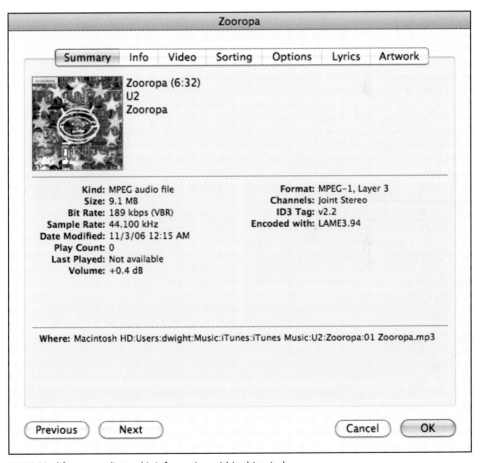

11.10 Modify your audio track's information within this window.

3. **Click one of the tabs at the top of the window to edit the information it contains.**

4. **Click OK when you finish editing the info.**

Adding album artwork to your music

You can add the album cover artwork to your music files in iTunes. Choose the Advanced menu and select Get Album Artwork; iTunes automatically scans your Library and adds artwork to your songs. You must have an iTunes login to perform this action, but it's easy enough to do; iTunes prompts you to create one if you aren't already logged in. An iTunes login performs several functions, including making it easy for Apple to access your billing and shipping information, and to unlock files you've purchased from iTunes.

Streaming radio

The Internet is teeming with radio stations for every genre of music and talk you can conjure, and iTunes is more than happy to stream many of those stations for your listening pleasure. Follow these steps:

1. **Select Radio in the sources pane on the left side of the iTunes window.**

Note You must have an Internet connection to use the Radio features in iTunes.

2. **Choose a music or talk genre from the list available (as shown in figure 11.11) and click the arrow to the left of it to see stations catering to your tastes.**

3. **Double-click a station in a genre to begin streaming its content to your Mac.**

Genius You can save links to your favorite Internet radio stations so that you can easily access them from your library instead of having to browse the various categories. Simply drag the name of the radio station and drop it into your Music folder in the Library. When you want to launch the station, just double-click its name.

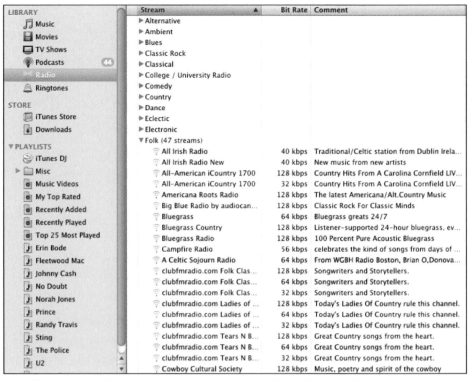

11.11 There is a veritable cornucopia of options to choose from in Internet radio.

Backing up your audio Library

Most people amass a huge volume of music and video after using iTunes for a while, and nobody wants to lose all that great entertainment and have to begin a collection from scratch. There are a couple of ways to back up your iTunes Library: Simply copy your iTunes folder to another computer or hard drive, or back up your files to CDs or DVDs.

To copy your iTunes folder

1. **Open a Finder window and click the name of your account in the sidebar on the left of the window.**

2. **Select your Music folder.**

3. **Drag the iTunes folder, shown in figure 11.12, to another hard drive or computer to begin copying it.**

11.12 The iTunes folder contains the files contained in your Library, unless you've specified a different location in the iTunes preferences.

4. **Should something happen to your iTunes Library, simply copy the backup iTunes folder to the Music folder in your home directory to restore it.** You may lose files you've added since your last backup, but that's better than losing everything.

To back up with CDs or DVDs, follow these steps:

1. **Choose File ⇨ Library ⇨ Back Up to Disc in the iTunes menu.**

2. **Decide whether to back up your entire iTunes Library or only items you've purchased from the iTunes Store (see figure 11.13).**

3. **Click Next.**

4. **Insert a blank CD or DVD to begin backing up.**

5. **ITunes will prompt you when you need to insert a new disc.** The number of discs needed depends on the size of your Library and whether you back up to CDs or DVDs (of course, DVDs can hold many times more data than CDs, so that's the best way to go if possible).

6. **To restore your backups, choose File ⇨ Library ⇨ Back Up to Disc, and select Restore.**

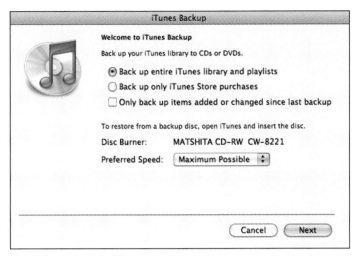

11.13 Determine what files in your iTunes Library you want to back up.

Converting audio formats

Sometime you may want to use your audio files with another device or share them with someone else. In some cases the device you or the person you are sharing the files with may not be able to use the audio file if it's in a particular file format. You can create a copy of your audio files in other formats while retaining the original file. Follow these steps:

1. **Choose iTunes ⇨ Preferences.**

2. **Click the General tab and click Import Settings to open the Import Settings window, as shown in figure 11.14.**

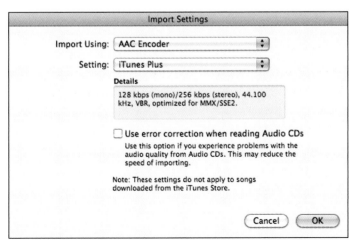

11.14 Select a new format for importing audio files into iTunes.

3. Choose a format from the Import Using pop-up menu and then click OK.

4. Select an audio file or files, and then right-click or Ctrl+click them.

5. Choose the Create *x* Version, with *x* representing the file format you selected in step 3.

6. The new version of the file appears in your iTunes library along with the original.

Creating ringtones for your iPhone

You can create ringtones for your iPhone using songs you've purchased from the iTunes Store, but it costs you about $1 to do so. Follow these steps:

 You must be connected to the Internet to create a ringtone.

Note

1. Choose iTunes ➪ Preferences.

2. Click the General tab and select the Ringtones check box.

3. Select the song from your Library you want to use for the ringtone.

4. Choose Create Ringtone from the Store menu.

5. iTunes opens an editing window at the bottom of its window, as seen in figure 11.15.

11.15 Find the perfect section of a song to use as an iPhone ringtone.

6. Choose up to a 30-second section of the song that you want to create the ringtone from.

7. Click Buy when you're ready to create your ringtone.

Using the iTunes Store

The iTunes Store is your one-stop shop for content such as music, movies, television shows, and podcasts of all kinds. New items are added to the iTunes Store all the time, and after you try it, you'll be hooked just as I am. To access the iTunes Store, simply click the iTunes Store icon in the Source pane, as shown in figure 11.16.

11.16 The iTunes Store is addictive, so be careful!

The categories of items you can get from the iTunes Store are listed in the iTunes Store section on the left side of the site. Table 11.3 lists the options offered by Apple.

Note

You must have an active Internet connection to use the iTunes Store; broadband is preferable.

Table 11.3 Items Available for Download or Purchase from the iTunes Store

Item	Description
Music	Download individual songs or entire albums.
Movies	You can rent or buy movies to view.
TV Shows	Watch your television shows on your own time instead of the networks' time.
Music Videos	See previews of and buy videos of your favorite songs.
Audiobooks	Purchase entire audiobooks and listen to them on your Mac, iPod, or iPhone.
Podcasts	Podcasts are radio shows or videos that you can subscribe to and download. I swear by my favorite podcasts!

continued

Table 11.3 continued

Item	Description
iPod Games	Buy games that you can play on your iPod.
App Store	Find lots of cool applications to use with your iPhone or iPod touch.

Finding music

You can browse through iTunes' vast collection of music, or you can do what I prefer to do: perform a search. When you have an idea what you're looking for, this is the fastest way to go:

1. **At the iTunes Store home page, click the Power Search link in the Quick Links section on the right side of the window.**

2. **Select Music in the Power Search pop-up menu.**

3. **Type any information you may have that can help you find what you're looking for into the Artist, Composer, Song, and Album fields (see figure 11.17).**

4. **Click Search to have iTunes look for items that match your criteria.**

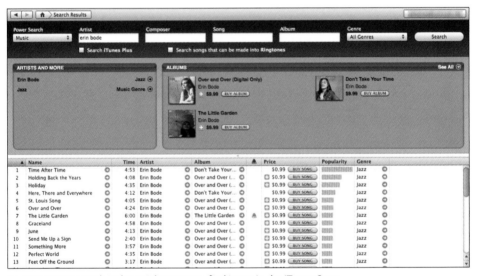

11.17 A power search is the quickest way to find items in the iTunes Store.

Renting or buying movies

That trip to the video store just got a lot shorter because you can use iTunes to rent or buy the latest releases as well as the classic films of yesteryear. This might not make the video store happy, but your automobile will thank you for the mileage you will save. Follow these steps:

1. **Click the Movies link in the iTunes Store section of the iTunes Store home page (left side of the window).**

2. **Browse the top ten lists to find the newest and most popular releases, choose a genre to browse through, or perform a Power Search to find your favorite movie.**

3. **Click the movie's title to open its page, which will be similar to figure 11.18.**

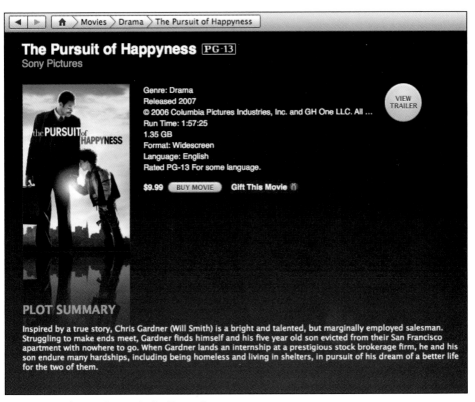

11.18 A typical movie's page in the iTunes Store

4. **Click the View Trailer button if you want to preview the movie before you rent or buy it.**

5. **Click Rent Movie or Buy Movie to do one or the other.** Notice that some movies can only be rented or may only be purchased.

6. **The movie downloads and is available for you to watch in the Movies section of your iTunes Library.**

Subscribing to podcasts

Podcasts are audio and video recordings you can download and listen to or view at your leisure. There are podcasts for almost any taste, ranging from the most popular talk shows to comedy, technology, and more. To subscribe to your favorite podcast, follow these steps:

1. **Click the Podcasts link in the iTunes Store section of the iTunes Store home page.**

2. **Find your favorite podcasts by searching in the different categories, performing a Power Search, or browsing the Top Podcasts lists.**

3. **When you find a podcast that strikes your fancy, click its link to go to its page, as I've done in figure 11.19.**

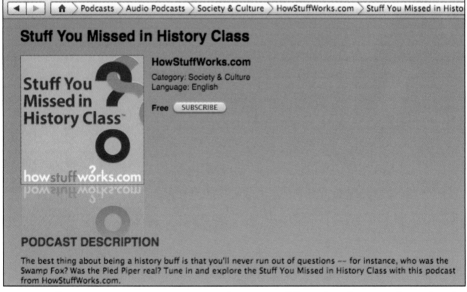

11.19 A podcasts iTunes Store page summarizes the content of the podcast for you and provides a list of the most recent episodes.

4. **Click Subscribe to have iTunes automatically download the newest episodes of the podcast.**

5. **Select Podcasts from the source pane to view your subscribed podcasts and to listen to or view them.**

Educating yourself with iTunes U

You don't have to be enrolled in a prestigious university to take courses from it. iTunes U provides online courses from some of the premier institutions in the world, and they are yours to take for free! Follow these steps:

1. **Click the iTunes U link in the iTunes Store section of the iTunes Store home page.**

2. **Browse the different categories, providers, and Top Downloads section to find content or a particular institution in which you are interested (see figure 11.20).**

11.20 Some of the finest institutions around provide content to iTunes U.

3. **Click the link for the institution or course you want to view.**

4. **Click the Get button for the audio or video course you want to take.**

5. **The course downloads and can be found in your Podcast's section of the source pane.** View or listen to it as you would any other podcast.

What Can Snow Leopard Do with Digital Photography?

n today's digital age, you simply can't have a computer, Mac or otherwise, without using it to catalog and share images. Fortunately, Snow Leopard offers several ways to have fun with digital photography. Photo Booth, while indeed functional, is still all about fun. Besides just making silly pictures, you can use Photo Booth to take video, and you can even use special effects with your pictures and video, including using your own custom backdrops. Because Apple is all about making your digital lifestyle easier, Snow Leopard also works with most digital cameras and scanners right out of the box. Image Capture is the tool Snow Leopard ships with to help you transfer images to and from your digital camera or to import files using your scanner

Getting to Know Photo Booth

Apple has moved the old-fashioned photo booths that we used to cram ourselves into with our friends on Friday nights at the mall to our Macs. Simple as it is, there are still a few features that could do with explaining. When I get anything new, I'm one of those people who actually likes to read the instructions and know what all the buttons and gadgets are for. Hence my insistence on you learning about the Photo Booth features that I've laid out for you in figure 12.1.

Single still picture   Video   Four quick snapshots   Camera button   Viewer window   Thumbnail bar

12.1 The Photo Booth main window in Snapshot mode

Taking Snapshots

Any kind of picture you take with Photo Booth is considered a snapshot, whether it's a still picture or a video. You can take three kinds of snapshots: single still picture, four quick snapshots (which are much more fun than you might think), and video (see figure 12.1). Use the snapshot-type buttons under the bottom-left corner of the viewer window to select the kind of snapshot you want to take.

Single snapshots

Single snapshots, or still pictures, are so easy to take it's ridiculous:

1. **Click the single still picture button under the bottom-left corner of the Viewer window.**

2. **Position yourself in front of your Mac's camera so that your image fits inside the Viewer window.**

3. **Click the Camera button.**

4. **Photo Booth begins its countdown from 3, flashes, and takes the picture.** That's it!

Taking four quick snapshots

Taking four quick snapshots lets you create different poses in rapid succession. Try it out:

1. **Click the four quick snapshots button under the bottom-left corner of the Viewer window.**

2. **Position yourself in front of your Mac's camera so that your image fits inside the Viewer window.**

3. **Click the Camera button to begin the countdown.** Get into your first pose before the first flash goes off!

4. **After the first flash, immediately change to your next pose and continue to do that through all four pictures.** You've only got about a second between snapshots, so you've got to move quickly!

5. **When all four snapshots are taken, you see a preview of your images, similar to figure 12.2.**

12.2 A preview appears in the viewer window so that you can see your four-up handiwork.

Creating video

The ability to make movies is a new feature in Photo Booth. To create that movie magic, follow these steps:

1. **Click the video button under the bottom-left corner of the viewer window.**

2. **Position yourself in front of your Mac's camera so that your image fits inside the viewer window.**

3. **Click the Camera button to begin the countdown.**

4. **Begin your video after the flash goes off.**

5. **When finished with the video, click the Stop button.**

Viewing your snapshots

All of your snapshots are stored in the Thumbnail bar at the bottom of the Photo Booth window. You can scroll through the list of snapshots using the right- and left-arrow keys on either side of the bar.

To view a snapshot, simply click it in the Thumbnail bar. It displays in the Viewer window.

To find a snapshot on your Mac, click the snapshot in the Thumbnail bar, and then press ⌘+R to open a Finder window displaying its exact location on the hard drive.

Genius

You can access your snapshots without having to open Photo Booth every time you need them. Photo Booth stores snapshots in the Photo Booth folder, which resides in the Pictures folder of your Home folder (Hard drive/Users/*your account name*/Pictures/Photo Booth).

Using Special Effects

You've only seen the tip of the Photo Booth iceberg. Photo Booth can do something the old photo booths at the mall could only dream of: add awesome special effects and backdrops!

Snapshot effects

To use visual effects like filters or distortions for your snapshots, follow these steps:

1. **Position yourself in front of your Mac's camera so that your image fits inside the Viewer window.**

2. **Click the Effects button to see the cool filter effects shown in figure 12.3.**

3. **Click the right arrow next to the Effects button to see the distortion effects, like those shown in figure 12.4.**

4. **Select the effect you want to use by clicking it, and then click the Camera button to take the picture.**

Effects button

12.3 These are the filter effects available in Photo Booth. You gotta love X-Ray!

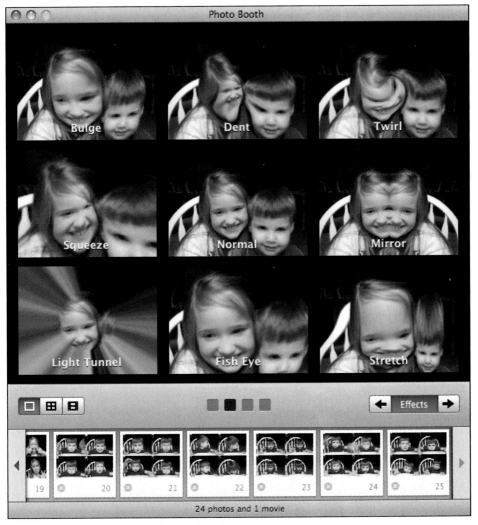

12.4 The distortion effects are a blast to play with.

Video backdrops

Video backdrops are really neat to use. They place a moving video of some exotic location behind you so that it appears like you're really there. Impress family and friends by creating a video of yourself in front of the Eiffel Tower, swimming with the fishes, or flying through the clouds!

1. **Position yourself in front of your Mac's camera so that your image fits inside the Viewer window.**

2. **Click the Effects button.**

265

3. Click the right arrow next to the Effects button twice until it brings you to the video backdrops.

4. Select the backdrop you want to use.

5. Step out of the frame when prompted until you see the backdrop you chose in the Viewer window.

6. Move into the frame of the Viewer window and click the Camera button to make your video, as shown in figure 12.5.

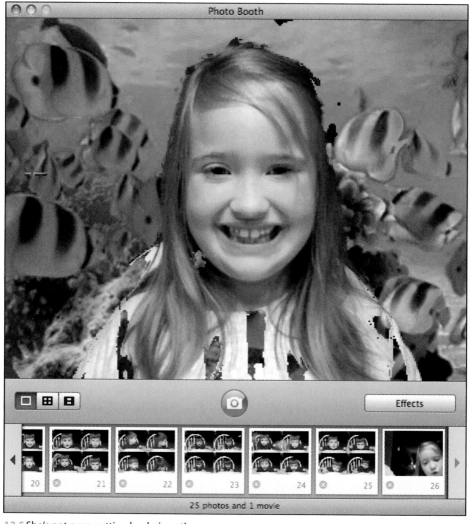

12.5 She's not even getting her hair wet!

Adding custom backdrops

My favorite feature of Photo Booth is the ability to use my own photos and videos as backdrops. To create a custom backdrop, follow these steps:

1. **Click the Effects button and then click the right arrow next to it three times to see the Custom Backdrop window.**

2. **Drag and drop a picture or video from the Finder, iPhoto, or iMovie into one of the Drag Backdrop Here windows.**

3. **Select the new backdrop to use it for your picture or video.**

Using your pictures and videos

What to do with all these great snapshots you've been taking? You can save your snapshots in iPhoto if you like, e-mail them to family and friends, or use them to represent you in an online chat session.

Click a snapshot in the Thumbnail bar that you want to work with. Notice in figure 12.6 that when you open the snapshot in preview mode, you now have several new icons underneath the Viewer window. Table 12.1 explains what clicking each icon does for you.

Table 12.1 Using Your Photo Booth Snapshots

Icon	Action
e-mail	Opens the Mail application and automatically creates a new e-mail containing the snapshot. Type the e-mail address of your intended recipient and send it right along.
iPhoto	Launches iPhoto (if you have it installed; iPhoto is not part of Snow Leopard, but is part of the Apple iLife application suite) and automatically imports the picture from Photo Booth.
Account Picture	Automatically opens the Accounts pane of System Preferences, selects your user account, and changes your account picture to the one you selected in Photo Booth.
Buddy Picture	Opens iChat and changes the picture that people you chat with will see.

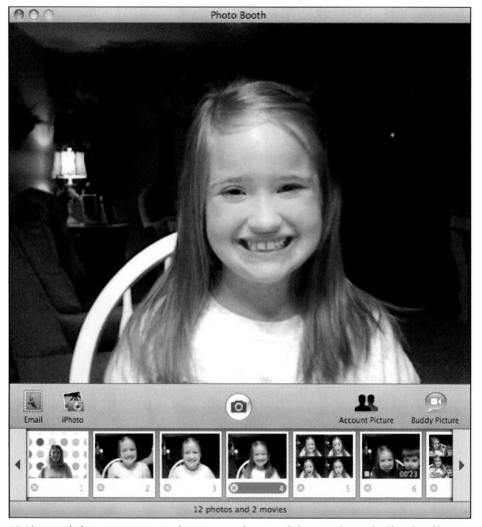

12.6 Icons to help you use your snapshots appear when you click a snapshot in the Thumbnail bar.

Printing Your Snapshots

You can print your snapshots from Photo Booth just as you can from any other application. To print your snapshots, follow these steps:

1. **Choose File⇨Print, or press ⌘+P.**

2. **When the print dialog opens, choose one of the options in the Photo Booth pane.** You can print the picture normally, or you can print proof sheets (either several different sizes of the same picture on the same page, or eight pictures of the same size).

Working with Image Capture

Image Capture is a great tool that may surprise you with its versatility. You can use it to do any of the following:

- **Transfer images from or to your digital camera**
- **Delete images from your digital camera**
- **Scan and import images with your scanner**
- **Share your digital camera or scanner with other users on your network**
- **Find shared devices on your network**

To open Image Capture, press ⌘+Shift+A from within the Finder, find Image Capture in the resulting Finder window, and then double-click its icon. If you don't have a digital camera or scanner attached to your Mac when you start Image Capture, you are notified in a dialog that no device is connected. If this is the case for you when you open Image Capture, read on to discover how to connect your device.

Note

You may wonder why iPhoto, Apple's amazing photo-organizing and -editing program, isn't covered in this book. iPhoto is actually part of the iLife application suite, which Apple sells separately from Snow Leopard. Because I'm concentrating on Snow Leopard in this book, Image Capture gets all the glory.

Connecting your device

If you haven't done so already, attach your device to the Mac with whatever connection its manufacturer recommends (most use USB). If Image Capture is already open, it should automatically
display a window when you attach a camera or scanner.

If you have multiple devices attached to your Mac, you can choose the device you want to use by
selecting it in the Devices menu.

Genius

Image Capture is versatile enough to import movies and MP3 files, as well as your
pictures, assuming your camera has the ability to record such files.

Using a Digital Camera

A digital camera is your window to the world around you, and allows you to keep your memories
for a lifetime. However, the memory cards the camera uses to store your precious keepsakes have
a finite amount of space, and therefore need to be emptied of their contents every now and again.
On the flip side, sometimes you may want to transfer images to your memory card. This is where
Image Capture makes its entrance.

Transferring images to and from your camera

As stated earlier in this chapter, when you connect your camera to your Mac with Image Capture
already up and running, a window opens (like the one in figure 12.7) that gives you access to and
a measure of control over your camera.

- **The Connecting this camera opens pop-up menu lets you choose an application to
open automatically when the camera is connected to your Mac.**

- **Select the Share camera check box to allow more than one application at a time to
use the camera.**

- **Click the List or Icons button (as shown in figure 12.7) in the bottom of the window
to change viewing options.**

- **Use the Rotate buttons (as shown in figure 12.7) to rotate images to your liking
before downloading them.**

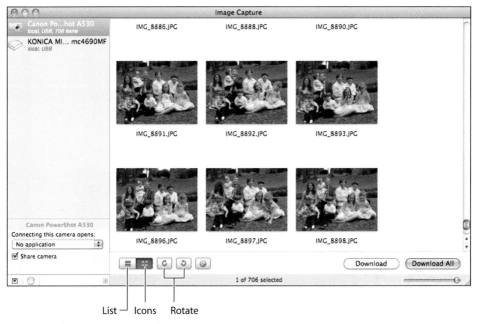

List ─ Icons Rotate

12.7 Control your camera using these options.

Download or Download All

Click Download All to do just that: download all the pictures and files from your camera. However, if you only want to download a few files, the Download button is your best option.

To import only certain files from your camera, follow these steps:

1. **Click the file you want to download from within the Image Capture window.** To choose multiple files, hold down the ⌘ key while making your selections, as shown in figure 12.8.

2. **Click Download to proceed with the transfer.** The files you downloaded can be found in the Pictures folder of your home directory.

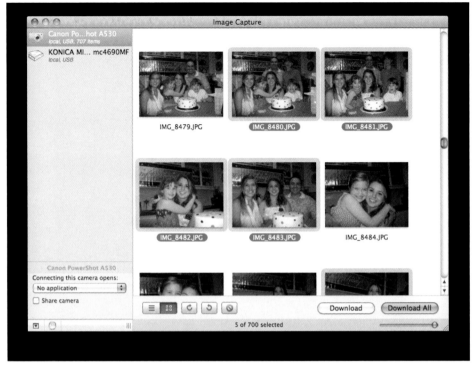

12.8 Select only the pictures you want to download, as opposed to downloading them all at once.

Transfer images to your camera

A really cool feature in Image Capture is the ability to transfer files to your camera, not just from it. To transfer files to your camera, follow these steps:

1. **Locate the file you want to transfer to your camera.** Be sure to position the Image Capture window so that you can see both the contents of your camera and the file you are transferring.

2. **Drag and drop the files you want to move to the camera into the Image Capture window, as shown in figure 12.9.** If you cannot drop files into the window, your camera doesn't support this functionality, or its memory card may be full (I learned that one the hard way).

The file is now copied to your camera, but the original remains intact.

272

12.9 Won't your camera be surprised when you transfer files to it instead of from it?

Deleting images from your camera

Sometimes you may only want to delete some of the images on your digital camera as opposed to all, but deleting individual images can be a chore. Image Capture sure comes in handy in this situation! To delete individual files from your camera, follow these steps:

1. **Select the files you want to remove from your camera.** Hold down the ⌘ key while clicking to choose multiple files.

2. **Click the Delete button at the bottom of the window.**

3. **Click OK to confirm the deletion, or click Cancel to stop it.**

Getting the Red Out

Image Capture is a great application for what it does, but if you need to touch up photos, such as removing the red in your subject's eyes or cropping part of the image, you need other software. iPhoto is the perfect application for such common tasks (and it is also great at organizing and sharing images). You can purchase it from Apple as part of the iLife suite of applications.

Using a Scanner

Your Mac can happily use Image Capture to import images and documents using a scanner. Simply connect your scanner to get started.

Note

You need to install your scanner's software before connecting the scanner to your Mac. The software probably came on a CD with the scanner, but it's always a good idea to visit the manufacturer's Web site for any updated drivers it may have released.

Scanning images

After you connect your scanner, Image Capture should open automatically. If not, open the Applications folder on your hard drive and double-click the Image Capture icon, and then choose the scanner from the list. Place the item you want to scan onto the glass of the scanner if it is a flatbed scanner, or into the feeder if it is a document-feeding scanner. This is where the fun begins!

Using the Image Capture options

The default scan window that opens offers a few basic options for scanning your documents into your Mac, as shown in figure 12.10.

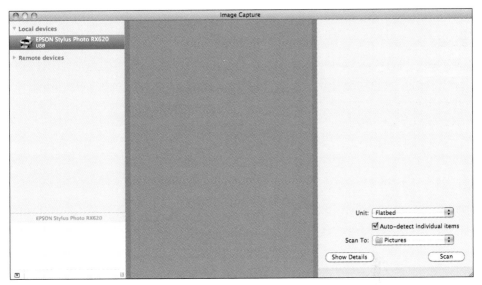

12.10 Image Capture's default scan window and its options

To scan an item using these options, follow these steps:

1. **Highlight the scanner under Local devices on the left side of the scan window.**

2. **Choose the type of scanner you are using from the Unit pop-up menu.** Most will be using a Flatbed scanner.

3. **Check the Auto-detect individual items box to have Image Capture automatically discern the contents of the scanned page, such as text or images.**

4. **Choose a location to store the scanned file using the Scan To pop-up menu.**

5. **Click the Scan button when ready to scan your document.** Once the scan is completed you can find the document in the location you chose in step 4.

Using your scanner's software options

Your scanner's software may offer many options that are not available in Image Capture's standard scan window. To access those features, follow these steps:

1. **Highlight the scanner under Local devices on the left side of the scan window, and then click the Show Details button in the lower right corner to see your scanner's options (figure 12.11).**

2. **Select the type of scanner you are using from the Scan Mode drop-down menu.**

3. **Choose what type of image you are scanning from the Document drop-down menu.**

4. **Decide which bit-depth to use for the scan (the higher the better).**

5. **Select the Resolution you want to use from its drop-down menu.** Resolution plays a major role in the quality of the image. Again, the higher the better, but your file sizes will also be much larger.

6. **Determine the size and orientation of your image.**

7. **Choose a location on your Mac where you want to save the scanned images by using the Scan To drop-down menu.**

8. **Name the file and select the format you want to use for the scanned image.**

9. **Your scanner may afford a host of other options, such as Image Correction, Unsharp Mask, etc.** If so, make any corrections you feel are necessary using these options.

10. **If you are using a document-feeding scanner, simply click Scan to begin scanning the pages and skip the rest of the steps.** If using a flatbed or transparency scanner, continue to step 11.

11. **Click Overview to see a preview of the item on the glass.**

12. **Click and drag your mouse over the portion of the preview that you want to scan, and then click Scan.**

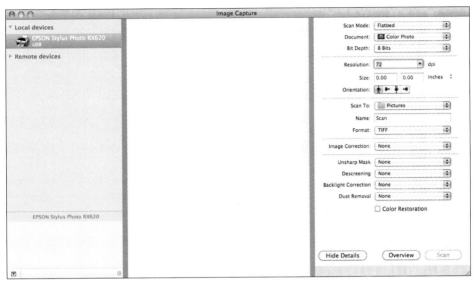

12.11 You will have more control over the quality of your scans using the software provided by your scanner manufacturer.

How Can I Share Files and Other Items?

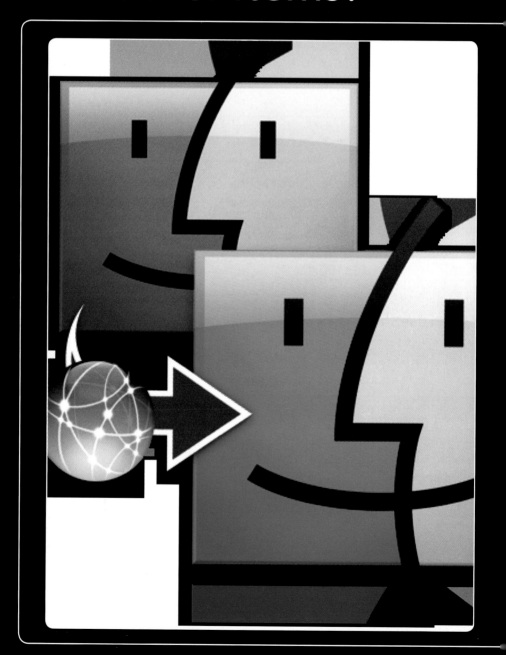

Apple taught Snow Leopard to share with others, and it does its job better than any other operating system around. As a matter of fact, no other operating system is as friendly with its competitors as Snow Leopard. Whether your network consists of mostly Windows PCs or Linux computers or is an all-Mac configuration, Snow Leopard happily shakes hands and exchanges greetings with its neighbors. You can share files, folders, printers, and even your Internet connection, using a variety of network protocols.

Using the Sharing System Preferences

The Sharing System Preferences is where all the action begins. That's where you go to enable and configure sharing of all types. Choose Apple menu⇨System Preferences and then click the Sharing icon to open the Sharing preferences window, shown in figure 13.1.

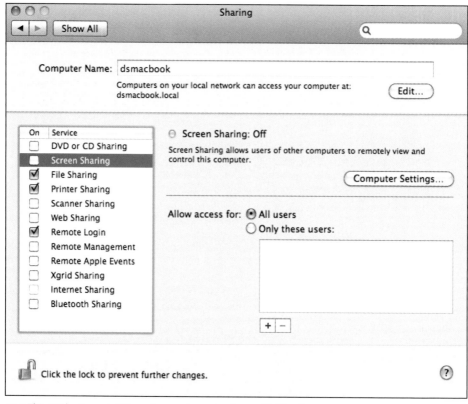

13.1 This is where you tell Snow Leopard how to share with friends.

First things first: If the Computer Name field is blank at the top of the Sharing pane, type a name for your computer. Other users can see your computer on the network using this name.

Your Mac can share many different items, but some don't demand the same amount of coverage as others. For that reason, Table 13.1 gives a brief overview of each sharing option, and the rest of this chapter is devoted to the areas of sharing that need a bit more attention.

Table 13.1 Sharing Preferences

Sharing type	Description
DVD or CD Sharing	Select this option to allow other computers to remotely connect to and use your Mac's optical drive. This option is helpful if you have a computer that doesn't have an optical drive built in, like the MacBook Air; you can share the optical drive from one of your other Macs so that the computer can utilize it.
Screen Sharing	Use this feature to allow users of other computers to remotely access your Mac so they can see your screen on their screen. They can also move and open items, such as folders and applications, on your computer.
File Sharing	Select this option to give other users access to folders that you are sharing from your Mac. There's much more about this later on in this chapter.
Printer Sharing	To share printers that you have created a queue for in your Print & Fax preferences, select the Printer Sharing check box. See more on this feature later in this chapter.
Web Sharing	You can create and store Web pages on your Mac. Select the Web Sharing check box to allow others on your network to access those Web pages from a Web browser on any computer. Your computer's Web site addresses are displayed once you enable Web Sharing.
Remote Login	Select this option to let users on other computers remotely access your Mac through a Secure Shell (SSH) in Terminal. Even though you can restrict which users have access, I would not recommend using this option due to security reasons, unless you are otherwise directed by someone in your company's IT department. See Chapter 15 for more information on using Terminal.
Remote Management	If you or your network administrators use Apple Remote Desktop to access your computer remotely, you must enable Remote Management. I discuss its options later in this chapter.
Remote Apple Events	Select this option to allow applications and users on other computers to send Apple Events to your Mac. Apple Events are commands that cause your Mac to perform an action, such as printing or deleting files. I don't recommend using this option unless you know what you're doing and trust other users on your network.
Xgrid Sharing	Select this option if you want to allow an Xgrid server on your network to remotely use your Mac's processing power. Large computing labs use this kind of setup to process gigantic tasks; using the processing power of other computers on the network can greatly help speed up those tasks. Basically, if you don't know what an Xgrid server is, you don't need to enable this option unless told to do so by your IT department.
Internet Sharing	You can share your Mac's Internet connection with other computers through Ethernet, AirPort, or FireWire. This comes in handy if only one Mac has access to the physical Internet connection in your home or office. If you enable this option, you must check which of the aforementioned connection types you are using to share.
Bluetooth Sharing	Use your Mac's Bluetooth connection to communicate with other devices, and then select this check box to share files. Learn more about Bluetooth later in this chapter.

Use Bonjour with Windows and Snow Leopard

Snow Leopard uses a network protocol called Bonjour that allows almost effortless networking between devices that are running Bonjour. Bonjour requires no configuration of any kind; devices that are using Bonjour simply see one another on the network. While Bonjour is built in to Snow Leopard, you might be pleased to know that Apple has developed Bonjour for Windows as well. See how simple networking can really be between Mac OS X and Windows by downloading and installing Bonjour for Windows from www.apple.com/downloads/macosx/apple/windows/bonjourforwindows.html.

File Sharing

File sharing is what most people think of when you mention sharing on a computer. Snow Leopard lets you decide which folders and volumes to share from your Mac, and you have control over who can access those shared items. Select the File Sharing check box to enable it on your Mac, just as I've done in figure 13.2.

Adding shared folders and users

The Shared Folders window lists the folders on your hard drive that are set up for sharing files. To add folders to this list, follow these steps:

1. Click the + button beneath the Shared Folders window.

2. Browse your Mac and select the folder you want to share.

3. Click Add to begin sharing items in this folder.

Next, you need to specify which users can access the folders you are sharing. Follow these steps:

1. Click the + button under the Users window.

2. Select a group of users from the list on the left pane and then choose the user from the right pane who you want to share the specified folder with, as shown in figure 13.3.

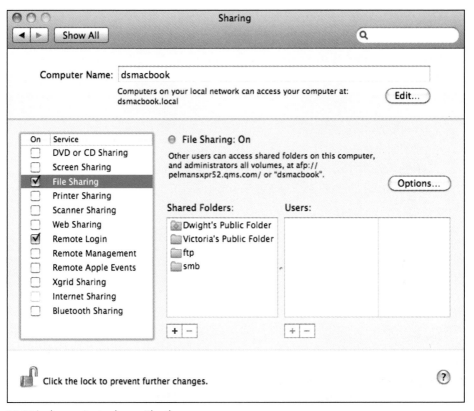

13.2 It's always nice to share with others.

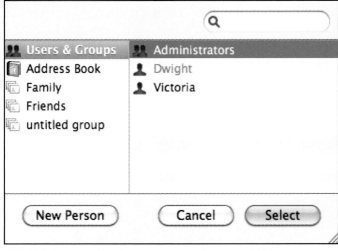

13.3 Click the user with whom you want to share your folder.

3. **Click Select to add the user to the list of authorized users.**

4. **Choose the user's name in the list and assign permissions to him or her by clicking the pop-up arrows, as shown in figure 13.4.**

   - **Read & Write.** This allows the user to modify and delete the files in the shared folder, as well as copy new files into it.

   - **Read Only.** This means the user can only see and open the files being shared in the folder.

   - **Write Only (Drop Box).** This only allows users to copy files into the folder; they can't see or open its contents.

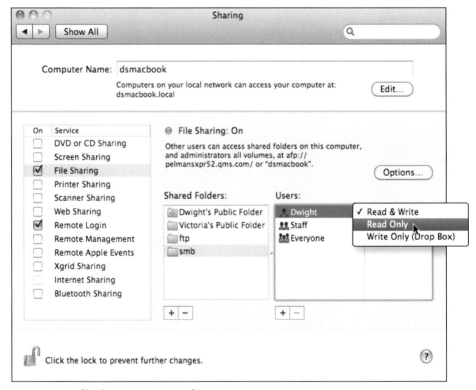

13.4 Assigning file-sharing permissions for a user

You can remove folders or users by highlighting them and clicking the – button under the appropriate window.

Enabling file-sharing protocols

Snow Leopard is very advanced in its sharing capabilities and can share using multiple protocols. Click Options in the lower-right corner of the File Sharing pane to see which protocols are available, as shown in figure 13.5. Table 13.2 briefly explains the protocols.

Selecting the check box next to the protocols you want to use enables them, allowing you to share items over your network with other users running the same protocols.

☑ **Share files and folders using AFP**

Number of users connected: 0

☐ **Share files and folders using FTP**

Warning: FTP user names and passwords are not encrypted.

☑ **Share files and folders using SMB (Windows)**

When you enable SMB sharing for a user account, you must enter the password for that account. Sharing files with some Windows computers requires storing the Windows user's account password on this computer in a less secure manner.

On	Account
☑	Dwight
☐	Victoria

Done

13.5 Select the check boxes next to the protocols you want to use for sharing your files.

Table 13.2 File-sharing Protocols

Protocol	Description
AFP	Apple Filing Protocol. This is an older network protocol that Snow Leopard uses for talking to ancient AppleTalk networks.
FTP	File Transfer Protocol. This is a TCP/IP protocol commonly used to transfer files between devices on a network or over the Internet.
SMB	Server Message Block, also called Microsoft Windows Network to former Windows users. This allows Snow Leopard to work seamlessly with a Windows-centric network. Select the check boxes next to the accounts you want to enable for SMB sharing. You must type the password for each account you enable.

Printer Sharing

When you share a printer from your Mac, you aren't physically sharing the printer; you're actually sharing the print queue that you created for the printer in the Print & Fax preferences. This means that when you share a printer, the clients who send jobs are sending them to your Mac, not directly to the printer. It's your Mac's responsibility to funnel the job to the printer after it has received it. Select the Printer Sharing check box to enable this feature for Snow Leopard, as shown in figure 13.6.

Printer sharing check box

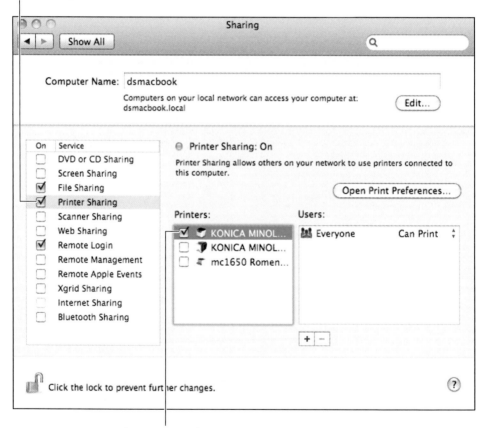

Select a printer to share

13.6 Share printers you have installed on your Mac using Printer Sharing.

Sharing with Mac OS X users

There's not much involved with sharing printers with other Mac OS X users. Simply select the check box next to the printer you want to share in the Printer Sharing pane, and the shared printer will be visible to users when they go to add a printer. See Chapter 6 for more information on add-ing a printer.

Sharing with Windows users

To share any printer on your Mac with other computers running Windows, follow these steps:

1. **Select the check box next to the printer you want to share in the Printer Sharing pane, as shown in figure 13.6.**

2. **Enable File Sharing by selecting the File Sharing check box in the Service list.**

3. **Click Options in the File Sharing pane.**

4. **Select the Share files and folders using SMB (Windows) check box.**

5. **Choose which accounts will access the printer and type their passwords.**

To add the printer to a Windows PC, follow these steps:

1. **Open the Printers and Faxes control panel if using Windows XP, or open the Printers control panel if running Windows Vista.**

2. **Click Add Printer and install a network printer.** See your Windows documentation for instructions on installing a network printer if you're unfamiliar with the procedure.

3. **Select the generic PostScript printer driver during the installation, even if the printer isn't a PostScript printer.** Anybody who understands printer drivers is probably slapping his forehead at this point, but here's the cool part: When the PC sends a print job, Snow Leopard automatically translates the PostScript code generated by the PC to the code the printer understands. That just goes to further prove how awesome Snow Leopard really is.

Note

The Windows user must be logged in as an Administrator account on the PC in order to install the shared printer.

Remote Management

When you first select the Remote Management check box, you are prompted to configure what level of access users of other computers can have to your Mac, as shown in figure 13.7. The options are self-explanatory.

After you enable Remote Management, you can add local users to the access list. Follow these steps:

1. **Click the + button under the access list.**

2. **Browse the list of available users, click the user you want, and click Select.**

3. **Configure the access options for this user as you did when you first enabled Remote Management.** You can change these options at any time by clicking Options.

All local users can access this computer to:
- ☑ Observe
  - ☐ Control
  - ☐ Show when being observed
- ☐ Generate reports
- ☐ Open and quit applications
- ☐ Change settings
- ☐ Delete and replace items
- ☐ Start text chat or send messages
- ☐ Restart and shut down
- ☐ Copy items

(Cancel) (OK)

13.7 Decide what users can do after they access your Mac.

Sharing through Bluetooth

The Bluetooth Sharing feature, shown in figure 13.8, lets you configure how your Mac will interact and share files with other devices running the Bluetooth protocol.

Once again, first things first: You must enable Bluetooth on your Mac in order to share files with other devices running the protocol. If Bluetooth is not already on, follow these steps:

1. **Click Bluetooth Preferences to open the Bluetooth preferences pane.**

2. **Select the check boxes next to On and Discoverable.**

3. **Click the Back button in the upper-left corner of the Bluetooth pane to go back to the Sharing pane.**

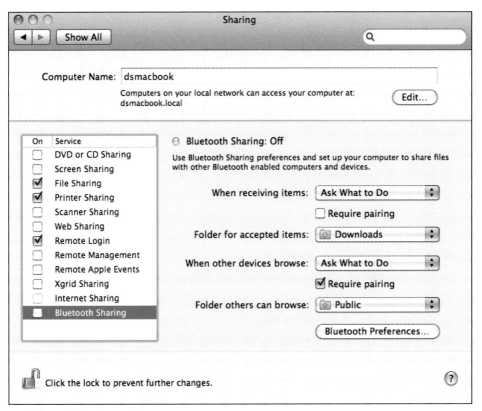

13.8 Bluetooth Sharing options

Table 13.3 briefly explains the options that are available in the Bluetooth Sharing pane.

Table 13.3 Bluetooth Sharing Options

Option	Functions
When receiving items	Decide how your Mac reacts when another Bluetooth device is trying to send an item to it. Select the Require pairing check box to require a password to be entered before any exchanges take place.
Folder for accepted items	Set the default folder for files received from other devices.
When other devices browse	Determine how your Mac reacts when another Bluetooth device wants to browse your shared folders. Select the Require pairing check box to require a password to be entered before any exchanges take place.
Folder others can browse	Set the default folder on your Mac that users of other Bluetooth devices can browse.

Note You must pair a device with your Mac in order to exchange files with one another. See Chapter 8 for instructions on pairing Bluetooth devices using the Bluetooth Setup Assistant.

Using Bluetooth File Exchange

Bluetooth File Exchange is the utility you use to browse and exchange files with other Bluetooth devices. Open Bluetooth File Exchange by pressing ⌘+Option+U in the Finder, and then double-click the Bluetooth File Exchange icon.

Send a file from your Mac

To send a file from your Mac to another Bluetooth device, follow these steps:

1. **Choose File ⇨ Send File, or press ⌘+O.**

2. **Browse your Mac for the file you want to send, highlight the file, and click Send.**

3. **Select the device you want to send the file to from the list in the Send File window, as shown in figure 13.9, and click Send.**

4. **The receiving device may prompt you to allow the incoming traffic from your Mac.** The transfer is complete once the receiving device has received all the data from your Mac.

13.9 Select the device you want to send a file to from the list of available devices.

Browse another Bluetooth device

You can browse another Bluetooth device to find files you want to copy, or to send files from your Mac to a specific location on the device. Follow these steps:

1. Choose File ⇨ Browse Device, or press ⌘+Shift+O.

2. Select the device you want to browse from the Browse Files list and click Browse.

3. Browse the folders on the device from within the Browsing window, as shown in figure 13.10.

4. **If you are sending a file, open the folder on the device in which you want to place the file, and click Send.** Browse your Mac for the file you want to send, select it, and click Send.

5. **If you want to get a file from the device, find the file, select it, and then click Get.** Name the file, choose where to save it, and then click Save.

6. **You may also delete a file from the remote Bluetooth device by highlighting the file and clicking the Delete button in the upper-right corner of the Browsing window.**

13.10 Browsing the directories, or folders, on my cell phone

How Can I Automate My Mac?

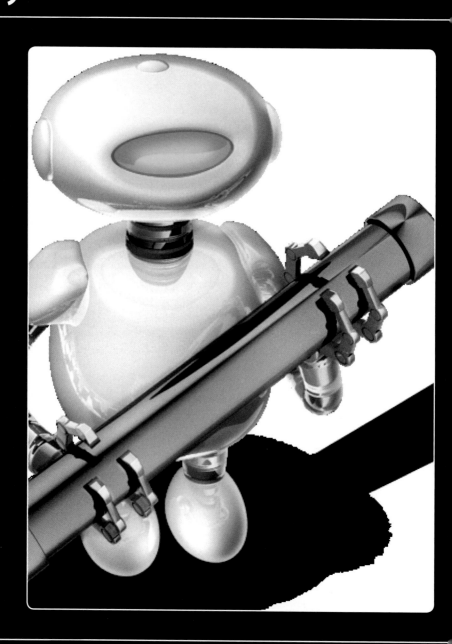

What if you could have your Mac perform daily, routine (and possibly mundane) tasks for you automatically? Sounds pretty tempting, no? Snow Leopard is fully equipped to make your Mac life more enjoyable through automation, using a handy application called Automator. Automator uses actions (another word for steps) to create workflows, which you can run anytime to complete repetitive tasks quickly and easily. Another way that Snow Leopard can help with your Mac housework is with Time Machine, Mac OS X's new backup utility. Time Machine can literally take you back in time to retrieve data that you may have lost in the present.

Getting Around in Automator

It's most helpful to know your way around Automator before trying to create workflows and actions. Open Automator by pressing ⌘+Shift+A in the Finder and then double-clicking the Automator icon. When Automator opens, make a selection in the Starting Points window, as shown in figure 14.1.

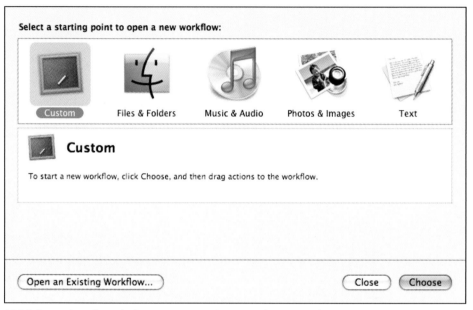

14.1 Select an item from the list to move onto Automator's main window.

For this example, select Custom and click Choose. You are now in Automator's main window; figure 14.2 points out Automator's most important features, and Table 14.1 gives a brief description of each.

Table 14.1 Descriptions of Items in Automator's Main Window

Item	Description
Library column	Lists the applications and other items that are available from which you can choose actions.
Action column	Lists the actions that are available for each application or item in the Library column.
Workflow pane	Allows you to arrange actions in the order they are to be performed.

Item	Description
Description window	Displays a brief explanation of the selected action.
Run	Runs the current workflow.
Stop	Stops the workflow that is running.
Step	Click to step through the currently running workflow.
Record	Records your keyboard and mouse events to help you create custom actions.
Media Browser	Lets you browse your Mac for audio, photos, or videos that you may want to include in your workflows.

Action column

Open the media browser

Stop the currently running workflow

Record user events

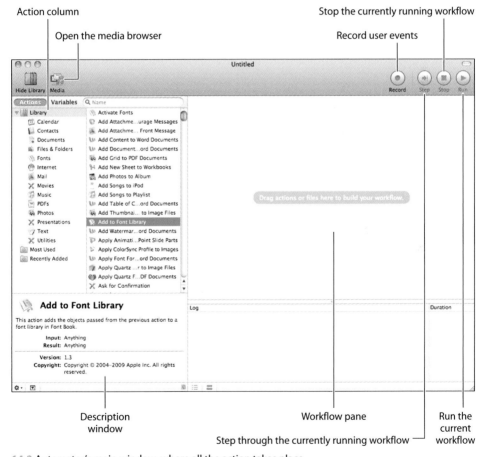

Description window

Workflow pane

Step through the currently running workflow

Run the current workflow

14.2 Automator's main window, where all the action takes place

Using Workflows

Workflows are groups of actions that are combined to help you accomplish a task. When you run a workflow, the actions in it are carried out in sequential order until the last action has been performed. The results, or output, of the first action become the input for the next action, and so on, until the workflow is completed.

Designing a workflow

Building a workflow from scratch is much simpler than you may think. To help you get started with Automator, I've created a new workflow and will walk you through creating that workflow step by step. Here's what I want to do with my new workflow:

1. **First, I want to rename images that I've saved from my camera using Image Capture, to a folder on my desktop called New Pics.** My camera automatically adds "IMG" to the beginning of every file and then numbers them sequentially. I'd like to name the files a little more descriptively, and Automator is the perfect tool to accomplish this task.

2. **Once my files are renamed, I want to open them in Preview so that I can check them out.**

3. **Next, I want my images to automatically print so that I can have a hard copy of each one.**

4. **Finally, I want to e-mail my new pictures to friends and family.**

Let's begin building the workflow:

Note

As I mentioned, my camera automatically saves files with an "IMG" prefix at the beginning of every filename, so that's the convention I use in this short tutorial. You may want to adjust the variable in step 3 below to match the default naming conventions of your camera.

1. **Tell Automator what files you want to interact with.** Select Files & Folders from the Library column and then drag and drop Find Finder Items into the Workflow pane, as shown in figure 14.3.

2. **Choose Other from the Search drop-down menu and select Desktop on the left side of the resulting window.** Click the New Folder button, name the folder New Pics, and then click the Open button.

3. **In the criteria section, leave the All pop-up menu alone, change the Any content pop-up menu to Name, leave the contains pop-up menu alone, and finally type** IMG **in the text field.** This tells Automator that you are looking for files whose names start with IMG.

4. **Tell Automator that you want to rename the items in the New Pics folder.** Select Files & Folders from the Library column and then drag and drop Rename Finder Items into the Workflow pane beneath the Find Finder Items action. A caution window appears; click Don't Add to proceed.

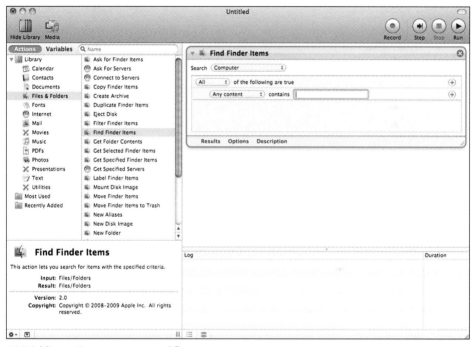

14.3 Adding actions to my new workflow

5. **Choose Make Sequential from the first drop-down menu, select the new name radio button in the Add number to option, and type the name you want to begin each of your files with in the text field.** I use *dwightpix* at the beginning of my picture files, as shown in figure 14.4. This action causes Automator to rename all files that start with "IMG" to files that start with *dwightpix* followed by a sequential number. However, I'm not quite finished renaming my files.

6. **Add the date the files were imported to my Mac to the end of the filenames.** Select Files & Folders from the Library column and then drag and drop Rename Finder Items into the Workflow pane beneath the previous Rename Finder Items action. Click Don't Add to proceed as before. The default criteria, as shown in figure 14.4, are appropriate for the needs of this example, so nothing needs to be changed in this action.

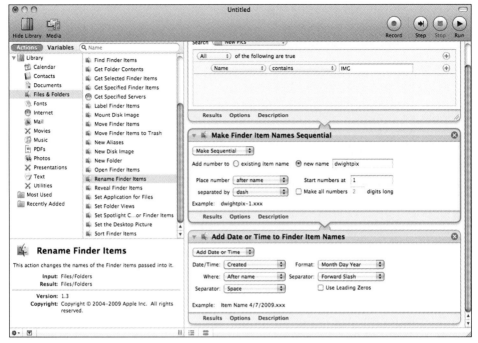

14.4 Renaming my files

7. **I want my renamed images to open in the Preview application so that I can see how they look.** Select Photos from the Library column, and then drag and drop Open Images in Preview to the Workflow pane beneath the second Rename Finder Items action. This causes Automator to start the Preview application (if it's not already running) and automatically display the new images in it.

Note

You may notice as you drag new actions into the Workflow pane that the actions that are already there move down a bit until the action you are dragging is beneath them. This just shows you that you can easily reposition actions in a workflow by simply dragging and dropping them into the order you need.

8. **Have Automator print hard copies of the photos automatically.** Select Photos from the Library column and then drag and drop Print Images to the Workflow pane beneath the Open Images in Preview action. Make any additional adjustments that you deem necessary; for example, I chose to center and scale my images to fit the page, as shown in figure 14.5.

298

9. **Have Automator open Mail and create a new mail message, automatically attach-ing the new images to the e-mail so that all you have to do is type the recipients' addresses and click Send.** Select Mail from the Library column and then drag and drop New Mail Message to the Workflow pane beneath the Print Images action. Type any items that you want automatically added to your new mail, such as the e-mail address or a subject, as shown in figure 14.5.

14.5 Automator automatically prints and creates a new mail message containing the new images.

10. **Click the Run button in the upper-right corner to run the workflow.** Automator per-forms the actions and warns you if there are any problems.

Saving your workflows

You will certainly want to save your workflows so that you don't have to create them every time you need them, which kind of defeats the purpose of Automator. You can save your workflows as workflows, applications, or plug-ins. Table 14.2 gives a brief explanation of each.

Table 14.2 Different Ways to Save Your Workflows

Save As	Description
Workflow	Simply saves the actions you brought together as a workflow. You can open the workflow in Automator to run or edit it.
Application	Saving a workflow as an application makes it a stand-alone document. Double-click the workflow application to launch it as you would any other application.
Services menu, Script menu, Print Workflow, Folder Action, iCal Alarm, Image Capture	Your workflow is saved as an application-specific plug-in that the application (such as Finder, iCal, or Image Capture) can use to automatically perform tasks.

To save your workflow as a new workflow, an application, or a plug-in type, follow these steps:

1. **Press ⌘+Shift+S.**

2. **Give the workflow a descriptive name.** Choose where to save it, and select a format from the Type pop-up menu.

3. **Click the Save button.**

To save an existing workflow that you are modifying, press ⌘+S.

Recording Your Own Actions

The coolest feature in Automator for Snow Leopard is the ability to create custom actions based on your keyboard and mouse events. Automator can record your keyboard and mouse events and execute them as part of a workflow.

For Developers and Scripters Only!

Scripters who write their own AppleScripts or developers who create their own applications will be delighted to know that they can develop their own actions that are specific to their needs. Xcode, which is an API (application programming interface) distributed by Apple with Snow Leopard, provides all the tools needed for programmers to make unique actions.

You can download the creations of some of these programmers by visiting www.apple.com/downloads/macosx/automator/.

To get started on your custom action, follow these steps:

1. **Open a workflow and click the Record button in the upper-right corner.**

2. **Perform the steps necessary to complete your action.**

3. **Click the Stop button shown in figure 14.6 when you are finished.**

4. **Click the Run button to test your new actions.**

5. **Edit actions in the list by deleting unnecessary actions, changing the timeout setting for each action, or modifying the Playback Speed.**

6. **Save your action as a workflow, application, or plug-in.**

Note To record your actions, you must enable access for assistive devices in the Universal Access preferences. To do so, choose Apple menu ➪ System Preferences, select Universal Access, and then select the Enable access for assistive devices option.

Note Before you start recording, make sure that your Mac is set up exactly the way it needs to be to perform the necessary actions. For example, if you are using an application as part of your action, you will want to have it open before beginning to record.

Stop button

14.6 Automator continues recording your actions until you click the Stop button.

Discovering Time Machine

One of the Snow Leopard features that Apple is most proud of, and rightly so, is Time Machine. Oh, there have been backup utilities out there made by third-party companies, even a few good ones, but Apple has delivered something above and beyond them in terms of simplicity and information retrieval.

Time Machine backs up your system behind the scenes, allowing you to do your work while it handles its business undetected in the background. Your initial backup will take quite a while, as Time Machine is backing up everything on your Mac's hard drive (again, it all happens in the background, so you can continue to use your Mac). After the initial backup, though, Time Machine continues to back up your files automatically every hour, only backing up items that have changed. Because it is only backing up changed items, the backups are much faster to perform.

Why it's important to back up your files

I wanted to take a small section of this chapter to simply preach to you the doctrine of backing up your computer. You have too many precious memories and too many important documents on your Mac to simply count on it to last forever (yes, even Macs do eventually have issues, as you'll see in Chapter 17). Take a few minutes out of your iLife, and perhaps spend a few dollars for an external hard drive, to get Time Machine up and going. Backing up your data is something that you will simply never regret doing.

Hardware requirements for using Time Machine

Time Machine can back up your data to any of these three configurations:

- **A network volume, such as a file or backup server.** This is a good idea for large networks.

- **An external hard drive, which is my recommendation.** Be certain that the data capacity of the external drive is large enough to save all the data on your Mac's hard drive.

- **A USB flash drive.** Be sure the data capacity of the flash drive is large enough to save all of your backup data.

- **A partition on your Mac's hard drive if the drive is indeed partitioned.** Partitioning a drive is the act of using a disk utility to divide a single hard drive into several sections, fooling the computer into believing that one drive is actually multiple drives. I do not recommend using this sort of configuration because if your hard drive has a problem, you've lost all of your data in spite of having backed it up.

The Apple Time Capsule

Time Capsule acts as both a wireless network router, like an AirPort, and a central backup point for all Macs running Snow Leopard and Time Machine. The Time Capsule automatically backs up every file from every Mac, wirelessly and in the background, eliminating the need to connect an external drive to your Mac. This is one serious backup tool, and I highly recommend getting your hands on one. Check it out by visiting www.apple.com/timecapsule/.

Setting Up a Backup Disk

There are a couple of steps necessary to get started with Time Machine: You need to format your backup drive, and then you need to tell Time Machine that it can use the drive for its backups.

Formatting a hard drive

You need to format any drive you connect to your Mac before you can use it with Time Machine. To format the drive (see the following Caution before continuing this procedure!):

1. **Open Disk Utility by pressing ⌘+Shift+U, and then double-clicking its icon.**

2. **Connect the drive to your Mac.**

3. **Select the drive in the list on the left of the Disk Utility window.**

4. **Choose the Erase tab near the top of the window, as shown in figure 14.7.**

5. **Set the Volume Format to Mac OS Extended (Journaled).**

6. **Click the Erase button, and then click the Erase button again in the verification window.**

7. **Once the formatting is finished, click the Eject button in the Disk Utility toolbar at the top, and disconnect the hard drive from the Mac.**

 Caution If this is a drive you've used before, be sure that you've copied all the data from it before performing a disk format on it. Once the formatting process has started, all data that was on the drive is lost forever.

Telling Time Machine about the backup drive

When you first connect an external drive (you may have to format it first) to your Mac, Time Machine detects its presence and asks if you want to use this drive for backups. If you say yes, Time Machine sets everything up automatically, and away you go. In most cases, this is fine; you are never bothered about it again, and Time Machine does its duty.

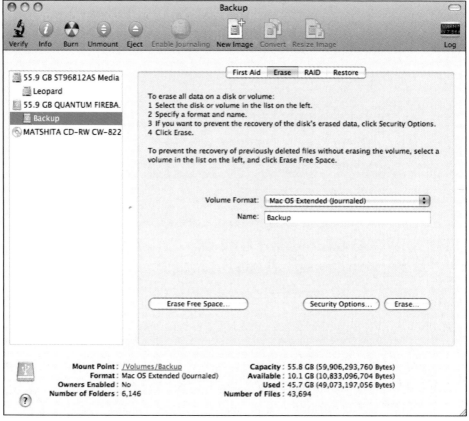

14.7 Click the Erase tab and select the volume format to get the drive ready for Time Machine.

You may be asking why you would say no to the question, if that were the case. Well, if this is a drive you've used in the past, or if it's a drive you want to partition, you may not want Time Machine hijacking it for its sole use. To manually set up a drive, follow these steps:

1. **Open the Time Machine preferences (shown in figure 14.8) by choosing Apple menu ⇨ System Preferences, and then clicking the Time Machine icon.**

2. **Click Select Backup Disk.**

3. **Choose a drive and click the Use for Backup button.**

4. **Time Machine begins a countdown for when it will perform the first backup, similar to figure 14.9.**

5. **If you want Time Machine to automatically begin backing up everything on the system, just sit back and relax.** However, if you want to only back up a portion of your hard drive, click the On/Off switch on the left side of the Time Machine preferences pane to toggle the switch to Off, and follow the directions in the next section of this chapter.

14.8 The Time Machine preferences allow you to manually configure how it works.

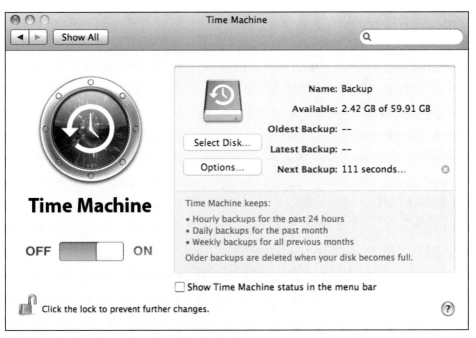

14.9 Time Machine is counting down to its first backup.

Selecting the Files You Want to Back Up

There may be several good reasons why you don't want Time Machine to back up every file on your Mac, one of which could be that there isn't enough storage space on the backup drive, or perhaps you simply don't want to back up all the information for each user on the computer. Whatever the reason, you need not fear, because I'm about to show you how to exclude information from your backup sessions. Follow these steps:

1. **Be sure Time Machine is Off so that it doesn't begin a backup process while you're choosing what not to back up.** Simply click the On/Off switch to toggle it on or off.

2. **Click Options in the middle of the preferences pane.**

3. **Click the + button in the lower-left corner of the Do not back up window.**

4. **Browse your Mac for folders and files that you do not want to include in the backup process, select them, and then click the Exclude button to add them to the list, which is shown in figure 14.10.** Refer to the Estimated size of full backup to see if your backup drive can store that much data. Click Done when finished.

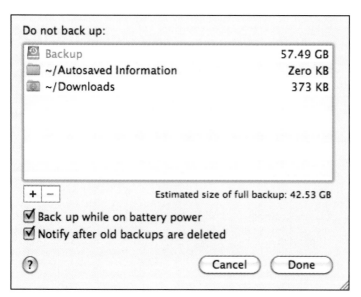

14.10 You can exclude files from being backed up by Time Machine.

Working with Backups

As mentioned, the entire backup process is handled behind the scenes, but that doesn't mean you can't check out what's going on, and even stop and restart a backup that's already in the works. Open the Time Machine preferences pane to see the progress of a backup procedure.

Manual backup

You don't have to wait for Time Machine to get around to backing up your system; you can start the process right now if you want. Follow these steps:

1. **Choose Apple menu ⇨ System Preferences, and click the Time Machine icon.**

2. **Select the Show Time Machine status in the menu bar check box.**

3. **Be sure Time Machine is On.** Toggle the On/Off switch, if necessary.

4. **Click the Time Machine icon in the menu bar.**

5. **Select Back Up Now, as shown in figure 14.11.**

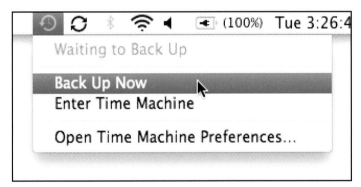

14.11 Select Back Up Now to back up your information immediately.

Caution When you manually select files to back up, you may not be backing up the preference files and other items necessary for Time Machine to completely restore your Mac should it fail.

Pause and resume a backup

You can stop and start backup processes if you need to. To pause a backup, follow these steps:

1. **Click the Time Machine icon in the menu bar.**

2. **Select Stop Backing Up.**

To resume the backup process, follow these steps:

1. **Click the Time Machine icon in the menu bar.**

2. **Select Back Up Now.** Your backup should begin where it left off. Nothing to it!

Genius

You can also use the Time Machine icon in the Dock to begin a backup, to pause or resume a backup, to open the Time Machine preferences, or to browse other Time Machine disks. Ctrl+click or right-click the icon in the Dock to see its menu.

Retrieving Information from Time Machine

Now that you know how to back up your system, it's time to learn how to retrieve that information should you ever need to do so. Let's see how to restore individual items and even an entire drive.

Restoring individual files

Time Machine lets you restore individual files and folders that you may have lost or simply want to get previous versions of. To do so, follow these steps:

1. **Open Time Machine by clicking its icon in the Dock, or press ⌘+Shift+A and double-click its icon in the Applications folder.**

2. **Time Machine opens and you see a Finder window, similar to that in figure 14.12.**

3. **Use the timeline on the right side of the screen, or the arrow buttons next to it, to navigate through time to the date the item you need was backed up.**

4. **Browse the files in the Finder window to find the item you want to retrieve.**

5. **Select the item in the Finder window, and then click the Restore button in the bottom-right corner of the Time Machine window.** The file is zipped forward in time to today, and Time Machine closes. You have to admit, that's one of the coolest things you've ever seen on a computer!

Restoring an entire drive

The ability of Time Machine to let you restore an entire drive is worth the price of upgrading to Snow Leopard all on its own. You can save countless hours by not having to reinstall the OS, as well as all the applications you had on the system. To restore a drive, follow these steps:

14.12 Traveling through time!

1. **Connect your backup drive to the Mac.**

2. **Start your Mac using the Snow Leopard installation disc.**

3. **In the Installer application, choose Utilities ⇨ Restore System from Backup, and then click Continue.**

4. **Choose your backup drive, and then select the backup with which you want to restore the computer.**

5. **Follow the instructions from that point to finish the restoration process.** The restoration process can take a while, but not nearly as long as starting from scratch.

Delete Files from Time Machine Backups

What if you want to delete a file from your backed-up folders, instead of restore it? Simple:

1. **Open Time Machine and use the Finder window and timeline to find the item you want to delete from the backup.**

2. **Select the file or folder you want to delete.**

3. **Click the Action menu (which looks like a gear) in the Finder toolbar and select Delete Backup.** To get rid of all references to the item in Time Machine, select Delete All Backups.

What Can I Do with UNIX Commands in Terminal?

Beneath the beautiful exterior of Snow Leopard beats the heart of a true UNIX beast! But don't act frightened; UNIX feeds off of fear. UNIX is the base software on which the bulk of Mac OS X Snow Leopard rests, and it provides time-tested reliability and stability that is unmatched by any other OS. Most of the functions you perform in Snow Leopard by clicking your mouse or by typing a keyboard shortcut are UNIX commands that you can easily execute through a command line. Windows and Linux users are familiar with the command-line concept, but most Mac users have never needed to venture into that territory. I attempt to alleviate any command-line anxieties in this chapter, as well as introduce some of my more-seasoned readers to the Snow Leopard version of a command-line interface.

Tinkering with Terminal

Terminal is your gateway to entering the command-line world of UNIX. In my opinion, in order to even think of yourself as a Mac OS X aficionado, you must have at least attempted some basic UNIX commands using the old-fashioned way. To take a step back in computing time, open Terminal:

1. **Click the Go menu and select Utilities, or press ⌘+Shift+U.**

2. **Double-click the Terminal icon to open a new Terminal window, as shown in figure 15.1.**

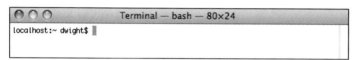

15.1 This is what computing looked like before the advent of the graphical user interface.

Terminal preferences

Terminal, like other applications, can be modified to work the way you want it to. Click the Terminal menu and select Preferences (or press ⌘+,) to open the Preferences window.

Startup

When you first open Terminal, it automatically opens a new Terminal window. The Startup options in the Preferences window, shown in figure 15.2, allow you to define the state that Terminal starts up in:

- **On startup, open:** Choose what settings to use for the new window or to open a series of windows called a window group (more on window groups a little later in this chapter).

- **Shells open with:** Determine whether to open Terminal in its default shell, which is called bash, or in a different shell. A shell is software that allows a user to interact with the UNIX services, and provides the commands that can be executed by the user. You can download and install other UNIX shells from the Internet. To use a shell other than bash, select the command (complete path) radio button and type the path to the directory the shell is located in.

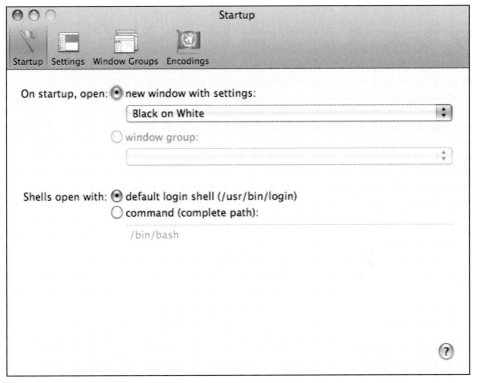

15.2 Decide how Terminal reacts when you first start it up.

Genius

If you are someone who uses Terminal quite a lot (you are an official, card-carrying geek if that's the case), it's a good idea to keep a shortcut to it in your Dock. That way, the comfort of the command line is within easy reach. I've used Mac OS X for years, and I like to keep the Terminal feature close by my side. You never know when the uncontrollable urge to chmod, mkdir, or ping might strike you!

Settings

The Settings section, shown in figure 15.3, lets you adjust the look and behavior of your Terminal windows. Table 15.1 gives a brief description of what each tab in the Settings section will let you modify.

The list on the left side of the Settings window contains preformatted window settings that you can choose. Set one as your default by highlighting the desired setting and clicking the Default button. Add or delete saved settings by clicking the + or – buttons, respectively.

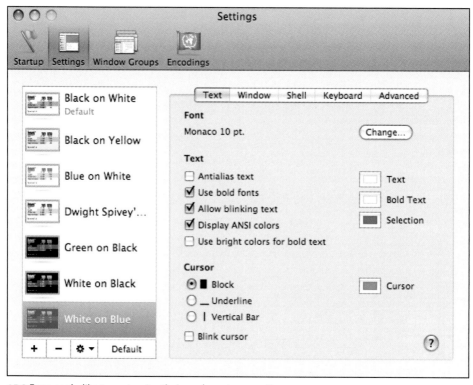

15.3 Even geeks like to customize their work environment!

Table 15.1 Options Available in the Settings Tabs

Tab	Options available
Text	Change the appearance of text, including the font used and the colors designated for certain types of text. You can also control how the cursor is displayed.
Window	Set the default title of windows, as well as what other information appears in the title bar, such as the dimensions of the window or the name of the currently active process. Choose the default background color of windows, the default size of new windows, and how far to allow a user to scroll back.
Shell	Have the shell issue a command by default as soon as a new window is opened, and tell Terminal how to behave when a user exits a shell, and whether it should prompt the user before closing the window.
Keyboard	Assign commands to shortcut keys to make entering commands even faster.
Advanced	Settings allow you to change the Terminal emulation, alarms, and character encodings.

Window Groups

Figure 15.4 shows the Window Groups tab, which allows you to delete, import, and export your window groups. Window groups are useful for users who utilize several windows, allowing them to run multiple tasks during their Terminal sessions.

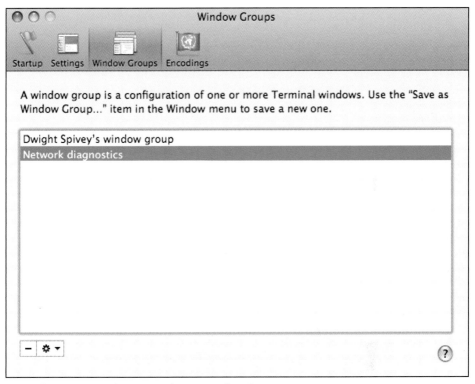

15.4 Delete, import, and export window groups from here.

Creating window groups causes Terminal to keep each window's individual settings intact, so that they are in the same state when you reopen them as they were when you closed them. To create a window group, follow these steps:

1. **Open the windows you will be working with and make sure they are set up in the format that you need.**

2. **Choose the Window menu and select Save Windows as Group.**

3. **Give the window group a descriptive name, like "Network diagnostics," and click the Save button.** Select the check box in the Save window to have this window group open automatically when you first open Terminal.

Encodings

Figure 15.5 shows the Encodings tab. These options allow you to enable and disable international character encodings so that Terminal can display international characters.

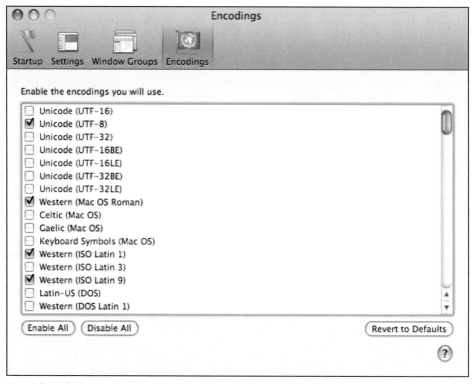

15.5 Select which character encodings that Terminal can use.

Tabbed windows

While some users may prefer to have several Terminal windows open at once, I like the simplicity of having one window running multiple tabs, as shown in figure 15.6.

To create a new tab, follow these steps:

1. **Choose Shell ➪ New Tab.**

2. **Select the setting for the new tab.** For example, choose Basic to select a default shell interface.

Close tabs by clicking the X in the upper-left corner of the tab.

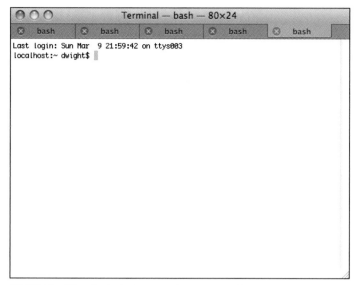

15.6 Tabbed Terminal windows are the way to go for me.

You can also save tabbed windows as a window group by choosing Window ⇨ Save Windows as Group, and giving the group a descriptive name.

Entering UNIX Commands

To effectively navigate in a CLI (command-line interface), you need to have an understanding of how UNIX views the structure of your files and folders on the hard drive. UNIX calls each folder on your Mac a directory and recognizes the disks as volumes. The beginning, or top, level of your startup disk is known as the root directory, which is represented by a / (slash).

Navigating a CLI

Let's begin learning how to get around in UNIX by opening a new window, if you don't have one open already:

1. **Choose Shell ⇨ New Window.**

2. **Select the setting for the new window.**

When you first display a Terminal window, it opens in your home directory, which is represented by a ~ (tilde). To move to another directory, type its path on the command line. For example, to move to the root directory of your hard drive, simply type **cd /** and press Return (cd stands for "change directory"). To move back from the root directory to your home directory, simply type **cd ~** and press Return.

Moving to a subdirectory can be a little trickier; however, knowing where directories are located on your drive will help immensely. Directories are separated by slashes when typing their path. For example, type the following to move to the Utilities folder on your hard drive, and press Return:

```
cd/Applications/Utilities
```

Common commands

You can bend Snow Leopard to your will using the Terminal just as you can with the mouse. Typing commands in the CLI executes functions that range from listing items in a directory to performing diagnostics on your network. As you learned in the previous section, entering and executing a command is as simple as typing it and pressing Return; that's it!

Table 15.2 lists some of the most commonly used UNIX commands and gives a brief explanation of the functions they perform.

Table 15.2 Common UNIX Commands

Command	Function
ls	Lists files in the current directory.
ls –a	Lists all files, including hidden files, in the current directory.
cd	Changes directories; type this command, followed by the path of the directory you want to change to.
man	Displays the manual page for a command.
su	Stands for "superuser," and temporarily enables the root user account, discussed later in this chapter. Type **su** followed by the command you want to invoke as the superuser, and then press Return. Enter the password for the root account when prompted.
mv	Moves or renames a file. Type **mv** followed by the name of the file (and in some cases, the path to the file) you want to move, and then enter the path and name of the file you want to move it to. This action creates a new file in the new location, and deletes the original.
rm	Deletes a file. Enter the command followed by the path and name of the file you want to delete.
rm –r	Deletes a directory and all of its contents. To use this command, type **rm –r** *directory name* (where *directory name* is the name of the directory you want to delete), and press Return.
pwd	Displays the path to the directory you are currently working in.
cp	Copies a file. Type **cp** followed by the path and name of the file you want to copy, and then enter the path and name of the file you want to copy it to. This action creates a new file in the new location, but also retains the original.
mkdir	Creates a new directory. Type **mkdir**, and then type the path and name of the new directory.

What's Up, Man?

There are literally hundreds of UNIX commands at your disposal in Snow Leopard, and each one of those commands could have several options that further expand their abilities. Needless to say, there's simply no way for me to explain the functions of all those commands here, but fear not; there's a UNIX command that can tell you everything you need to know about all the other commands: man. In a Terminal window, type **man**, followed by the name of the command you need more information about, and press Return to see the man (or manual) page for that command. A command's man page describes what the command can do and what options are available for it.

When you first open the man page for a command, you can only see a few lines of the page. To navigate through the man page, follow these steps:

1. **Press the up and down arrows on your keyboard to scroll up or down one line at a time.**

2. **Press the space bar to move to the next page.**

3. **Press Q to exit the man page.**

It's a bird! It's a plane! It's superuser!

There is a very special account that you can use both in Terminal and in Snow Leopard that is separate and above all others: the superuser, or root, account. The root user is the end-all and be-all account that has the final say over every other account on the system, including Administrator accounts.

Apple hides this powerful account from most users, and for good reason: If you are using the root user account and make just the right mistake at just the right time, you can totally junk your Mac. As a matter of fact, the root account is disabled by default in Snow Leopard. However, there are some things you can do with root, such as access folders of other user accounts, that you just can't do with an Administrator account. If you are feeling especially brave, you can enable the root account by following these steps:

1. **In the Finder, press ⌘+Shift+U to open a Finder window directly into the Utilities folder.**

2. **Double-click the Directory Utility icon.**

3. **When Directory Utility opens, click the lock in the bottom-left corner of the window, and then type an Administrator account name and password.**

4. **Choose Edit and select Enable Root User.**

The default password for the root account is blank, and this simply won't do. To change the password

1. **Choose Edit ⇨ Change Root Password from the menu.**

2. **Type a password in the Password field, as shown in figure 15.7, and retype the password in the Verify field.** Click OK when finished.

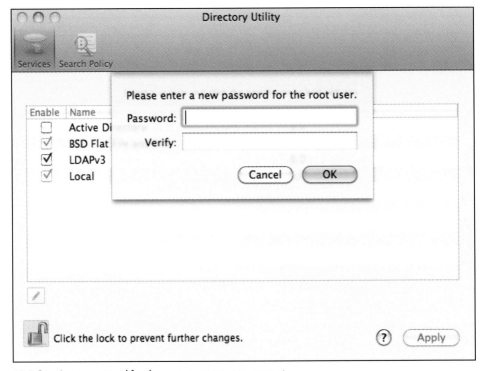

15.7 Creating a password for the root, or superuser, account

Expand the Abilities of Snow Leopard by Using X11

Because the Snow Leopard version of UNIX, Darwin, is a fully compliant and certified UNIX variant, it can compile and run the full gamut of your UNIX applications. There are thousands of applications, many of them using graphical user interfaces, that you can run side by side with your Mac OS X applications using X11, also known as the X Window System. X11 is an optional installation that can be performed with your Snow Leopard installation disc. Apple has an excellent online resource for discovering X11 and learning how to use it to expand your Mac OS X Snow Leopard experience; check it out at http://developer.apple.com/opensource/tools/runningX11.html.

Some X11 applications of note include OpenOffice.org and Fink.

Snow Leopard UNIX Tricks

There are several ways to customize the way you work with your Mac, but there are also many more that are not as obvious as making a change in the System Preferences. That's where Terminal comes in, providing you with access to Mac OS X's internals so that you can really dig deep with your changes.

Each one of these commands requires the Terminal application, so go ahead and open it before you begin. Be sure to press Enter after each line you type to execute the command.

Changing the Dock from 3-D to 2-D

Many a Mac user still pines away for the old two-dimensional look of the Dock that reigned in Mac OS X 10.4 and previous versions (figure 15.8). Well, pine no more with this simple UNIX trick.

```
defaults write com.apple.dock no-glass -boolean YES
killall Dock
```

15.8 The Dock appears in 2-D when you execute this command.

Adding a message to the login window

You can personalize the login window with your own message, using the Terminal and a little know-how.

```
sudo defaults write /Library/Preferences/com.apple.loginwindow LoginwindowText
    "Your Message"
```

Type your user account password when prompted to execute the command.

Changing the format of screenshots

The default format of screenshots is PNG, but you can change that format with a simple command in Terminal.

```
defaults write com.apple.screencapture type jpg
```

Notice the jpg at the end of the line; this is the format type. You can enter any format type you want here (as long as the format is supported by Snow Leopard).

Enable the path view in Finder

I like to know where I am in the hard drive's directory path when I browse in the Finder. While there are a couple of other ways to achieve this, my favorite is to view the path at the top of the Finder window, as shown in figure 15.9.

```
defaults write com.apple.finder _FXShowPosixPathInTitle -bool YES
```

15.9 This command shows the directory path in the top of the Finder window.

Using transparent icons for hidden applications

If you have lots of applications open at once, but choose to hide the ones you aren't using, this tip is for you. This trick causes the Dock to display applications that are hidden with a transparent icon.

```
defaults write com.apple.Dock showhidden -bool YES
killall Dock
```

Enable double scroll arrows

This simple trick places double arrows at both ends of the scroll bar, which makes for less mouse movement for you.

```
defaults write "Apple Global Domain" AppleScrollBarVariant DoubleBoth
```

Setting a screen saver as your desktop picture

How cool would it be to have an animated desktop picture? This trick lets you use a screen saver as your desktop picture.

```
/System/Library/Frameworks/ScreenSaver.framework/Resources/ScreenSaverEngine.
   app/Contents/MacOS/ScreenSaverEngine -background
```

Finding Additional UNIX Information

UNIX adds a whole other dimension to Snow Leopard that many regular users will never discover, but believe me, there are hidden treasures in UNIX that you may find are well-worth discovering. Here are some additional resources to learn more about UNIX and how to utilize its commands and applications alongside your other Mac OS X applications and utilities:

- **www.apple.com/macosx/technology/unix.html**
- **http://images.apple.com/macosx/pdf/L355785C_UNIX_TB.pdf**
- **www.apple.com/opensource/**
- **http://developer.apple.com/opensource/**
- **www.unix.org**

All of these links are accurate at the time of this writing. The Internet is chock-full of more UNIX goodness, so feel free to scour it for all the command-line enlightenment you can stand.

Can I Install Windows on My Mac?

Now that all new Macs are equipped with Intel processors, you can install Windows XP or Vista on your Mac just as you would on any other Intel-based PC. If you are switching over from a Windows computer to the wonderful world of Mac, having Windows installed on your Mac can make the transition a little smoother. However, if you are like every other Windows convert I know, you will find yourself booting up into Windows less and less as you become more familiar with Snow Leopard.

Understanding Boot Camp

Boot Camp is simply a tool provided with Snow Leopard that helps step you through the process of installing Microsoft Windows on your Mac. It is a very simple utility but one that performs some very big jobs, such as

- **Partitioning your hard drive**
- **Booting from the Windows installation disc**
- **Installing drivers in Windows that you need in order to use the hardware that comes with your Mac, such as your built-in camera (if you have one)**

Benefits of installing Microsoft Windows

If you're a longtime Mac fan, you may be dubious about the title of this section, but former Windows users probably understand the upside of having Windows at their fingertips. Here are a few of the most obvious benefits:

- **Some companies use software that runs only on Windows.** If you work for one of those companies but are one of the smart folks who insist on having a Mac, you can have the best of both worlds.
- **Windows converts probably have a lot of Windows-only software — including games — that they don't want to just trash because they now have a Mac.** Boot Camp enables them to keep their software.
- **On increasingly rare occasions, you may run across a Web site that only works with a Windows operating system version.** Those sites are no longer off-limits to Mac users.
- **Some new Mac users may have printers that only work with Windows (this is also becoming increasingly rare).** Installing Windows ensures that they won't have to chuck the printer, which can be pretty painful if you have a stockpile of consumables (such as toner and ink) tied up in the device.

What you need in order to install Windows

Here are the requirements that must be met before installing Windows on your Mac:

- **At least 10GB of space available on your hard drive.**
- **Your Mac must have an Intel processor.**

- **You must install all firmware updates available for your Mac.** Run Software Update (choose Apple menu ⇨ Software Update), or go to the Apple support Web site for your particular Mac model to find out if there are any updates for your computer.

- **A Mac OS X Snow Leopard installation disc.**

- **At least 1GB of memory if you are installing Windows Vista.**

- **A Windows installation disc.** You can install Windows XP Home or Professional editions, or Windows Vista Home Basic, Home Premium, Business, or Ultimate.

Note You must install a 32-bit version of Windows, unless you have a Mac Pro or MacBook Pro introduced in early 2008 or later, in which case you can install a 64-bit version. If you are installing Windows XP, it must be Service Pack 2. You cannot install versions prior to Service Pack 2 and upgrade after the fact; the install disc must contain Service Pack 2 already.

Genius If your Windows XP installation disc doesn't include Service Pack 2, Google the search term "slipstream Windows XP Service Pack 2 disc" to find several sites with instructions for creating a bootable installation CD that does include Service Pack 2.

Using Boot Camp to Install Windows

Open the Boot Camp Assistant to get started:

1. **From within the Finder, press ⌘+Shift+U to open the Utilities folder.**

2. **Double-click the icon for Boot Camp Assistant to see a window like that in figure 16.1.**

3. **Click Print Installation & Setup Guide to do just that, assuming you have a printer.** This guide is necessary to have, and you need to print it if you can, or have access to it.

4. **Click Continue.**

Caution The Print Installation & Setup Guide is necessary to have in order to continue with this chapter. This chapter is only meant as a brief tour of installing Windows, not a comprehensive guide. The Setup Guide is 26 pages long and is chock-full of information that you must have before continuing any further. If you can't print it, run it or view it from the Apple support Web site on another Mac (www.apple.com/support/bootcamp/).

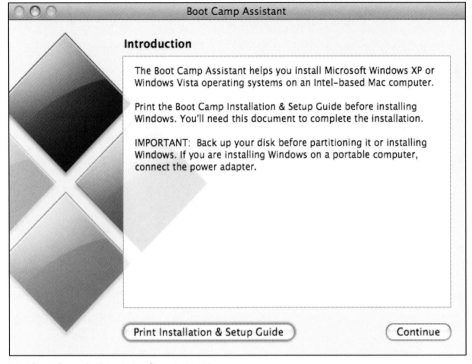

16.1 Boot Camp Assistant standing at attention

Partitioning your hard drive

Boot Camp Assistant now wants to help you partition your Mac's hard drive. Partitioning your drive essentially marks off a section of your hard drive and fools Snow Leopard into thinking your Mac has two hard drives installed instead of one. This partition will be used exclusively for Windows, so keep this in mind when deciding how much disk space to allocate to it, since you cannot recover that space for Mac usage.

Note

If you already partitioned your Mac's drive at some other time, you may simply see a window asking if you want to create or remove a Windows partition or start the Windows installer. Because you are installing Windows in this chapter, choose to start the Windows installer and click Continue.

At this point, you need to decide how much of your Mac's hard drive to allocate to Windows. There is no set number that I can recommend to you for the size; it depends entirely on your needs. Vista calls for at least 16GB of drive space to install it and XP needs at least 2GB. Keep in mind that you will also need additional space to install applications and to store files. To divide the drive, click and drag the little dot between the Mac OS X and Windows boxes to the left or right to increase or decrease the size for each partition, as shown in figure 16.2.

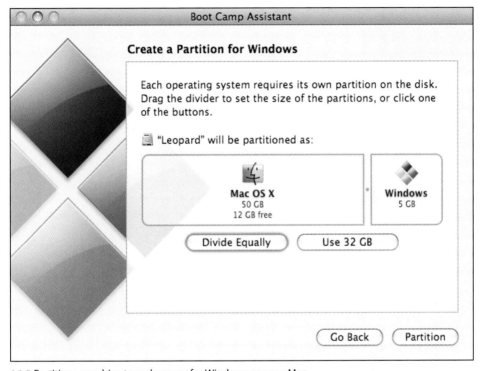

16.2 Partition your drive to make room for Windows on your Mac.

If you have a lot of Windows applications that you plan on installing, you might do well to click Divide Equally. Click Use 32GB if you want to automatically set the Windows partition to that amount. You would do so if you were using the FAT format when installing Windows and need to use the maximum amount of space that this format allows. Follow these steps:

1. **Set the size of your Windows partition and click Partition.** Boot Camp Assistant checks your hard drive for any potential problems and then continues the process.

2. **When it finishes partitioning your hard drive, Boot Camp Assistant tells you to insert the Windows installation disc.** Do so and then click Start Installation, as shown in figure 16.3.

16.3 Click Start Installation to begin installing Windows.

Windows installation

By now, your Mac should have booted into the Windows installer disc, which is where I pick up:

1. **Follow the instructions on your computer for installing Windows, being sure to follow along with the Boot Camp Installation & Setup Guide you printed earlier.**

2. **At a certain point, you are asked on which partition to install Windows.** Be certain to choose the one labeled BOOTCAMP! This is key to your success or failure.

3. **Select the partition format you want to use for Windows (either NTFS or FAT32).** If you're installing Vista, NTFS is your only option. If you install XP, consider using FAT32; you can easily transfer files between the Mac and Windows partitions because Snow Leopard can natively read the FAT32 file system, but not NTFS.

4. **Once Windows is installed, your Mac reboots into Windows.**

Don't Be Afraid to Ask for Help!

When you first boot your Mac into Windows following the Boot Camp installation, you see the Boot Camp Help window. Use this resource! It has invaluable information on how to use your Mac and its hardware, such as the keyboard, with Windows software. There are some differences when using a Mac compared to using PC hardware, but nothing that you can't easily overcome by reading through a Help window.

5. **Eject the Windows installation disc by choosing the Start menu in the bottom-left corner and selecting My Computer.** Click the drive containing the Windows installation disc to highlight it, and then click the Eject this disk option in the Systems Tasks (the upper-left corner of the window).

6. **Insert your Mac OS X Snow Leopard installer disc; the Boot Camp installer program runs.** Follow the instructions on your screen and never cancel any part of the installation! Remember to read the guide! Your Mac restarts when the installation is completed and you have finished your Windows installation process.

Note

If you are prompted by a message saying the software hasn't passed Windows Logo testing, click Continue Anyway.

Note

If you are using a MacBook Air, you need to install Windows and the Boot Camp drivers using a compatible external drive that's connected directly to your computer.

Choosing a Startup Disk

Now that you have a Mac with two operating systems on it, you need to decide which one will be its default: Snow Leopard or Windows? You can easily select either of the two disks to be your default startup disk, and you can just as easily switch between the two operating systems.

From Windows

To select a startup disk from within Windows, follow these steps:

1. **Click the Start menu and select Control Panel.**

2. **Choose Classic view to see all the control panels that are installed.**

3. **Double-click the Boot Camp icon.**

4. **Under the Startup Disk tab, shown in figure 16.4, select the operating system that you want to boot into by default, and then click OK.** Click Restart if you want to reboot right now.

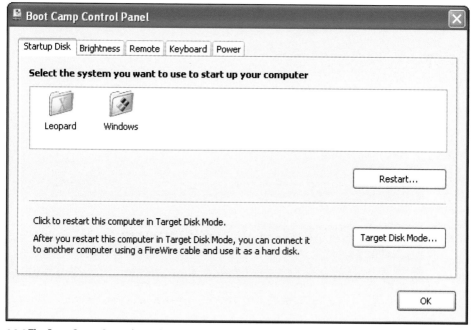

16.4 The Boot Camp Control Panel in Windows

From Snow Leopard

To select a startup disk from within Snow Leopard, follow these steps:

1. **Choose Apple menu ⇨ System Preferences.**

2. **Click the Startup Disk icon.**

3. **Select the operating system that you want to be your default from the list, as shown in figure 16.5.** Close the System Preferences unless you want to reboot the Mac now, in which case you would click Restart.

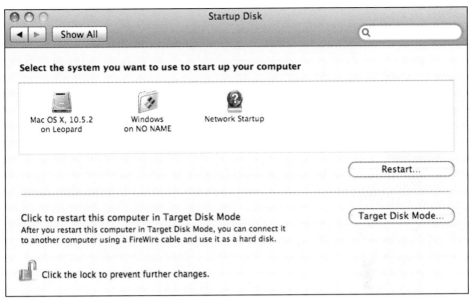

16.5 Select the disk partition you want your Mac to boot into by default.

Removing Windows from Your Mac

When you get tired of Microsoft's operating system taking up a large chunk of your hard drive, you may want to know how to safely remove it. Easy enough:

1. **Open the Boot Camp Assistant by pressing ⌘+Shift+U from within the Finder and double-clicking its icon.**

2. **Click Continue.**

3. **Select the Create or remove a Windows partition option and click Continue.**

Caution

If you wipe out your Windows partition, all of your Windows content will be lost permanently. So if you have important files or documents on the Windows side, you'll want to back these up before restoring your Mac's drive.

4. **Click Restore (as shown in figure 16.6) to completely wipe out your Windows partition and restore your Mac's drive back to a single partition.**

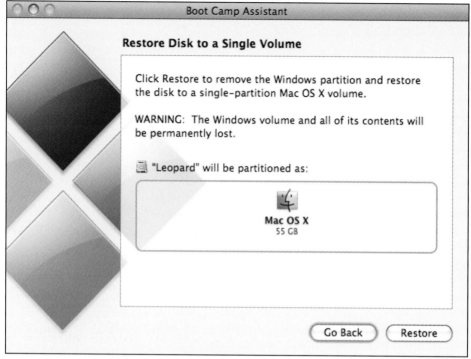

16.6 Easily restore your hard drive to a single partition.

An Alternative Method for Running Windows on Your Mac

You may be happy to know there is another way to install and run Windows (and other operating systems) on your Mac that doesn't require you to partition a section of your hard drive. My biggest beef with the Boot Camp method is that the partition you create for Windows has a fixed size: It won't increase or decrease, which could waste lots of space on your hard drive if you don't use all of the partition, or it may not be large enough to contain all of your data. My second beef is that I'm limited to either installing Windows XP or Vista, and not older versions of Windows or an alternative OS like Linux. Thankfully for folks like me, there is another way: virtualization. Virtualization is a method that allows you to install multiple Intel-capable operating systems on your Mac at the same time (as many as your hard drive or external drives will hold) and run them simultaneously within Mac OS X. There are several software packages out there that can help you achieve this dream, some of which I mention here. These applications help you to create virtual machines that are virtual, or pretend, hard drives that you can install operating systems on. These virtual machines access your computer's hardware and run at almost native speeds. Another great upside to virtual machines is that they can be made to expand or contract based on the amount of data they contain, which prevents you from wasting hard drive space.

Note I do not endorse any one of the upcoming software titles over another. All three have their pros and cons, and one may suit me better than it suits you. The two titles that you have to pay for offer free trials you can download, while the third option is free to begin with, so there's no reason not give each one a go and determine which you like best for your needs.

Parallels Desktop for Mac

Parallels Desktop for Mac, from Parallels, was the first viable virtualization option for Macs with Intel processors. The latest release (as of this writing), version 4, introduced many new and powerful features, such as the ability to access devices across operating systems, 64-bit operating system capability, and up to 50 percent better performance than the previous version, which allows you to run multiple virtual machines at the same time even more efficiently than before (as shown in figure 16.7).

For more information, and to download a trial copy of Parallels Desktop for Mac, visit www.parallels.com/products/desktop.

16.7 Parallels Desktop for Mac in action

VMWare Fusion

VMWare Fusion, shown in figure 16.8, is the brainchild of VMWare, one of the most trusted virtualization applications in the PC and Linux markets for years. In 2007, VMWare decided it was time to apply its knowledge of virtualization to the Mac platform, and a wonderful competition (from the consumer's standpoint) began with Parallels, which resulted in both companies making great leaps in their software's capabilities to try and outdo one another. This competition caused VMWare to gain a significant chunk of ground technologywise between versions 1 and 2 (the most current as of this writing). Features such as Unity View (the ability to run Windows programs as if they were native Mac applications) and Data Sharing (you can drag and drop files between operating system windows) make VMWare a viable option for anyone needing to run multiple operating systems on his or her Mac.

To learn more about VMWare Fusion and to download a trial copy, visit http://vmware.com/products/fusion.

16.8 VMWare Fusion running Windows XP within Mac OS X

VirtualBox

If you want to use Parallels Desktop for Mac or VMWare Fusion, you have to shell out some cash. Don't have any to spare? Don't worry; you're not completely without options. As a matter of fact, Sun Microsystems has provided you with a very nice option that not only supports multiple operating systems, but it's also free: VirtualBox. VirtualBox doesn't have all the bells and whistles that accompany the other two apps mentioned here, but if you simply need the ability to run Windows, Linux, or other Intel-based operating systems within Mac OS X, VirtualBox, shown in figure 16.9, can get the job done. Check it out at www.virtualbox.org.

16.9 VirtualBox running Internet Explorer within Mac OS X

Do You Have Any Troubleshooting Tips?

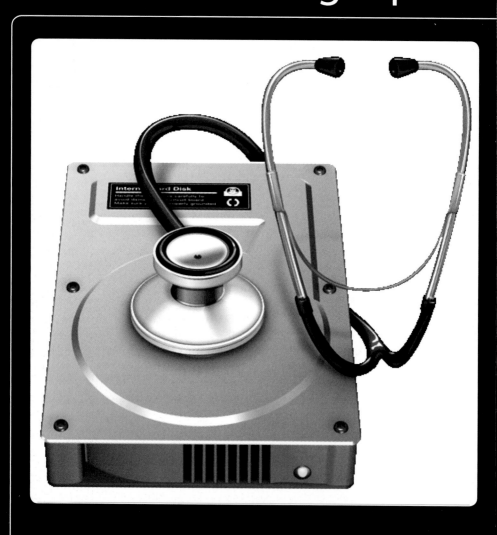

Macs have a well-earned reputation for being as rock-solid reliable as it gets in the tech realm, but nothing, not even Cupertino engineering, lasts forever. Things happen, and hopefully with this chapter I can point you to the help you need, if not lend a hand in resolving the issue altogether.

hay already be beyond the basics in your experience. However, by nature, any troubleshooting chapter must begin with the basics, so let's dive right in.

Restarting your Mac

Most issues with your Mac are fairly simple to resolve. As a matter of fact, the simplest resolution to most problems is to simply restart your Mac. Restarting is something that most computer user have had to do at some point, and it's always the first recourse to take when you notice quirky things beginning to happen. To restart your Mac, follow these steps:

1. **Choose Apple menu ⇨ Restart.**

2. **Snow Leopard asks if you are sure you want to restart (see figure 17.1).** Click Restart to restart the computer.

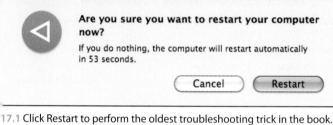

Are you sure you want to restart your computer now?

If you do nothing, the computer will restart automatically in 53 seconds.

Cancel   Restart

17.1 Click Restart to perform the oldest troubleshooting trick in the book.

Hopefully your woes are gone once your Mac boots back up; if not, the rest of this chapter should help you get to the heart of the matter.

Backing up your Mac

I cannot stress enough the importance of backing up your information before continuing any further. Maintaining a backup of your files prevents you from losing them should something cata strophic happen to your Mac, not to mention the peace of mind it fosters. I've learned the hard way to back up my files, and I hope to prevent you from experiencing the same nightmare I've dealt with.

Chapter 14 covered the use of Time Machine for keeping an external hard drive continuously updated with your backed-up files. While Time Machine is an easy way to keep your backups current, it's not the only way you can back up your Mac.

- **Purchase backup software.** Why lay down your hard-earned cash for a backup application when you have Time Machine as part of Snow Leopard? Time Machine is a great utility, but it may not be enough or offer enough control for some users, and that's where third-party applications come into play. Here are a few I've personally used:

  - **Intego Personal Backup (currently my favorite choice).** Visit www.intego.com/personalbackup for information and to download a free trial.

  - **Carbon Copy Cloner, by Bombich Software.** This one has been a tried-and-true app for a very long time on the Mac platform. Learn more about CCC at www.bombich.com/software/ccc.html.

  - **Retrospect.** This is another longtime backup stalwart that I remember using as far back as Mac OS 8. Download a trial, and even find a comparison to Time Machine, at www.retrospect.com/products/software/retroformac/.

- **Back up the old-fashioned way: manually.** Simply attach an external hard drive, install an internal drive, use a flash drive, or connect to another computer, and then drag and drop your files to it.

Make Sure You Are Up to Date

There could be a bug in your operating system or application software that is causing your problems. Check to be sure you are using the latest versions of your Mac's firmware and Snow Leopard by running Software Update:

1. **Choose Apple menu ⇨ Software Update.**
2. **If Software Update finds new versions of your firmware or software, install them to see if this resolves your issues.**

If the problems you are experiencing are related to a particular application, visit the Web site of the application's developer to see if there are any updates to the software or if there are any known issues with it. Table 17.1 lists the addresses of some of the most popular Apple software vendors and a list of their more popular products.

Table 17.1 Third-Party Apple Software Vendors

Company	Popular applications	Support site address
Adobe	Photoshop, InDesign, Illustrator, Acrobat	www.adobe.com/go/gn_supp
Quark	QuarkXPress	www.quark.com/service/desktop/support/
Microsoft	Word, Excel, PowerPoint, Entourage	https://www.microsoft.com/mac/default.mspx
Mozilla	Firefox, Thunderbird	http://support.mozilla.com/
Intego	VirusBarrier, FileGuard	www.intego.com/support/
Intuit	TurboTax, Quicken, QuickBooks	www.intuit.com/support/
FileMaker	FileMaker Pro, Bento	http://filemaker.com/support/index.html
Roxio	Toast, Popcorn	www.roxio.com/enu/support/default.html

Startup Issues

When your Mac won't start, it's a pretty scary time. I won't insult your intelligence by telling you there's nothing to worry about, but most of the time this can be solved with a few quick-and-easy steps. If you told me you had startup issues, the first question I would ask you is if the Mac literally won't power up, or if it is getting hung up in the boot process. Let's take it from there.

Your Mac won't power up

Here are a few questions and tips to try if your Mac simply won't power up at all:

- Is the power cable connected?

- Does the power outlet you are connected to work with other devices?

- If you are using a laptop, is the power adapter connected or are you running off the battery? Is the battery charged? Will the Mac work with the power adapter connected?

- Is the Mac itself powering up, but the display isn't coming on? If so, you could have a bad display. Try connecting another display to your Mac to determine if that is the issue. If a new display doesn't work, or if your display works with another computer, your Mac's video card could be having problems.

- Have you added any devices (such as an external hard drive) or parts (such as memory) to your Mac, either internally or externally? If so, remove or reconnect the device or part and try to boot again. You may have a defective device, cable, or part.

- If all else fails, you should try to reset the System Management Controller (SMC). There are three ways to reset the SMC, depending on the model of your Mac:

  - For Mac Pros, iMacs, and Mac minis, shut down the computer and remove all its cables (mouse, keyboard, power cord, everything). After waiting at least 15 seconds, reconnect only the power cable, mouse, and keyboard (in that order) and then push the power button.

  - For MacBooks and MacBook Pros, remove the battery and unplug the power adapter if it is connected. Hold the power button down for at least 5 seconds and release. Install the battery and connect the power adapter, and then press the power button.

  - For MacBook Air, connect the power adapter to the computer. Holding down the Shift, Option, and Ctrl keys on the left side of the keyboard, press the power button once. Wait at least 5 seconds before pushing the power button again to turn on the computer.

Note   If you have a PowerPC Mac, you need to reset the Power Management Unit (PMU). Search the Apple Web site for instructions on how to do so for your particular model.

Your Mac is hung up at startup

Believe it or not, sometimes it is even more maddening to start up your Mac but not be able to boot into Mac OS X than it is simply not being able to turn on the computer at all. All sorts of things can occur: You may see a folder with a blinking question mark, the screen may be stuck at the gray Apple logo with the spinning gear, a blue screen may appear but nothing happens past that point, and so on. These issues can hopefully be resolved by following one of these next few steps:

- **Force your Mac to restart.** Hold down the power button for several seconds until the Mac turns off. Restart the Mac and see if it boots normally.

- **Reset the parameter RAM, which is also known as zapping the PRAM.** Snow Leopard stores information about your Mac in the PRAM, such as speaker volume levels, time zone settings, display settings, and the like. Restart your Mac and immediately press ⌘+Option+ P+R simultaneously. Continue to hold down all four keys until you hear your Mac's startup sound at least two times (give it three, just for good measure). Release the keys after the second or third startup sound, and hopefully you will be able to start up normally.

- **Start up your Mac in Safe Mode by holding down the Shift key immediately after the startup sound.** Don't let go until you see the gray Apple logo.

◉ **Boot your Mac using your Snow Leopard installation disc, and select Disk Utility from the Utilities menu.** Click the icon of your hard drive in the left column of the list, and click the Repair Disk button in the lower-right corner of the window. Once the repair is completed, reboot your Mac to see if it starts normally.

If you're still having no luck getting your Mac started up at this point, it's time to take some drastic measures. Contact Apple technical support at this point, as your Mac may need a bit more hands-on expertise.

Handy startup keyboard shortcuts

Apple has come up with a toolbox of startup keyboard shortcuts that allow you to start up your Mac and perform specific tasks, such as choosing a different startup disc. Table 17.2 lists the shortcut key combinations and the tasks they facilitate.

Table 17.2 Startup Keyboard Shortcuts

Task performed	Key combinations
Start up from a disc	Insert the disc into your Mac's optical drive and press C until the disc begins to boot.
Choose a startup disk	Press and hold Option as soon as you hear the startup sound. Release the button after you see available startup disks. Select the disk you want to boot from.
Start in Safe Mode	Press the Shift key as soon as you hear the startup sound, and don't release it until you see the spinning gear under the gray Apple logo.
Start up in Target Disk mode	Press and hold T immediately after the startup sound, and release when you see the FireWire logo on your screen.
Zap the PRAM	Press and hold ⌘+Option+P+R immediately at startup, before you hear the startup sound. Release the keys after you hear the third startup sound.
Start in Single User mode	Press ⌘+S immediately after the startup sound. You may release the keys once you see the command line screen.
Start up in Snow Leopard instead of Mac OS 9	If you have an older PowerPC Mac with Mac OS 9 and Mac OS X installed on the same disk, you can force the Mac to boot into Mac OS X by pressing ⌘+X at startup.
Eject a disc at startup	Hold down the mouse button or the eject button on your keyboard at startup.

Isolating Software Troubles

You're typing away in your favorite word processor and all of a sudden you see the wait cursor, known fondly as the "spinning wheel of death." The application crashes, and you lose about an hour's worth of nonstop typing because you forgot to save your document as you were going along. Or you are performing a banking transaction in your favorite Web browser when the browser freezes on you, and you find out that your transaction was lost in the process of your browser crashing. What to do if you have an application that just won't behave? I've taken the liberty of listing some questions and tips for troubleshooting a software issue:

- **Have you installed the latest updates for your software?** If not, visit the Web site of the application developer to see if there are any updates.

- **Did the issue occur only after you installed an update (either an application or a Mac OS X update)?** Check with the application developer for any known issues with the update, and explain the issue you're experiencing.

- **Do you experience problems with only one document?** There may be an element in that particular document, such as a font or graphic, that is corrupted and causing the issue. Try creating a new document; copy and paste elements from the old document into the new one and see if your issues are resolved.

- **Do you get a specific error message?** If so, consult the application's documentation or the manufacturer's Web site for help in interpreting the message.

- **Is the issue related to a software/hardware combination, such as a certain scanner or camera with a particular application?** For example, if you have a problem with Image Capture crashing when you try to import images from your camera, check to see if you can import images with some other application. If other applications also have this issue, then see if another camera will work. If other applications do not exhibit the problem, it's quite likely that the single misbehaving application is the culprit.

- **Discard the application's preferences files.** Consult your application's documentation or contact the manufacturer to find out where the application stores its preferences in Snow Leopard. When you restart the application, new preference files are created.

- **Is the application frozen?** If so, force the rogue application to quit by pressing ⌘+Option+Esc. Select the offending application from the list in the Force Quit Applications window and click Force Quit.

Unfortunately, if the issue at hand hasn't cleared up by now, you may need to reinstall the application. Again, be sure to contact the manufacturer or read the documentation that the application came with to see if there are any special instructions that you need to follow to properly reinstall the application.

Utilizing the root account

Sometimes the problem may be that something has become corrupted in your user account. The way to find out is to log into a different account and see if the issue persists. I prefer to use the root account, which gives you complete control over the Mac. Follow these steps:

1. **Open Directory Utility, which is found in the System/Library/CoreServices folder.**

2. **Click the lock icon in the lower-left corner (see figure 17.2), and type your user name and password when prompted.**

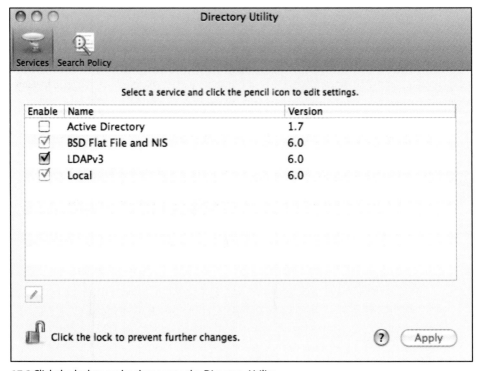

17.2 Click the lock to make changes to the Directory Utility.

3. **Choose Edit ⇨ Enable Root User to enable the root account.**

4. **Type the root account password twice to confirm it.** Do not forget this password!

5. **Quit Directory Utility.**

6. **Log out of the account you are currently using.**

7. **In the login window you will see an entry called Other.** Click Other, type **root** for the user name, and then type the password you assigned to the root account in step 4.

8. **Click Log In in the lower-right corner to log into the root account.**

9. **Test your issue while logged in as root. If the symptom persists, it is a systemwide problem.** If the issue does not present itself while logged in as root, you've isolated the problem to the account you were using.

Deleting preference files

Most applications you will ever install on your Mac create preference files somewhere on the system. These preference files tell the application how it should behave, what customizations you've made to how it works, what passwords may be necessary for someone to use it, and lots of other information it may need to function properly. If these preference files (there may be more than one, depending on the application) have been corrupted, your application may engage in some very odd behaviors and may not even be able to start up at all.

1. **Contact the developer of the application to find out what preference files are used by the app and where you can find them on your Mac.**

2. **Find the preference files and delete them.**

3. **Reopen the offending application and the preference file(s) will be correctly rebuilt.**

Killing a process

If your Mac seems to be super sluggish, there may be an errant application hogging up all the memory. When this happens you could restart your Mac, which effectively kills all processes and starts over. What if you have other tasks running that you need to leave alone? Apple made Activity Monitor for just such occasions.

1. **From the Finder, press Ô+Shift+U to open the Utilities folder.**

2. **Double-click the icon for Activity Monitor.**

3. **Browse through the processes list (see figure 17.3) and see if there are any taking up a large percentage of the computer's cycles.** To see the percentage being used by each process look under the % CPU heading.

4. **Highlight the offending process and click the Quit Process button in the upper left of the window to stop the rogue process in its tracks.**

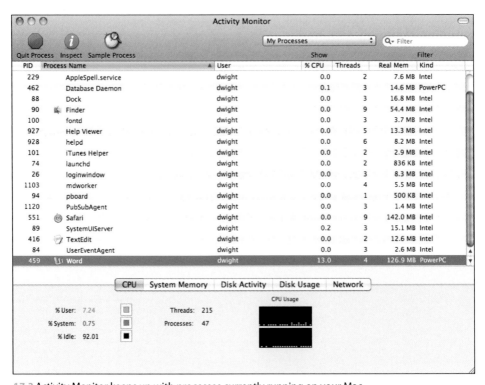

17.3 Activity Monitor keeps up with processes currently running on your Mac.

Correcting permissions issues

Every file in Mac OS X has a set of permissions assigned to it, which tells Snow Leopard exactly who can access the file and how that person can use it. Sometimes these permissions can get a little out of sorts and need to be repaired in order for your Mac to function in its normally spectacular way. Here are some symptoms to look for:

- You are unable to empty a file from the Trash.
- An application can only be launched by one user account, even though it is installed for use on all accounts.
- You cannot open a document that you know you should to be able to open.
- The Finder may restart when you are trying to change permissions for a file.
- You are unable to open folders on your Mac or the network that you are supposed to have access to.
- An application crashes when you try to print from it.

There are several other issues that may be related to permissions problems as well, but these are the most common.

Repairing permissions is thankfully an easy task to accomplish. Follow these steps:

1. **From within the Finder, open Disk Utility by pressing ⌘+Shift+U and double-clicking its icon.**

2. **Select the drive that contains the files with the permissions issues.**

3. **Click Repair Disk Permissions in the lower-left corner of the First Aid tab, and the process of repairing the permissions will begin, as shown in figure 17.4.**

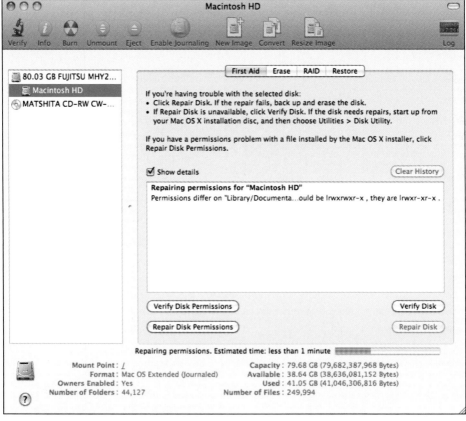

17.4 Restoring permissions to their proper states

Note   You can also run Disk Utility from the Snow Leopard installation disc, which is especially helpful if you can't boot up with the disk in question. Boot your Mac using the installation disc, choose Utilities ➪ Disk Utility, and run the repairs as described in the previous steps.

When All Else Fails, Reinstall

When the dust settles and you've done all that I've mentioned already — and you may have even dug further into the issues than this book does — but the Mac still won't work properly, it's time to completely back up and reinstall Snow Leopard. See Chapter 14 for help on backing up your system and Chapter 1 for instructions on installing Snow Leopard over an existing copy of Mac OS X.

Note

If you're in the United States and aren't comfortable with reinstalling Snow Leopard without taking a few more stabs at resolving the issue, give Apple Technical Support a call at 1-800-APL-CARE (1-800-275-2273). If you are outside the U.S., visit Apple's Technical Support contacts Web site to find support numbers for your country: www.apple.com/support/contact/.

Appendix A

Mac Online Resources

The Internet is an awesome tool for finding more information regarding Mac OS X and all other things Mac. The plethora of sites dedicated to the Mac are capable of keeping you up-to-date with all the latest Mac news, software updates, issues other users are experiencing, help with trouble-shooting, the most recent rumors, and the latest and greatest tips and tricks for squeezing all the juicy goodness you can get out of Mac OS X.

Official Apple Sites

Apple's site should be any self-respecting Mac user's first stop in their quest for more information about their Mac. Here are some helpful links to the most important sections of their site.

www.apple.com/mac/

This is your portal into all things Mac-related on Apple's site. From here you can check out the latest hardware and software Apple has to offer.

www.apple.com/macosx/

This is Apple's Mac OS X site, solely dedicated to the best operating system on earth.

www.apple.com/downloads/

Visit this site to find all the latest software downloads from Apple and the Mac community.

www.apple.com/support/

The Mother of Mac Support Sites, this is where you should go first when troubleshooting an issue with your Mac.

www.apple.com/itunes/

Need to get your Mac groove on? This site will take you to iTunes and iPod nirvana.

discussions.apple.com

This site is where you can connect with other Mac users about issues, tips, and all the neatest tricks regarding your Apple hardware or software.

www.apple.com/usergroups/

Would you like to join up with other local Mac users to discuss all things Mac? If so, then a Mac usergroup is right up your alley. Go here to find the Mac usergroup in your area, and then get involved.

http://guide.apple.com/

This is a great help with finding software and hardware that's compatible with your Mac.

http://support.apple.com/specs/

This is hands down the best site for finding specifications for almost any Apple product.

More Mac Sites

The Web is packed with third-party sites catering to the needs of Mac users. Here are a few of my favorites, in no particular order.

www.macworld.com

You can find all sorts of Mac stuff here, from how-to articles to reviews of the newest products. The premier Mac news and reviews site.

www.appleinsider.com

Rumors are a part of life for many Mac fans, and this site relays all the online gossip regarding Apple's latest and greatest offerings.

www.macintouch.com

One of my favorites since the 1990s (I'm dating myself a bit), this is a great source for Mac news and reader reviews.

www.macnn.com

News, podcasts, reviews, blogs, and forums can be found on this Mac news site.

www.macosxhints.com

This site is great for Mac OS X tips and tricks, from the simplest to the most difficult to implement.

www.microsoft.com/mac

Find all the latest updates for your Microsoft applications, and learn how to better use those you currently work with.

http://mactimeline.com/

A great history of Apple's updates and when they were offered to users, this site will probably best benefit the nerdiest of us Mac users (obviously including myself), but I've included it for all the Mac nerds-to-be as well.

http://macscripter.net/

All you wanted to know about scripting for your Mac, and more! Applescript and Automator are favorite topics on this site.

www.macfixit.com

A great site for learning about your Mac's hardware, how to solve hardware issues when they crop up, and find hardware tutorials to learn how things work on your Mac.

http://macosrumors.com

Another of the great rumor sites, this one has been in my bookmarks since the days of Mac OS 8.

www.versiontracker.com

Find the newest versions of your favorite third-party software, and discover the newest offerings from the best Mac developers around.

http://db.tidbits.com

This is another tried and true site for fans of the Mac that faithfully caters to the news and tips needs of other Mac users. It's also been around since before Noah.

Appendix B

Mac Shortcut Keys

Through all the years that computers have been around, the remaining constant has always been the keyboard. While it has gone through some subtle changes, the basic layout of the keys has remained the same since man first walked upright (which is ironic since we have to lean over to use them). The keyboard can be quite an efficient tool for quickly executing tasks on your Mac, and this section lists some of the more common keyboard shortcuts.

Finder Shortcuts

Use the shortcuts in Table B.1 to switch Finder window views, open a new Finder window, eject a disc, duplicate files and folders, maneuver through Finder's Sidebar, and manage your Trash.

Table B.1 Finder Shortcuts

Shortcut	Description
⌘+A	Select all items in the current window
⌘+D	Duplicate the selected item
⌘+E	Eject the current disc
⌘+F	Display the Find dialog box
⌘+I	Open the Get Info window for the selected item
⌘+J	Show the View options
⌘+L	Create an alias for the selected item
⌘+N	Open a new Finder window
⌘+O	Open the selected item
⌘+R	Show the original item for the current alias
⌘+T	Add the currently selected item to the Sidebar

continued

Table B.1 continued

Shortcut	Description
⌘+W	Close the current Finder window
⌘+Delete	Move the selected item to the Trash
⌘+1	Switch the active window to Icons view
⌘+2	Switch the active window to List Flow view
⌘+3	Switch the active window to Columns view
⌘+4	Switch the active window to Cover Flow view
Shift+⌘+A	Go to the Applications folder
Shift+⌘+C	Go to the Computer folder
Shift+⌘+D	Go to the Desktop folder
Shift+⌘+G	Display the Go to Folder dialog box
Shift+⌘+H	Go to the Home folder
Shift+⌘+I	Go to the iDisk folder
Shift+⌘+K	Go to the Network folder
Shift+⌘+N	Create a new folder in the current Finder window
Shift+⌘+U	Go to the Utilities folder
Shift+⌘+Delete	Empty the Trash (with the confirmation dialog)
Option+Shift+⌘+Delete	Empty the Trash (without the confirmation dialog)
Option+⌘+N	Create a new Smart Folder in the current Finder window
Option+⌘+W	Close all open Finder windows

Application Shortcuts

Table B.2 shows you how to cycle through your current application's icons, how to open the application's preferences, and how to maneuver through windows without resorting to your mouse.

Table B.2 Application Shortcuts

Shortcut	Description
⌘+Tab	Cycle forward through active application icons with each press of the Tab key; release ⌘ to switch to the selected application
⌘+,	Open the current application's preferences
⌘+H	Hide the current application
⌘+`	Cycle forward through the current application's open windows
⌘+M	Minimize the current window to the Dock
⌘+Q	Quit the current application
Shift+⌘+`	Cycle backward through the current application's open windows

Shortcut	Description
Shift+⌘+Tab	Cycle backward through active application icons with each press of the Tab key; release ⌘ to switch to the selected application
Option+⌘+H	Hide all applications except the current one
Option+⌘+M	Minimize all windows in active application to the Dock
Option+⌘+Esc	Display the Force Quit Applications window

Startup Shortcuts

Table B.3 details shortcuts you can use for alternate booting techniques.

Table B.3 Startup Shortcuts

Shortcut	Description
C	Press and hold to boot from the inserted CD or DVD
T	Press and hold to invoke FireWire Target Disk mode
Option	Press and hold to display the Startup Manager
Shift	Press and hold before the Apple screen comes up to boot into Safe Login mode
Shift	Press and hold after the Apple screen comes up but before login to bypass login items
Shift	Press and hold after login to boot into Safe Login mode

Restart and Shutdown Shortcuts

Table B.4 gives you some different options for the various dialog boxes you see when you restart or shut down your Mac.

Table B.4 Restart and Shutdown Shortcuts

Shortcut	Description
Control+Eject	Display the Restart/Sleep/Shut Down confirmation dialog box
Power	Display the Restart/Sleep/Shut Down confirmation dialog box
Shift+⌘+Q	Log out (with confirmation dialog box)
Option+Shift+⌘+Q	Log out (without confirmation dialog box)
Option+⌘+Eject	Put your Mac into Sleep mode (without confirmation dialog box)
Control+⌘+Eject	Restart your Mac (without confirmation dialog box, but you can save changes in open documents)
Control+Option+⌘+Eject	Shut down your Mac (without confirmation dialog box, but you can save changes in open documents)

continued

Table B.4 continued

Shortcut	Description
Control+⌘+Power	Force your Mac to restart (without confirmation dialog box, and you can't save changes in open documents)
Power	Press and hold to force your Mac to shut down (without confirmation dialog box, and you can't save changes in open documents)

Safari Shortcuts

Table B.5 details the shortcuts you can use to maneuver through Safari windows, manage your bookmarks, send e-mails, and perform Google searches.

Table B.5 Safari Shortcuts

Shortcut	Description
⌘+I	E-mail the contents of the current page
⌘+L	Select the Address bar text
⌘+N	Open a new window
⌘+O	Open a file
⌘+R	Reload the current page
⌘+T	Open a new tab
⌘+W	Close the current tab
⌘+D	Add the current page to the Bookmarks
⌘+n	Open the nth item on the Bookmarks bar, where n is a number between 1 and 9
⌘+}	Select the next tab
⌘+{	Select the previous tab
⌘+.	Stop loading the current page
⌘++	Make the text bigger on the current page
⌘+0	Make the text normal size on the current page
⌘+-	Make the text smaller on the current page
⌘+[	Navigate back
⌘+]	Navigate forward
Shift+⌘+H	Navigate to the Home page
Shift+⌘+T	Toggle the Tab bar on and off (works only if you have one tab open)
Shift+⌘+W	Close the current window
Shift+⌘+I	E-mail a link to the current page
Shift+⌘+K	Toggle pop-up blocking on and off
Shift+⌘+L	Run a Google search on the selected text

Shortcut	Description
⌘+Return	Open the Address bar URL in a background tab
Shift+⌘+Return	Open the Address bar URL in a foreground tab
Shift+⌘	Click a link to open it in a foreground tab
⌘	Click a link to open it in a background tab
Option+⌘	Click a link to open it in a background window
Shift+Option+⌘	Click a link to open it in a foreground window
Option+⌘+D	Add the current page to the Bookmarks (without the Bookmark dialog box)
Option+⌘+B	Display the Bookmarks window
Option+⌘+L	Display the Downloads window
Option+⌘+A	Opens the Activity window
Option+⌘+Return	Open the Address bar URL in a background window
Shift+Option+⌘+Return	Open the Address bar URL in a foreground window

Miscellaneous Shortcuts

Use the shortcuts in Table B.6 to cut, copy, and paste materials, undo recent actions, manage the dock, and capture screenshots.

Table B.6 Miscellaneous Shortcuts

Shortcut	Description
⌘+X	Cut the selected objects or data
⌘+C	Copy the selected objects or data
⌘+V	Paste the most recently cut or copied objects or data
⌘+Z	Undo the most recent action
F12 or Eject (depending on your keyboard)	Press and hold to eject an inserted disc
Fn+Control+F2	Give keyboard control to the menu bar
Fn+Control+F3	Give keyboard control to the Dock
Option+⌘+D	Toggle Dock hiding on and off
Option+Volume up/down/mute	Display the Sound preferences
Option+Brightness up/down	Display the Display preferences
Shift+⌘+3	Capture an image of the screen
Shift+⌘+4	Drag the mouse to capture an image of the selected area of the screen
Shift+⌘+4	Press Spacebar and then click an object to capture an image of that object

Glossary

access point A network device that allows two or more Macs to connect over a wireless network.

Address Book Application for maintaining lists of personal contacts and their pertinent information, such as their phone numbers, e-mail addresses, street addresses, and relevant Web pages.

administrator A powerful user account that has the ability to make permanent changes to your Mac's operating system. An administrator can perform many functions, including (but not limited to) creating and deleting other users (even other administrators), installing software for system-wide use, installing device drivers, and the like.

AFP Apple Filing Protocol. A network protocol used to share files and network services among Mac computers.

AirPort Apple's range of wireless networking products. AirPort uses the industry standard 802.11 protocol.

Apple menu Click the Apple icon on the left side of the *menu bar* to see this menu, which is home to a few key commands, such as Software Update and System Preferences. This menu also includes Sleep, Restart, Shut Down, and Log Out commands.

AppleTalk A networking protocol developed by Apple for communication among computers, servers, printers, and any other devices running the protocol. A hallmark of AppleTalk is its ease of use.

application Software that you can install on your Mac. Applications are designed with specific purposes in mind, such as word processors, Web browsers, e-mail clients, page layout, and so on.

application menus This is the part of the *menu bar* that sits between the *Apple menu* icon and the *menu extras*. This section of the menu bar displays the menus associated with the current application.

application preferences The options and settings that you can configure for a particular application via the Preferences command. See also *system preferences*.

backup The process of creating copies of your data. Having recent backups prevents losing all of your information should your Mac experience serious hardware problems.

Bluetooth A wireless networking technology that allows you to communicate between two devices when the devices are within range of each other.

Bonjour A service discovery protocol implemented in Mac OS X. Formerly known as Rendezvous, Bonjour allows for the automatic discovery of other devices running the protocol. There is no setup needed; devices running Bonjour simply discover one another and can then share services. For example, a Mac running Bonjour can discover and print to a printer that's also running Bonjour, without having to know the printer's IP address.

bookmark An Internet site saved in a Web browser so that you can access the site quickly in future browsing sessions.

BSD Berkeley Software Distribution. UNIX-based operating system that was developed by the University of California, Berkeley. Mac OS X runs on a derivative of BSD called Darwin. *See* Darwin.

Carbon A set of APIs (Application Programming Interfaces) that allows a developer to write applications that can run on Mac OS X as well as earlier versions of the Mac OS.

Cocoa A set of APIs (Application Programming Interfaces) that helps developers write programs specifically for Mac OS X. Cocoa applications can be created with a great set of tools provided by Apple, and can implement services that allow them to integrate with other applications that are installed.

ColorSync Apple's color management technology that uses other industry-standard technologies, such as ICC profiles, to keep color consistent among applications, your Mac, and input (scanners and cameras) and output (displays and printers) devices.

Command (⌘) The Command key is located next to the spacebar on the keyboard. This key can be used in conjunction with other keys to perform certain tasks. For example, pressing ⌘+P causes an application to open its print dialog box.

Command-line interface A text-only interface used to display information for the user and to send commands to the computer.

compression The process of making a file, or a folder containing many files, smaller in data size.

Cover Flow A Finder view that shows a split screen, with a List view of the contents on the bottom, and a preview of the current item on the top.

CUPS Common UNIX Printing System. The printing system used by most UNIX-based operating systems, including Mac OS X. Apple purchased CUPS in 2007.

Darwin The name of the flavor of BSD UNIX that Mac OS X is based on. Darwin is developed by Apple and is the core of your Mac's operating system services, such as networking and file systems.

Dashboard An application that runs other mini-applications, called widgets. Dashboard can be accessed by pressing the F12 key on your keyboard or clicking its icon in the Dock.

Device Driver Software developed by a hardware device's manufacturer that allows the operating system to interact with that hardware.

DHCP Dynamic Host Configuration Protocol. A protocol used to automatically assign IP addresses to client computers in a network environment.

disk image A file that acts exactly like a physical disc would on your Mac. Disk images are created by Disk Utility, and you can place items into it just as you would any other directory. Many application installers that you download from the Internet use disk images to transport their data. Disk Utility mounts disk images just as it would an actual CD, DVD, or hard drive.

discoverable Describes a device that has its Bluetooth feature enabled so that other Bluetooth devices can connect to it.

Dock Located at the bottom of your screen, the Dock is a great place to store links to items or applications you use more frequently than others.

Drop Box A directory in your home folder that can be used by others on your network to share files with you. They can drag-and-drop files into your Drop Box, but cannot view its contents.

Eject Press this key (or, on some Macs, hold down the key for a second or two) to eject the currently inserted CD or DVD.

Ethernet The most common network standard in use today, Ethernet links computers together via a system of cables and hubs, or routers. Data transmission speed can range from 10 to as fast as 1,000 megabits per second, depending on the cabling and hardware used.

event An appointment or meeting that you've scheduled in iCal.

Exposé Allows the user to press the F9 key to see all open windows at once, F10 to see only the windows associated with the currently active application, or F11 to hide all open windows. The button configurations vary between some Mac models and keyboards.

fast user switching A Mac feature that allows more than one user to be logged into their accounts at once. Fast user switching leaves your programs running when you log out, and reinstates them just as they were when you log back in.

file system A technology used by the operating system to keep track of the files stored on a disk, such as a hard disk.

Finder The one application that you can interact with that is running all the time on your Mac. The Finder is what you use to navigate your Mac's disks for files, folders, applications, other volumes, and so on.

Firewall Software that protects your computer or network from outside intrusion.

FireWire A high-speed serial bus standard developed by Apple for the speedy transmission of large amounts of data. Also known as IEEE 1394, FireWire is cross-platform and can transmit between 400 and 800 megabits per second, depending on which version your Mac's hardware supports.

font A complete set of characters for a particular typeface that defines how the typeface appears on the Mac's display and on printed documents.

FTP File Transfer Protocol. An IP protocol used for transferring, creating, and deleting files and folders located on an FTP server.

group A collection of Address Book contacts. See also *smart group*.

guest operating system An operating system that runs inside a virtual machine using virtualization software.

HFS+ Hierarchical File System. The default file system for Mac OS X, which uses a hierarchical system for storing and organizing files and folders.

home directory This is the directory that contains all of a user's personal documents and files. Every user account created on your Mac is assigned a home directory. These directories are located in the Users folder at the root of your hard drive.

HTML HyperText Markup Language. The programming language used to render the graphics and text of a simple Web page.

HTTP HyperText Transfer Protocol. A protocol responsible for linking and exchanging files on the Internet.

iCal Your Mac's default scheduling application.

iChat A Mac application that you use to converse with other people in real time by sending each other online text messages.

iDisk Online file storage that comes with a MobileMe account.

iLife A suite of applications that you can install on your Mac and that includes programs such as iDVD, iPhoto, and iWeb.

Image Capture The Mac application that you use to connect to a device such as a digital camera or digital camcorder and download the device's photos or videos to your Mac.

iTunes Your Mac's default media player application.

iWork A productivity suite that comes with three programs: Pages, a word processor; Numbers, a spreadsheet program; and Keynote, a presentation program.

Java Cross-platform software development environment used on most computer operating systems and many handheld devices. Java is also frequently used to display dynamic information on Web pages.

JPEG Joint Photographic Experts Group. Perhaps the most common format for pictures on computers and the Internet. JPEG can compress the data size of the image while still retaining reasonable image quality.

kernel The central component of Mac OS X's UNIX underpinnings. Its main responsibility is the management of the system's resources. The kernel makes sure that each process running is allocated the proper amount of computing resources, such as memory, it needs to complete its task.

LAN Local Area Network. Network that is confined to one particular area, such as in a small office or home business.

LPD Line Printer Daemon. An industry-standard protocol for printing via TCP/IP over a network.

login items The applications, files, folders, network shares, and other items that start automatically when you log in to your user account.

Mail Mac OS X's default e-mail application. Mail can handle multiple e-mail accounts of varying protocols, such as IMAP, POP, and even Exchange.

menu bar. This is the strip that runs across the top of the Mac screen and it includes the *Apple menu* icon, the *menu extras*, and the *application menu*.

menu extras These icons appear on the right side of the *menu bar*, and the number of icons you see depends on the configuration of your Mac. You use these icons to see the status of certain Mac features (such as your wireless network connection) and to configure other features, such as the Mac's sound volume and Bluetooth functionality.

modifier key A key that you press in conjunction with one or more other keys to launch some action. On the Mac, most keyboard shortcuts involve the *Command* (⌘) key.

open source The software development method that allows for free access to source code, and the modification and redistribution of the code.

OpenGL Developed by Silicon Graphics, OpenGL is a cross-platform application programming interface (API) used for producing two- and three-dimensional graphics.

pair To connect one Bluetooth device with another by entering a passkey.

partition A portion of a hard drive's space that has been separated from the rest of the disk. Your Mac views each partition as a separate hard disk, and you can use the partition for anything you want, such as installing Windows or storing particular types of files.

permissions Every file and folder on your Mac is owned by a user account. Permissions are access rights given to the owner and other users of the Mac. Without the right permissions, another user may not view or access the file or folder owned by another user.

preferences file A document that stores options and other data that you've entered using an application's Preferences command.

Preview An application that ships with Mac OS X that is used for viewing PDF files and images. Preview is capable of opening more than 25+ file formats, including almost all of the popular image formats.

printer queue Stores print jobs for your printers. Whenever you print a document the print data goes to the printer queue that was created when you originally installed the printer on your Mac. The printer queue passes the data from Mac OS X to your printer. If there is a problem, the print data will be stored in the printer queue and wait until such time that it can resume printing.

protocol A set of standards or rules that govern the communication of information between two computers.

Quartz A graphics service in Mac OS X responsible for rendering two-dimensional graphics.

QuickTime Apple's default multimedia framework designed for the creation and handling of various digital media formats in the areas of video, sound, and animation.

QuickTime Player Your Mac's default digital video player.

Safari Your Mac's default Web browser.

Safe Boot To start your Mac in Safe Mode.

Safe Mode A startup mode where your Mac doesn't load most of its behind-the-scenes components.

Sidebar The pane on the left side of any Finder window that offers a number of shortcuts to objects such as devices, network shares, and local folders.

sleep mode A low-power state where your Mac uses only marginally more electricity than if it were powered off altogether, while still preserving all your running applications, windows, and documents.

smart folder A kind of virtual folder where the contents depend on the criteria you specify, and your Mac adjusts the contents automatically as your files change.

smart group A collection of Address Book contacts where each member has one or more things in common, and where Address Book adds or deletes members automatically as you add, edit, and delete contacts.

smart mailbox A Mail folder that consolidates all of your messages that meet one or more conditions, and where Mail Book adds or deletes messages automatically as you receive and delete messages.

SMB Server Message Block. Protocol used primarily by Windows computers for accessing shared files, printers, and other network services. Mac OS X has the built-in ability to communicate with Windows-based PCs through SMB.

SMTP Simple Mail Transfer Protocol. Protocol that is used mainly for sending e-mail, but rarely for receiving e-mail.

Spaces An application that allows you to work with multiple desktops on which you can run applications and view documents. You can use each space for a different task, which is a good way to keep yourself organized.

Spotlight The Mac feature that you use to search for files, folders, applications, Mail messages, images, and other data.

synchronization A process that ensures that data such as contacts, email account, and events on your Mac is the same as the data on other devices such as cell phones, other computers, and PDAs.

System folder Located at the root of the hard drive, this folder contains the core components needed to boot your Mac system and run it efficiently after the boot process occurs. Your Mac will not be able to boot correctly if this folder is tampered with (such as by changing its name), so it's best to steer totally clear of this folder.

system preferences The options, settings, and other data that you've configured for your Mac via the System Preferences application.

TCP/IP Transfer Control Protocol/ Internet Protocol. Set of industry-standard protocols used for communications via the Internet. TCP's job is to keep up with the packets of data being sent, while IP is the actual vehicle for delivering the packets.

Terminal A program used for accessing the command-line interface of Mac OS X.

TextEdit Your Mac's default word processor.

Time Machine A Mac application that you use to create and access backups of your files.

user accounts Every person who uses your Mac needs an account to access personal files and folders, and these are called user accounts. Each user account contains folders dedicated to that user alone, and no other users, even administrators, can access them without permission.

utility Utilities are software applications dedicated to managing and tuning your Mac's software and, to some degree, hardware. Each utility has its own specialty; for example, Grab's function is to capture screen shots, and that's all it does. Some utilities may perform a variety of tasks, but the tasks are designed around a specific theme, such as Disk Utility, whose functions pertain to disks (formatting, mounting, and so on).

virtual machine Software files that virtualization applications, like Parallels Desktop for Mac or VMware Fusion, recognize and utilize as if they were separate computers. You can install virtually any Intel-based operating system on your Mac using virtual machines. The virtual machine runs within Mac OS X, allowing you to use Mac OS X and the OS on the virtual machine at the same time.

virtualization Running a guest operating system (such as Windows on a Mac) in a virtual machine.

widget Mini-applications that are launched with Dashboard. Widgets typically concentrate on one particular task, such as local weather, movie show times, sports scores, recent news, and the like.

Index

The Genius is in.

Macs
PORTABLE GENIUS

978-0-470-29052-1

Mac OS X Leopard
PORTABLE GENIUS

978-0-470-29050-7

iPhone 3G S
PORTABLE GENIUS
Also covers iPhone 3G!

978-0-470-52422-0

Final Cut Pro
PORTABLE GENIUS

978-0-470-38760-3

iMac
PORTABLE GENIUS

978-0-470-29061-3

MacBook Air
PORTABLE GENIUS

978-0-470-38108-3

MacBook
PORTABLE GENIUS

978-0-470-29169-6

MacBook Pro
PORTABLE GENIUS

978-0-470-29170-2

Switching to a Mac
PORTABLE GENIUS

978-0-470-43677-6

iPod & iTunes
PORTABLE GENIUS

978-0-470-38259-2

iLife '09
PORTABLE GENIUS

978-0-470-41732-4

iPhoto '09
PORTABLE GENIUS

978-0-470-47569-0

The essentials for every forward-thinking Apple user are now available on the go. Designed for easy access to tools and shortcuts, the *Portable Genius* series has all the information you need to maximize your digital lifestyle. With a full-color interior and easy-to-navigate content, the *Portable Genius* series offers innovative tips and tricks as well as savvy advice that will save you time and increase your productivity.

Available wherever books are sold.

WILEY
Now you know.